Staying Small Successfully

Staying Small Successfully

A Guide for Architects, Engineers, and Design Professionals

Second Edition

Frank A. Stasiowski, FAIA

John Wiley & Sons, Inc.

New York   Chichester   Weinheim   Brisbane   Singapore   Toronto

Copyright © 2001 by John Wiley & Sons, Inc. All rights reserved.

Published simultaneously in Canada.

For ordering and customer service, call 1 (800) CALL WILEY.

Library of Congress Cataloging-in-Publication Data

Stasiowski, Frank, 1948–
    Staying small successfully / Frank Stasiowski.—2nd ed.
       p.   cm
    Includes bibliographical references and index.
    ISBN 0-471-40773-9 (cloth : alk. paper)
    1. Architectural services marketing—United States. 2. Engineering services marketing—United States. 3. Design services—United States—Marketing. I. Title.

NA1996.S75 2001
720'.68—dc12

                                                    2001024236

Printed in the United States of America

10 9 8 7 6 5 4 3 2 1

Inspiration

Attitude is everything! Success in a small business takes courage combined with relentless action at a pace that outstrips your competitors' ability to beat you. Remember: Energy outperforms quality 90 percent of the time. Go for it!

Contents

Foreword

WOW!

That's how I describe the dramatic impact Frank's philosophies have had on my firm's performance in a very short time. When I took over management of a small design firm three years ago, we appeared comfortable with mediocrity in both the approach to our practice and financial results. We knew we had the talent and expertise to do better but were hesitant to change and didn't know where to start. Like most design professionals, I was not schooled in business practices and was searching for a definitive source of best-practice tools specifically targeted to design firms in order to lead my company forward. I found that source in Frank's design industry tools, outlined in *Staying Small Successfully.*

My firm started investing in Frank's intellectual capital one step at a time at a fairly steady pace. We revitalized our annual strategic planning session by focusing on the elements of a plan: purpose, marketing, project delivery, human resources, finance, and ownership transition. This year, we added another key element—information technology. We've found that when the plan is communicated effectively, the energy created during planning sessions permeates the entire organization. The belief we have in our plan is measured in the excitement we see in the forward movement the plan generates. We recently wrapped up a strategic plan update meeting where 80 percent of the initiatives assigned for the last quarter were completed successfully. Boy, are we happy!

It took courage to enact the changes necessary to achieve the results we wanted. Changes included focusing on fewer primary markets in a larger geographic region while learning to say *no*. We hired a marketer for the first time and developed a process to recruit and hire talented people, then train them in Frank's winning philosophies. Our contingency plan for an economic downturn enables us to calmly attack that potential situation on all fronts. A leadership transition plan is in place that creates clarity of purpose and buy-in from our leaders.

The performance results are amazing! The final PMSM Architects financial numbers for the past year show:

- a total revenue that ranks second since incorporating in 1964
- 61 percent growth in total revenue over the past two years
- a profit that ranks #1 since incorporation and a 98 percent increase over the previous high

As a business-centered practice, we're excited about the results of our investment. More important, the positive financial results have increased staff morale and creativity while allowing us to more clearly focus on our design process because we know we're operating more efficiently and effectively than ever before. We now embrace change and look forward to our future. Thanks to Frank and his philosophies, embodied in *Staying Small Successfully*, all I can say is *Wow!* Read this book and follow Frank's advice; then you can say *Wow* too!

Jim Moore
Managing Partner
PMSM Architects
Santa Barbara, California

Acknowledgments

In working on this, the revised version of *Staying Small Successfully*, it became clear that I owe a debt of gratitude to the small businesses profiled in the book, like Perteet Engineering and Talbot & Associates, who think outside the box to create movement away from traditional ways of doing business. It was the wrongs that I've witnessed in my own life—failed ownership transition and the lousy leadership I experienced as a young architect—that inspired me to go into the business of consulting and educating for change and innovation.

This book could not have come to fruition without the tremendous work effort of Allison Tilly Carswell, the staff of PSMJ Resources, and our team of talented consultants, who provided ideas and input for the text.

Thank you.

Introduction

When I first put pen to paper to create this manuscript in 1991, the architecture, engineering, and construction (A/E/C) world felt much smaller than it does now. Many of the owners I interviewed for the original *Staying Small Successfully* focused their efforts on wooing and winning clients relatively close to home. With fewer staff members than the big guys in the industry, this approach made sense. There just weren't many options, outside of opening a branch office, for expanding a firm's geographic reach.

NEW OPPORTUNITIES FOR SUCCESS

One of the major drivers behind revising *Staying Small Successfully* was to share with small firm practitioners the tools available today that prevent size from being a limiting factor in winning big jobs. Arrangements like partnering and strategic alliances, coupled with Internet resources widely available at low costs, have blown open the door to a much vaster A/E/C world.

In a recent PSMJ Resources, Inc., poll of firm principals,[1] 50 percent of respondents planned to grow revenues through strategic alliances. This is good news—but it could be better. The survey also revealed that the majority of growth factors considered by firm owners were traditional, more-of-the-same strategies, such as adding clients, obtaining more work from existing clients, and reaching out to clients in new geographic areas.

PSMJ Resources' lead researcher Bill Fanning summarized the results in this way: "More-of-the-same tactics can satisfy everyone's growth expectations only if the construction market continues to expand. And while construction is expected to grow, most projections fall far short of participants' projections. Thus, firms may be forced to look to the more difficult strategy of expanding their capabilities to meet their growth projections (which are 15 percent increase in revenue, 11 percent increase in staff)."

WE'RE IN AN INDUSTRY SEA CHANGE

Entrepreneur-led, successful firms have always found ways to do business a little differently. Truth be told, the innovators and wildly successful owners I've encountered recently broke out of the box of thinking in terms of more of the same years ago. So what are they doing differently?

These firm leaders understand that they're practicing during a remarkable time in the A/E/C marketplace. We are in the midst of an evolutionary period. In the 1991 release of this book, technology did not figure prominently in the state of affairs in A/E/C. We were still struggling with how to install computer-aided design and drafting (CADD) into our workplaces. We're still struggling with CADD today, but the issues are different. How can we take advantage CADD's timesaving, productivity-enhancing features? How can we use CADD to do more, to automate more functions, to take over more of the design process?

The trend in this thinking involves the decreasing importance of the individual in basic design services. What is the answer for the small-firm practitioner who has paid the bills by being a technically competent, quality-minded professional?

IDENTIFY YOUR SMARTS

As players in a service industry, we must assume the role of visionaries not only for our own practices but for our clients as well. Staying small successfully in this environment means taking a step away from what everybody else is doing. It means replacing the emphasis in your firm on quality drawings and good communication (which is what every client expects from every A/E/C provider) with an emphasis on anticipating needs.

Today, the most important mission of my work is to reveal to A/E/C firm owners and leaders like you the unparalleled power of harnessing and taking advantage of the intellectual capital—or unique smarts—in your organization. As you make your way through chapters in this book about fundamental firm operations, success philosophies, and management wisdom, don't forget to frame them in your mind as the support structure for leveraging your intellectual capital.

The biggest favor you can do yourself before, during, or after reading *Staying Small Successfully* is to answer one fundamental question: What do I know about this business that people will pay for? Here's a tip: It's not your design skills!

Think about your depth of experience in your niche market. If you specialize in restaurant design, you should be able to walk into a meeting with a potential client and enlighten him about what his facility needs. This is business consulting, and it's not only the future of A/E/C, it's the present!

DEVELOP LEADERS IN YOUR FIRM

The firms I've encountered that stand head and shoulders above the rest in terms of fees generated, staff commitment, and promise for the future are the ones whose leaders think like business consultants and look for this trait in others. Leaders of high-achieving firms aren't afraid to bring in the very best employees they can find, then groom them to take over.

Instilling leadership characteristics in your employees—whether you're a firm of five or five hundred—will differentiate your operation from others. This topic is addressed throughout this updated version of *Staying Small Successfully*. It is at the heart of keeping your vision and your firm going strong for years. It is the *Staying* in the title of this book.

BE PROUD OF WHO YOU ARE

In the introduction to the first edition of *Staying Small Successfully*, I concluded with a sentiment I want to reiterate here: Never apologize for being a small practitioner. With the changes in our field, the small firm practitioners are, at times, better positioned to bring value to a client than are some of their large competitors.

There are many benefits to being a streamlined operation of few employees: exposure to all aspects of a project, true relationship development between your firm and the client, no bureaucracy for poor performers to hide behind. These add up to competitive advantage for your firm in an industry looking for A/E/C professionals to function as business consultants with the know-how and resources to put clients first and anticipate their needs. The last—but not least—factor in the equation is the fire of your entrepreneurial spirit. Use it to ignite your team and your clients to success!

REFERENCE

1. *PSMJ A/E Pulse,* November 2000.

Planning and Strategy

Of the thousands of small firms that exist in the United States today, one common element appears to be prevalent in all firms that are not successful—the lack of planning. At one time, Harvard Business School performed a study of 1000 graduates.[1] Of the 1000, 80 percent had never written down any planned goals. Of the 20 percent who had written them down, 17 percent had done so only once. The remaining 3 percent, however, had written down their plan goals annually and then updated them monthly throughout the course of the year. The results were that the income of the 3 percent that wrote down their goals regularly superseded the income of the 80 percent that had no planned goals—by 400 percent. The results suggest that the physical act of writing down a plan is a powerful motivator toward achieving success.

You can trace most management problems directly to poor planning. Without planning, your organization moves slowly, awkwardly, and without direction. You will benefit from the tips, techniques, methods, and other materials in this book only if you recognize the importance of planning to your success.

One important characteristic of successful planning is flexibility. Successful firms plan regularly, then adjust, modify, update, criticize, mold, and work on variations of business plans.

Planning is:

- Participatory
- Ongoing
- Critical to your success

Planning is not:

- One-time
- A written text
- Elaborate or involved

In October 1999, a PSMJ Resources poll showed that of 85 firms surveyed, 100 percent conducted an annual planning meeting. The majority of firms (80 percent) held the meeting offsite for two days (56 percent). Only 20 percent of respondents held planning meetings that lasted longer than 2 days. Also of interest, 48 percent of respondents held meetings during the workweek, 40 percent on a combination of workdays and weekends, and 12 on a weekend. Attendees at the firms' annual planning meeting include principals (100 percent), department heads (52 percent), administrative managers (40 percent), and project managers (32 percent). Only 24 percent of responding firms used an outside facilitator.

In the same survey, those polled reported developing plans for marketing (84 percent), updated strategic plan (84 percent), annual budget (72 percent), annual business plan (62 percent), and technology plan (52 percent). The 16 percent of firms who don't annually review their strategic plan are placing the future of their firm in peril. Their strategic market position—that market share that a company can obtain in selling its service or product—may be dwindling due to lack of attention. Within the total marketplace, how much business will your company obtain? This chapter shows you (1) how to assess your place in the market, (2) where to go, and (3) how to translate your vision of the future into an action-oriented strategic business plan. Many of the ideas presented in this chapter explaining the strategic plan are discussed in greater detail in later chapters. The concepts are introduced here within the framework of the strategic plan.

Most design professionals today conduct their practices using technologies and professional policies heavy with tradition. To succeed—and, if desired, to grow—a professional firm must be able to recognize and absorb the dynamic forces that shape its environment. This may mean laying aside the traditional lines of thought on running a design firm.

THE NEED FOR VISION

Before outlining your strategic plan, you must decide who you are and where you want to be in 5, 10, even 15 years. Many companies operate without this type of clear vision. They just happen to be in business. But consider the individuals who have succeeded as a result of their commitment to a vision. Ted Turner persisted with his idea for cable news channel CNN, despite being turned down by dozens of banks, because he had a vision that it would work. He was $30 million in debt, but he succeeded and became one of the world's richest men. Turner's vision was clear, he stuck to it, and he did not give up when no one else believed in him.

Innovative persons who are leaders break with traditional ways of thinking. They act outside the mainstream and eat, sleep, breathe their vision, sometimes to the point of obsession. Others say such individuals were clairvoyant, knowing of their success ahead of time. Their energy, however, combined with passion, drove these people to succeed. Moreover, you cannot have 15 visions—only one. Focus on your vision as you read the rest of this book to maximize its benefit to you.

A clear vision will allow you to stretch yourself, to succeed beyond your capacity, and to survive failure.

DEFINING A VISION

WHAT'S ALL THIS ABOUT VALUES?

I used to think of values as fluff. No more. When honed to their essentials, they're real markers for building the right strategy.

We usually start by focusing the discussion on professional values such as leading-edge innovation, customer intimacy, and process enhancements. We agree to treat top-line revenue growth and bottom-line profitability as prerequisites for all strong organizations.

When we ask our work teams to pare the lists to only the most meaningful values, the rich debate begins.

One observation of ours is that most deeply held values have the charge they do for a reason. For example, if the firm had an authoritarian founder, the next generation is likely to value collaboration and teamwork. If the firm made its mark as a production firm emphasizing process efficiency, the next generation is more likely to value innovation.

Ellen Flynn-Heapes, *PSMJ's Strategic Planning Manual,* ©1997, p. 23.

One method of developing a vision is to emulate a hero or champion. General George Patton emulated Napoleon. He had studied French and knew a scholar who compiled the memoirs of Napoleon. Patton carried these memoirs wherever he went. Despite the great differences in military technology, he would ask himself, before he made a move, how Napoleon would have acted in the situation. An example of an architect with a vision is Moritz Bergmeyer. While his firm never grew to more than 35 people, he was able to sell it a few years ago to buy a ski resort in Wyoming to fulfill his dream of building a community in the mountains. (See Fig. 1-1.)

As you work to define your champion, run down this checklist:

1. What biographies have you read lately?
2. My vision is to be like _____.
3. Study this person: discover his or her traits and methods; learn how he or she lives or lived and was perceived prior to greatness.
4. How can you pattern your image after this person?
5. List tasks and thinking patterns that will allow you to act and think like your champion.

Take, for example, well-known architects such as Richard Meier, I. M. Pei, Philip Johnson, Frank Gehry. Why do they receive so much publicity?

When you look at any of the great architects or engineers, notice that they break with tradition. They don't follow the norm. Consider: Who are their clients? How do they get to those clients? Then set up your personal and office image so your clients and prospects will see you as the kind of person they want to work with. It is good to follow norms, to stick with tradition, to read the textbooks

Developing a Vision by Emulating a Model

Firm: *Bergmeyer Associates*

Staff: *32 (when sold)*

Specialty: *Architecture, planning, and project development*

Address: *286 Congress Street*
                 Boston, Mass. 02210
                 www.bergmeyer.com

Bergmeyer Associates gained prominence after it redeveloped and converted over 60 warehouses on the historic Boston waterfront. Specializing in such projects, the firm gained experience in planning, design, and development of mixed-use (residential and commercial) waterfront projects and marina facilities. According to Moritz Bergmeyer, the firm's success can be traced to a vision he had several years ago.

The firm began as a partnership in 1970. Bergmeyer split with the partner to form his own company in 1973. After growing steadily to 13 to 15 people, the size of the firm hit a plateau for several years. Despite the steadiness of the company, Bergmeyer was analyzing a troublesome problem. "I was looking for a way to get away from being viewed as the boss and a pain to employees, being looked at negatively. A lot of architects are like martyrs, and if you're in the mode of being a martyr, it's not a good place. It's as bad as being an alcoholic because you feel sorry for yourself all the time, and you think everyone's going to take advantage of you," Bergmeyer says. "I spent a lot of time looking at this problem and hiring consultants, but I couldn't find any answers."

A sudden attitude change took place within Bergmeyer, inspired by a meeting with William Gore, founder of Gore-Tex, at a leadership conference in Tarrytown, New York. Gore and several other high-tech executives were talking about solving the very problem Bergmeyer himself couldn't solve. They talked about creating profit centers, giving employees the room to make decisions, and profit sharing. The profit centers were fairly autonomous and were responsible for managing themselves—negotiating contracts, making a profit, hiring and firing personnel. The firm was simply there to provide overall goals, information, work environment, marketing, support, and other administrative functions.

The notion of giving autonomy to employees went against the traditional thinking in most design firms at the time, Bergmeyer says, mostly in the area of sharing financial information. However, once he developed a financial system to monitor each profit center on a monthly or sometimes even weekly basis (described later in this chapter and in Chapter 7, "Managing the Bottom Line"), the concept took off.

"I got people to feel like they were owners, not employees, and because of all the information sharing, they saw why it was so important to meet budgets and deadlines." Naturally, when Bergmeyer sold the firm, he sold it to the employees. There are now five principals, and the associates also own company stock.

"The person I really admired was Bill Gore of Gore-Tex, because he solved the problem I wasn't able to solve on my own. That was to deal fairly with people, share profits, giving people more accountability and respect."

Not surprisingly, the attitude change, information sharing, and profit centers launched the firm to success. "The firm made more money that year than it ever had. It grew 35 to 40 percent each year. That was the fun part of it.

Figure 1-1
Source: Moritz Bergmeyer. Used with permission.

on business management. But those who do are not always the ones who achieve great success. Sometimes individuals with less business knowledge take an idea to fruition with their unrivaled passion.

Study those who have passion, then develop your own unwritten plan to be like the person or firm you envision. Figure 1-2 profiles the role of the CEO in a small business firm.

Success is relative. If you are an engineer with three employees, your vision of success may be to keep this staff profitably employed. You need not aim to become the richest or the most renowned architect in the world. Your vision can be much smaller—to stay small successfully.

THE CONCISE WRITTEN VISION

Partners of small firms often have difficulty in describing and writing down a vision because they think they are writing down "the answer." In fact, many successful firms have no written plans, but they have clear vision. They engage in a planning process instead of a plan.

The planning process also involves your key people. Review with them what you want your firm to be; ask them how to get there. Get them to believe in you. Your ability to motivate others will establish whether or not you are a leader. If you are a leader, people will believe in your concept and help you carry out your vision.

The next step is to convert your vision into a concise written statement. For a small firm, that means one or two sentences. Figure 1-3 profiles a firm that worked to maintain its vision despite changes in the organization. Once you've created a written vision statement, hone it. Every plan is written in pencil, to be erased, changed, and modified. Work hard to avoid filling your vision statement with cliché words—for example, creative, innovative, design-oriented—that don't inspire action. Figure 1-4 contains sample one-sentence vision statements. Write only enough so that you don't overwhelm your employees with paper. Eschew the 40-page plan.

ELEMENTS OF A PLAN[2]

The strategic planning process is made up of six main elements. Coordinate these elements so there is no conflict among them. Follow the order below. If you don't, you will create conflict among the items. The six elements are

Role of the CEO in a Small Business Firm

"How should we spend our time?"

PERSONNEL
Recruiting
Initial salary level
Employment letter
Position description
Annual evaluation
Technical development
Promotions
Daily greetings
Periodic lengthy chats
Reprimands
Dismissals
Exit interviews
Human resources committee
Response to morale changes
Response to walk-ins

FINANCE
Signing payroll checks
Expense logs/checks
Time report
    —Production ratios and trends
Accounts payable
Aging report/collections
Project budget reports
Borrowing/negotiating lending rate
Salary reviews/adjustments
Quarter review with accountant
Quarter review/financial statement to bank
Trends/statistics/ratios overall
Annual planning
    —Operating budget
    —Marketing goal
    —Major purchases
    —Building lease

—Profit goal
—Bonus goal
—Accumulation goal
Bonus distribution

SPONTANEOUS OTHER
(marketing, administrative, etc.)
Backlog
—Contracted
—Potential
—Individual workload
Project problems/client sensitivities
Corporate programs/fringes
Policies/procedures
Project meetings
Long-range planning
Management committee
Proposals/fee development/negotiation
Contract review/signature
Services/diversification
Ownership transition
Marketing development
Technical development
    —Self
    —Managers
    —Staff
Corporate survey/evaluation/response
Corporate structure
Professional liability insurance
    —Review/application/renewal
Maintenance marketing/feedback
Mail sort
Reviewing/hiring consultants
Acquisition/mergers
Working conditions
Equipment/tools

Figure 1-2
Source: Michaels Engineering. Used with permission.

Keeping Your Vision Alive

Firm:	*Perteet Engineering, Inc.*
Staff:	*70*
Specialty:	*Transportation—studies, design, and construction management*
Address:	*2707 Colby Avenue, Suite 900*
	Everett, Wash. 98201
	www.perteet.com

From its founding in 1988 until 1997, Perteet Engineering's vision and business strategy was to stay small. Owner Rich Perteet had decided that all growth would stop at 25 employees because of the ease of management and good profitability achievable with that number.

Today, Perteet Engineering numbers 70 employees. What happened? As Perteet explains, "We kept nudging up on the number 25. With 23 employees, I had key people come to me who wanted to stay with the firm but were looking for challenges. We had to grow to offer them new opportunities and the ability to become owners."

In 1997, Perteet Engineering acquired a small survey group. Thus began the firm's two "challenging and fun years of explosive growth." The roster of employees grew from 23 to more than 50 during that time. With 70 employees today, Perteet reports that his firm still feels small. "It's funny. In this environment, at 70, we're a small firm. It used to be that at 19 we were a small firm."

With the increase in staff size, however, and a desire among his firm's eight shareholders to continue growth, Perteet recognized the need for a renewed strategic plan and vision for his firm. In early 2000, Perteet Engineering created a strategic plan with goals, objectives, steps to success, accountability, and procedures for keeping the firm healthy well into the future.

One of the cornerstones of this effort was the articulation of the firm's vision in a Purpose Statement and a Growth Statement. Firm leaders who participated in the strategic planning session collaborated to create the statements. Perteet describes these as "live" statements that will change to accurately reflect the goals and mission of the firm. Currently, the Purpose Statement is under review in light of Perteet Engineering's intention to enter into strategic alliances to compete more effectively. Perteet's employees brought the issue forward, believing in the importance of keeping the statement accurate.

Perteet Engineering's Purpose Statement
"Perteet Engineering, Inc., is a firm sought out by clients who want to move people and goods in the most effective way."

Perteet Engineering's Growth Statement
"Perteet Engineering, Inc., will grow by seeking larger and more challenging projects with more diverse clients and services in a wider geographic area."

Figure 1-3

Sample Vision Statements

To be the largest firm in the country.

To be the world's most noted expert in Victorian theater redesign.

To work in various corners of the world.

To have a firm culture that attracts the top engineering talent in the nation.

To be the wealthiest architect in the world.

To be known as the country's most successful small firm doing facilities management.

To emulate I. M. Pei.

Choose a single statement that crystallizes your focus and direction. This vision is, as it appears, a massive wish. This statement is the impetus for the rest of your planning process.

Figure 1-4

1. *Purpose*—Why are you in business? What's special about the work you do? What are you trying to accomplish? What is your mission?
2. *Marketing plan*—Is there a market for what you want to sell? Who are your clients and potential clients? How do your competitors and potential competitors approach the market? How will you gather information? How will you sell your products or service?
3. *Delivery system*—How are you organized to deliver products and services to your clients?
4. *Finance*—How do you set up and maintain easily used systems that give you the data you need?
5. *Human resources*—How do you staff your firm?
6. *Leadership/Ownership transition*—How do you identify and prepare future leaders? How do you assure an orderly ownership transition?

Purpose A firm's purpose must be translated into *mission statements* and *firm culture*.

Mission Statement The mission statement should capture the essence of what you want your business to be. It should be unique, succinct, and tailored to the exact service your firm provides. It shouldn't be a middle-of-the-road, generic statement ("XYZ Associates is a unique architectural firm"). Instead, state specifically what the firm is trying to accomplish; identify your core drivers. For example, "We work only for hotel clients that are going to build major hotels in the next 20 years."

To uncover your core drivers, ask:

- What makes us tick? What do we get excited about?
- What priorities really guide our decision making?
- What do people talk about, think about?
- How do we spend our time?
- What would we *not* want to change about our company?
- How do we want people to describe our company?

Core drivers might include:

- Innovation
- Being really close to customers
- Being fast and efficient
- Following the marketplace wherever it takes you
- Making as much money as possible
- Teamwork
- Empowerment for employees
- Superior client counseling ability

Culture Statement A culture statement should answer questions such as:

- Is the firm a single or multiple corporate culture?
- Do we believe in our people more than our clients or our clients more than our people?
- How do we keep the team together?
- How important is loyalty?
- How important is hard work? Is it more important than performance? Or do we put performance first and hard work second?
- How important are family, friends, and outside life to the interests of the firm?
- Do we believe in hiring cheap labor or having a united, balanced family?
- How will we serve our markets?
- What business are we in?
- What is our product or product mix?
- What is/are our market(s)?
- What is our competitive advantage?
- What is our strategic role?

A culture statement will help define your firm's purpose, which all employees should understand and work toward. Figure 1-5 is a sample culture statement from an actual design firm. Another approach is to tailor culture statements for each function, as shown in Figure 1-6. Although CH2M Hill is a large company, its culture statement appears here because it is one of the most well-defined culture statements the author has encountered. The statement clarifies each aspect of the business. Few small firms take the time to define their culture statements so well.

Sample Culture Statement

Shared Values

The following are values that we share:

1. We serve with love.
2. Honesty and professionalism are fundamental to each of us.
3. Quality is the true criterion for evaluating our work.
4. Teamwork is the way we work.
5. The perception of our clients is reality to us.
6. Through generalized training and experience, we, as individuals, choose to become specialists.
7. We have fun.
8. We reward performance and correct nonperformance.
9. All that we do with and to the environment must contribute to its maintenance or improvement.
10. We support individuals and their families in their responsibility to achieve their fullest potential in a way that does not disable others.

Figure 1-5

Although CH2M Hill is a massive firm, even the smallest firms can use its culture statement as a guide to emulating CH2M Hill's success.

Marketing Plan and Direction The key goals outlined in the marketing plan should be clear, concise, and measurable. Typical marketing plans are well researched, with comprehensive data about clients in the market and targets for dollar volume. As well as containing measurable goals, large-firm marketing plans specify strategies and techniques for attacking the market, from call reporting to presentation strategies to proposal strategies. Well-researched plans contain detailed personnel plans, including staff members' roles and how they should be involved in the marketing effort.

The smaller firm lacks the resources to do this research on the scale a large firm such as Skidmore Owings & Merrill or Black & Veatsch would, but you may compensate for this by means of elementary research. Consider calling 25 potential clients to find out how much they will spend in the next year, adjust the findings to reflect the number of clients in the market, then estimate the percentage of those dollars you can capture. (See Fig. 1-7.)

Objective market research can be purchased by hiring a consultant to provide marketing research or by buying prepared marketing research.

Many firms make the mistake of writing elaborate, long, highly literate marketing plans. These are cumbersome and seldom followed. It is much better to have a one- to two-page plan that is measurable and easily tracked by all in your firm. (For more information about creating a marketing plan, see Appendix B.)

Next, make sure you share the plan not only with other principals, the marketing director, and other top people but also with every employee in the company, from partner to receptionist and bookkeeper. If your firm's administrative assistant understands how your vision translates into the marketing plan, then he or she will be able to correctly answer questions on first contacts from client prospects. This way, everyone becomes a part of the marketing plan, thinking about sales and marketing wherever they go. Successful firms disseminate the marketing plan and allow staff to share the information and the vision.

Make the marketing plan an integral part of the firm, not something that sits on a shelf. This need not mean that you must hand every employee a physical copy of the plan. A partner may outline the marketing plan at a semiannual meeting. For such cases, it is best to emphasize the key targets in the discussion and distribute a single piece of paper that illustrates them.

Measurable Goals Saying "We want to be the biggest and best firm and do more hospitals" is not effective. A marketing plan should be specific; for example, "We want to go after 75 university science buildings and libraries in the next nine months." This type of statement is measurable because it includes statistical information.

Focus Firms that solicit clients in a few distinct markets, as opposed to soliciting every project on the horizon, tend to be more lucrative. Thomas Wirth Landscape Architects, a six-person firm based in Sherborn, Massachusetts, successfully focuses on small, signatory gardens. Although Wirth has designed many large commercial landscape projects, focusing on the small projects he prefers has carried him to success; he is the landscape architect for public television's "The Victory Garden" and has written a book entitled *The Victory Garden Landscape Guide.* A description of this firm and further discussion of the importance of focusing your practice appear in Chapter 2.

A Well-Defined Tailored Culture Statement

CH2M Hill, Inc.
6060 South Willow Drive
Greenwood Village, Colo. 80111-5142
www.ch2m.com

Culture Statement

We believe that each CH2M Hill employee must understand what the organization stands for. And so, presented in this publication are our beliefs and values. These ideas represent the collective thoughts of our founders and employees.

Business

CH2M Hill is a professional services firm focusing on engineering design and related services in water, wastewater, and hazardous waste management as its core business, while expanding its business in energy and transportation.

Ownership

CH2M Hill is an employee-owned corporation with broad ownership existing throughout the organization. Employee ownership enhances the opportunities offered by the firm and the employees' shared commitment to the firm's success. We believe our ownership program is a key element in sustaining our commitment to excellence.

Corporate Ethics

We must be profitable, but we desire to make a profit by undertaking projects that are challenging and that contribute to the safety, health, and well-being of the public. The quality and integrity of our work are of overriding importance to us. We strive for technical excellence and innovative solutions.

Our clients are critical to our success, and our aim is for clients to receive full value for our services. We strive to be a good corporate citizen in those communities where we work.

Employee Philosophy

We strive to recruit, develop, and retain outstanding people in our profession. We provide them with challenging assignments, a stable environment, and career opportunities, and we reward them with merit incentives and ownership.

We endeavor to maximize the strengths of our employees so that each is productive to the optimum extent of his or her abilities.

We recognize that family goals are as important as career goals and that the support of family members is integral to creating an atmosphere of productivity and contribution.

Management Philosophy

Our management philosophy is based on participative decision making and is supported by open, frequent, and nonhierarchical communications on all aspects of the firm's and the individual's performance.

We encourage informed decision making at all levels in the organization, and we support individual market development initiatives or research interests at any level, provided these are aimed at improving the firm's long-term competitive position in markets we have identified as being of interest.

We promote leadership among our employees, and we grant authority and responsibility to individuals and teams of individuals to achieve the goals of the firm.

Organization

We are a matrix organization, balancing the maintenance of technical excellence and quality through our discipline structure with a decentralized, close-to-the-client geographic structure. These strengths are embodied in our project teams, which combine technical and local knowledge in the unique blend required by each of our clients.

Growth

Our growth resulted from continued high-quality performance and client satisfaction, expansion in our major markets, increased market share in our core businesses, expanded geographic penetration, selected acquisitions, and new services to meet client needs.

Profit and Financial Condition

We operate at a sufficient level of profit to provide for a reasonable net operating income relative to labor income, and manage operations to ensure a sound, long-term financial condition.

Figure 1-6
Source: CH2M Hill. Used with permission.

Low-Budget Market Research

1. Call 25 clients in your market area.
2. You find that those 25 people project a total of $4 million in fees in the next calendar year.
3. You have 10 people in your firm. Three other firms in your marketplace serve the same clients. The total in all firms is 63 people.
4. As you have 10 people in your firm, you represent roughly one-sixth of the total market.
5. Multiply 1/6 by the total fees for the next year: $1/6 \times \$4$ million = $666,666
6. Your targeted market share for the next year should be $666,666.

Note: All of this information depends on the validity of the information you obtain in the telephone calls. If you get good information, you have valid market research. If the information is invalid, so is your research.

Figure 1-7

Cost and Organization   Include your marketing costs and an organizational chart in your marketing plan. By including costs, you are narrowing down your plan to *strict, measurable* goals.

Delivery System   The delivery system, or organizational makeup, of a firm is a source of constant debate. In typical organizational charts, principals are at the top, project managers and staff below them.

Basic organizational types are market-focused teams (studio), departmental, and matrix. Organization comes about because of a common, basic conflict in architecture and engineering practice—that between quality control and client service. These often opposing issues are relevant even in a one-person firm. The person must decide whether or not to spend more time on a project or to stop the project. The frequently opposing forces of providing good client service versus higher and improved quality are what drive larger organizations to develop organizational plans as they move from 1 to 2 people to 5 to 10 people to 20 to 25 people. The earliest of these organizational plans is the development of teams to serve the client (market-focused). As teams grow, companies often move into matrix and departmental organizations, each of which is described below.

Market-Focused Teams   To achieve a market-focused organization, clearly define the relationship between the client and your firm. Instead of dividing staff by discipline (e.g., interior designers, landscape architects, mechanical engineers, electrical engineers), create teams, each serving a particular client. In this type of organization, project managers become the most important entities. (See Fig. 1-8.) A market-focused team approach will produce a more client-driven organization, better able to serve the client. Market-focused teams are better for small firms; other organizational types are better for large firms.

Departmental   In a departmental structure, the whole staff focuses inter-
Organizations   nally (as opposed to externally toward the client, like market-focused teams) on the quality of the department's work. This encourages competition with other departments, to the detriment of the project. For example, the mechanical engineers are departmentally focused on mechanical engineering, but they are not thinking about the client. See Figure 1-9 for an illustration of the departmental approach.

Another disadvantage of the departmental structure is that the project manager's authority is diminished by the role of department managers, who tend to be senior, powerful members of the firm. Where the project manager has less

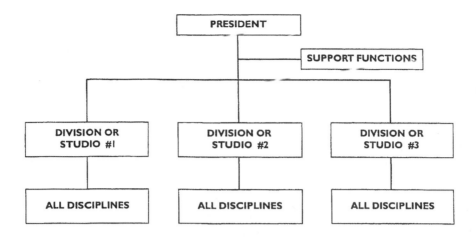

Figure 1-8. Market-focused team organization.

power, the client's budget and schedule suffer. So does quality control, because drawings go from one department to the next without continuity. Finally, the department becomes more important than the project, the firm, or the client.

Departmental organizations are successful when a project stays in one department. Obviously, there are advantages to the departmental approach—it helps when working with clients that are massive departmental agencies, such as the federal government and other large bureaucracies. Generally, small firms shouldn't have departments. As a small firm, if you start growing, don't grow with departments, grow with teams.

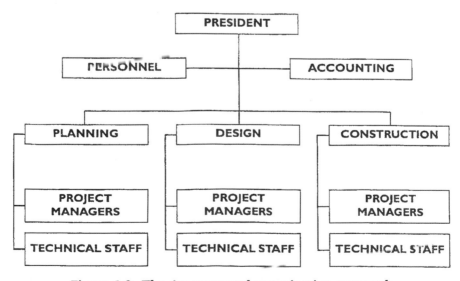

Figure 1-9. The departmental organization approach.

Matrix Organizations A matrix organizational structure seeks to balance power among the project leaders/managers and department managers. Both managers are equal, and each staff member has two bosses—the architectural or engineering department manager and the project manager. The staff's time is split 50–50 between the two bosses.

In a matrix organization, the scales are usually tipped in favor of the person with the most power. If the department manager pays the staff, gives raises, and promotes, then the project manager has little control. The staff's allegiance is to the department. This is the case in the majority of design firms using a matrix approach, and they are really departmental organizations. On the other hand, if the project manager has more power, then the staff becomes more project-oriented and, hence, client-oriented. Unfortunately, this is the exception, not the rule.

The only way a pure matrix can exist is if both the department heads and the project managers have equal power. Figure 1-10 shows the matrix type of organizational structure.

The matrix is not good for the small firm for the following reasons:

1. A matrix organization requires that energy be focused internally instead of on clients. Small firms cannot take this risk.
2. There is a loss of accountability. Typically, the matrix arrangement finds people blaming others when things go wrong and taking credit when things go right.
3. Most small firms offer only one service. Matrix works best in a multidisciplinary environment where three to four services are offered.
4. Personnel planning is difficult. With project managers—who know the demand for staff—often in a different organizational structure from department heads—who manage the resources to get the work done—staffing projects appropriately can be next to impossible.
5. Matrix management requires higher overhead to maintain than do other types. The cost of increased management time is generally too great for smaller firms.

The matrix structure generally first appears in firms of 40 to 50 people in a multidisciplinary environment. The exception may be a 30-person firm that provides architectural, mechanical, and civil engineering services. In such

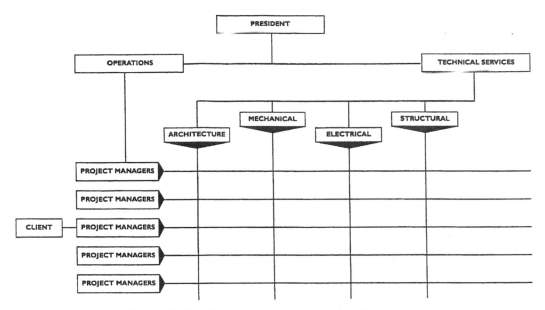

Figure 1-10. The matrix organizational structure.

cases, the smaller organization moving toward a medium size may find this type of structure useful.

Financial Plan The next element of a strategic plan is a financial plan. Begin by targeting revenues and expense and keep it simple.

Moritz Bergmeyer, a successful Boston architect described earlier in this chapter (see Fig. 1-1), sold his design firm in 1988 to buy a ski resort in Wyoming. This individual strove for success from the very beginning. Bergmeyer never had a "financial management system" and, instead, decided to zero in on a few key elements of financial planning to measure his firm's success. Bergmeyer's key measures included the utilization ratio and ratios of employee salary to overall revenue to measure productivity (explained in Chapter 7); return on equity; net profit before taxes; next year's target for gross and net revenue; percent of total revenue allocated to salaries; computer operations, and overhead. These key elements are presented in more detail in Chapter 7. The main point here is that Bergmeyer requested a one-sheet report from each profit center. By keeping his approach simple, he was able to identify problems quickly.

Standardization Successful firms have a clear financial direction. They standardize the terms and conditions of their financial system. The typical design firm draws up a contract any way the client wants it—lump sum, percentage of construction, hourly or unit-based, to name a few calculations. You should aim for a narrower standard, perhaps one or two ways. With proper legal advice, develop your own consistent contracts, a standard approach to contracting, a consistent way of negotiating, a single invoice format. Avoid allowing clients to control you with their different ways of operating.

Do you simply turn away a client who refuses to use your contract? In many cases, small firms use this go/no-go criterion: they will not work with clients who will not do work their way. If a firm presents a lump sum contract and the client says, "No, we want to pay you hourly," the response might be, "I'm sorry, we simply don't want to work with firms who won't do it our way." There is usually some negotiation, however, and the small firm should convince the client that its way is best. Still, it may come down to saying "This is the way we want to do it—take it or leave it." Successful smaller firms must know when to walk away from clients who dig in their heels and detrimentally affect the company's business success. This is one of the toughest strategies that a small firm must employ, because it is incredibly hard to walk away from real work just because a client's contract procedures do not meet your standard.

Employee Involvement Involve all employees in financial planning and its execution. Disseminate financial information within your firm. This way, the staff is motivated to compare budget versus actual costs routinely. Involve project managers from approval of each job through fee collection.

You may look at this as a divulgence of private information. As football great Fran Tarkenton said, "People like to know the score" so that when they are carrying out their plays, they know the impact on that score—in business, the budget.

If your players do not know the firm's finances, you are hurting your overall chance of success. Obviously, you run the risk of information being passed to a competitor, but the benefits of an open culture, one that involves all employees in the control of their destiny via the use of valid numbers, far outweighs the risks involved.

Profit The norm profit for design firms, according to PSMJ Resources' *2000 A/E Financial Performance Survey,*[3] is 13.5 percent. Typical firms with profits in this range start out the year saying "We want to achieve 15 percent profit." Successful firms project much higher profits. This represents a philosophical difference in the financial planning effort. Such firms avoid mediocrity in their financial planning. For instance, they select utilization rate goals of 75 to 80 percent, as opposed to the norm of 64 percent (see Chapter 7 for definitions). They target for return on equity in the 33 percent range, compared to a norm of 20 percent. Net bottom-line profit before taxes is projected at 25 to 35 percent rather than the 13 to 15 percent typical to the industry.

Therefore, establish targets that are hard to reach and then stretch to get there. If you aim for 30 percent net bottom-line profit and achieve 22 percent, you are still ahead of the average firm. (See Chapter 7 for a section on profit and profit planning.) Figure 1-11 is a chart showing typical-profit firms versus high-profit firms from PSMJ Resources' *2000 A/E Financial Performance Survey*. The top 25 firms that responded to the survey had numbers that were actually double those shown in the upper quartile column.

Finally, do not tolerate staff who are skeptical of your goal to achieve high ratios and who aspire merely to a modest 10 percent project profit. Every member of the firm must believe in and work toward the profit goals you set for the firm.

Human Resources Plan   Success in human resources involves the ability to staff your organization with employees who believe in what you are doing and the skill to motivate them to stay.

Key Profit Performance Results

	Lower Quartile	Median	Mean	Upper Quartile
Net Profits Before Incentive/Bonus Payments and Income Taxes (as % of Net Revenues)	7.67%	13.49%	15.33%	21.76%
Net Profits Before Incentive/Bonus Payments and Income Taxes (as % of Gross Revenues)	5.92%	9.86%	12.23%	17.90%
Net Profit Before Taxes (as % of Net Revenues)	1.35%	5.00%	5.91%	9.23%
Net Profit Before Taxes (as % of Gross Revenues)	1.15%	3.84%	4.66%	7.42%
Net Profit (as % of Net Revenues)	1.02%	3.58%	4.5%	6.72%
Net Profit (as % of Gross Revenues)	0.86%	2.73%	3.61%	5.44%
Contribution (Gross Profit) Rate (as % of Net Revenues)	60.82%	64.91%	65.00%	68.40%
Contribution (Gross Profit) Rate (as % of Gross Revenues)	43.56%	50.26%	50.26%	57.83%
Profit (before Incentive/Bonus and Taxes) per Total Staff	$4,495	$8,175	$7,307	$11,609
Profit (before Incentive/Bonus and Taxes) per Project Manager	$22,277	$40,129	$44,178	$82,691
Profit (before Incentive/Bonus and Taxes) per Partner/Principal	$48,888	$103,000	$115,043	$186,043

Figure 1-11

Human resources is not only recordkeeping and keeping track of vacation and sick time but also recruiting and filling your organization with the right kind of people. It takes a plan.

This plan should correspond to your financial and marketing goals and organizational structure. It should address staffing, recruitment, position planning, performance appraisal, career planning, training, compensation/rewards/benefits (see Chapter 6), employee assistance, and records. All of these elements, which in larger firms fall under the jurisdiction of the human resources director, must become the responsibility of one of the principals, who performs these functions on a part-time basis.

Figure 1-12 shows a sample organizational chart for the human resources division of a design firm. The chart applies to firms of all sizes.

As with other plans, your human resources plan should not be an elaborate document detailing every process. Instead, it should focus on the kinds of people you need to attract and the methods you should use to attract them.

Staffing and Recruitment Staffing activities include promoting your firm through methods that reflect your firm's personality. For example, if you are looking for a receptionist, how does your newspaper

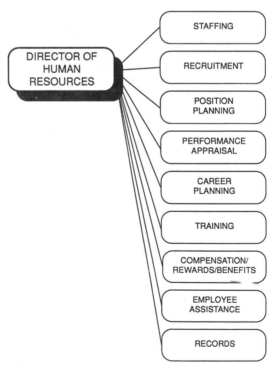

Figure 1-12.   Organizational chart of the Human Resources Division. Used with permission.

ad stand out from the crowd so you attract people who are better than the norm? Write an ad that sets you apart from the others. Ask for "a virtuoso on the phone." You will get fewer resumes, but they will be top people.

At the professional level, recruitment may also involve attracting good people from your competitors. While the ethics of this continues to be debated, good employees gravitate to firms that offer challenging work, a pleasant workplace, and attractive pay, not necessarily in that order. Make them an offer. (See Chapter 6.)

Position Planning In position planning, create clear job descriptions with no task associations. Focus on accomplishment, not method. When you list tasks, you allow employees a loophole whereby they can claim an assignment is not listed in their job description.

Performance-oriented job descriptions are driven by accomplishment. Example: "Your projects will achieve 32 percent profit next year." How the employee achieves the goal is up to him. For an illustration of a standard performance-oriented job description, see Figure 1-13. Goal-oriented job descriptions are clear. They also simplify the performance appraisal.

Performance Appraisal Measure performance using five criteria:

1. *Actual performance*—Did you complete contract documents on 80 percent of your projects on schedule?

2. *Work ethic*—Did you report to work on time? Do you work hard? Do you put in the effort to do your job?

3. *Effectiveness*—Is the work you do effective? Do you get your work done?

4. *Loyalty*—Are you loyal to the organization? Are you loyal to the vision that we have as a company? How is that loyalty measured?

5. *Emotion*—Do you have the right emotional fit with our group? Are your morals the same as ours? That is: Do you really psychically fit with our team?

Avoid performance appraisal systems where employees are numerically rated on forms. Successful smaller firms tend not to have forms but to prefer informal relationships with the staff. Appraisals are direct and regular, sometimes occurring daily as people perform their jobs. Reviews are constant. Forms should be a record of the performance appraisal, rather than the performance appraisal itself.

Career Planning and Training Your firm should encourage training and establish training goals. Government statistics show that the average spending for training and education across all industries is 1.2 percent

Performance-Oriented Job Description

Position: *Department Manager*

Accountable to:

Responsible for:

General Responsibility

The primary responsibility of the Department Manager (DM) is to make sure that the Department operates in such a way as to meet its responsibilities to:

1. The customers
2. The Company (including other Departments)
3. The employees

In addition, the DM should develop ways of improving the Department's (and the Company's) strategies and operations.

Specific Responsibilities

Marketing

1. Support Company marketing objectives and priorities.
2. Develop marketing objectives and plans for Department in coordination with other Departments.
3. Manage the implementation of Department marketing plans.
4. Assist own Group Managers in exploiting marketing opportunities.
5. Support other Departments in exploiting marketing opportunities.
6. Identify how the Company can improve its marketing capabilities.
7. Ensure that Department generates marketing reports.
8. Approve proposals initiated by own Department.
9. Identify how the Company can improve its technical capabilities, and support such efforts.
10. Approve technical reports issued by own Department.

Personnel

1. Supervise and review Group Managers and support staff assigned to Department.
2. Assist and train Group Managers of own Department in obtaining, training, assigning, utilizing, and releasing technical personnel.
3. Determine Department requirements for Group and Project Managers and make promotion and/or hiring recommendations to the President.
4. Review planned salaries of Department members with Administration Department for consistency and for contractual implications.
5. Recommend to the Scientific Career Committee qualified employees within their Departments for promotions into the Technical Specialist or Principal Scientist positions.

Other
1. Identify routine and special facilities needed by the Department.
2. Conduct special projects as assigned.

Specific Authorities

Marketing
1. Negotiate and agree upon job tasks and schedule with technical customer.
2. Provide informal cost estimates to the customer.
3. Agree with other DMs on people utilization for proposal purposes.

Technical
1. Approve all aspects of technical approach.
2. Assign/reassign project management responsibilities within own Department and between Departments (by agreement with other applicable DMs).
3. Establish appropriate technical liaison with the customer.

Personnel
1. Approve promotions to Senior Analyst and salaries for Department members only.
2. Approve transfers within groups of own Department.

Firm Description

This is a multidisciplinary professional service firm that conducts research and provides technical support to federal government, state government, and commercial customers. Their services consist primarily of operations research, naval welfare analysis, engineering analysis and feasibility studies, planning computer modeling, environmental analysis, and the development of technical documentation. This firm is located in the Northeast.

Figure 1-13

of revenues. PSMJ Resources data show that design firms, however, spend a median of .35 percent on training—about one-fourth the national average.[4] Exceptional firms allocate five times that amount. Encourage employees to become better trained, to attend continuing education programs, masters-level classes, and so on. This motivates the staff to stay with you. See Chapter 6, "Compensation," for more information on career planning programs.

To encourage continuing education in your firm, consider these points:

- Hire people who are motivated to be educated. You cannot force someone to want to become better educated.
- Put control in the hands of the employee, not the firm. Allow employees to take courses that may or may not be directly related to the firm's activities.

Compensation/ Insist on fair compensation planning. Do not compensate
Rewards/Benefits people arbitrarily; aim for equity in positions and bonus
plans tied to performance not company profits. Award hard
working employees, not all. Pay 75 percent of the bonus
money to the top third, 25 percent to the middle third, and no
bonus money to the bottom third. Reward the top people and
penalize the nonperformers. (For more details, see Chapter 6.)

Flexibility Many job-seekers expect employers to allow work schedules
that are adapted to suit their lifestyles. Recognize this
expectation; don't insist on traditional patterns. Do you provide child care or work schedules that revolve around children's school patterns? Consider offering evening, flextime,
and part-time hours. Student and team employment (two
people sharing one job) are other examples of flexible work
arrangements. Such accommodation of employees' personal
responsibilities will motivate them to perform and to stay.

Recordkeeping Plan your recordkeeping so all your records are succinct.
The easiest way for small firms to maintain records is to
adapt a standard industry format such as the CSI MASTER-
FORMAT. This format corresponds to the chapter allocation
of all project resources under the CSI numbering system.
Other standards, such as the UNIFORMATII system, can be
useful in setting up your records as well. Adapting such a
system will put you in the industry mainstream without sac-
rificing efficiency, and your records will be easily translat-
able from discipline to discipline as you network with other
firms in the marketplace. Many client organizations keep
their records in the CSI or similar format.

CSI MASTERFORMAT
1. General requirements
2. Site work
3. Concrete
4. Masonry
5. Metals
6. Wood and plastics
7. Thermal and moisture protection
8. Doors and windows
9. Finishes
10. Specialties
11. Equipment
12. Furnishings
13. Special construction
14. Conveying systems
15. Mechanical
16. Electrical

Leadership and The problem with leadership transition in a service business
Ownership such as architecture or engineering is that you cannot just
Transition sell your firm and leave. Clients who buy your service count
on having you there, especially if you built up the practice.

Leadership selection is one of the most overlooked
functions in design firms. You must ask such questions as:

- Who will carry on your vision into the future?
- What kind of person must you hire as leader to guarantee your firm's future success?

Some firms cannot function without their original leadership, especially if they are star-driven. Address the issue,
whether or not you solve it. It is better to have a plan that
rejects leadership transition than to vacillate on this issue.
Be clear about your plan for selecting, training, and cultivating new leaders.

One architect in Tennessee boldly skipped over a generation of 40- to 50-year-olds to pick a new president who was
33. He risked losing 10 or 15 employees in order to make
clear who he wanted as the future leader of the firm.

Leadership Selection Define the criteria for leader selection in the firm. Include
Criteria well-described steps leading to the top position. When
clearly stated, the leadership selection plan lets junior
employees know where they stand and what it takes to get to
the next rung.

Be careful, however. Many misconceptions about what
makes a good leader and how to transition a firm into new
hands are buried in the good intentions of a firm principal
scanning his operation's horizon for potential heirs.

The concept of loyalty—and oft-stated reason for promoting individuals—has many risks as a leadership criterion. Loyal followers seldom make good leaders—they lack
the wherewithal and hunger to take your firm to new
heights. Similarly, turning your firm over to a group of dedicated associates can be disastrous.

In the attempt to reward talent and good service and to
treat employees "equally," many principals have killed the
firms they struggled to build. Creating a group management
situation in your firm on your departure is akin to fostering
communism in the worst sense. In no time, your firm will
flounder due to lower profitability, lack of leaders' ability to
act quickly, slow organizational change, and internal focus
that cripples relationships with existing and potential clients.

While this may sound disheartening, there is great news
for firm principals facing the prospect of choosing a new
leader: You can discriminate in ownership selection. Don't
feel obligated to choose one person or a group of people for

Leadership Qualities and Attributes

This list of 15 traits was developed by employees of Setter Leach and Lindstrom, Inc.

1. Courage
Leaders have the courage to do what they believe is right rather than what is convenient, popular, or least painful. They have the courage to admit mistakes and the courage to recognize their need for lifelong learning and development. Leaders have the courage to create vision; they challenge the status quo. Leaders deal with change and make it a positive force in their organizations. Change entails risk. A leader experiments and takes risks and allows others in the organization to do the same.

Leaders have the courage of their convictions. The work they do will take years to accomplish and, often, results are not immediately evident. One must be patient and tenacious—always moving forward in the face of doubt and unknowns. Immediate gratification is not the leader's way.

Leaders have the courage to be vulnerable.

2. Introspection
Leaders understand their power and know how and when to use it. They also understand the potential of power to seduce and corrupt. To stay on course, a leader must be able to listen to dissent, constantly evaluate and measure. Ego is not enough; self-esteem is not sufficient. Leaders need to be in touch with how their behavior and attitudes affect people's lives.

3. Stewardship
It is imperative for the survival of an organization that leaders see themselves as stewards. They treat their position not as an inheritance from past leaders but as a trust for future leaders. They accept the principle of servant-leadership. Leaders are dedicated to high principles—fairness, integrity, honesty, service, quality, authenticity, excellence.

4. Intelligence
Intelligence is required for dealing with complex, abstract, strategic, interpersonal, and cross-disciplinary issues and problems. Intelligence takes several forms and includes linguistic, logical, visual, and practical intelligence. Leaders constantly work at mastering new forms of intelligence.

5. Passion
Leaders must want (or need) to lead. They seek leadership positions for the opportunities to serve and to make a difference, and not solely for personal gain.

6. Resilience
Leaders have the ability to bounce back from setbacks—often their own. They accept mistakes and learn from them. They must have the ability to cope with uncertainty, inconsistency, chaos, and confusion. Leaders live well with confusion and are nourished by difficulty and ambiguity. They evaluate which risks to take and which to avoid.

7. Influence
Leadership is an influence relationship. Leaders must have the skills to align people toward a common and shared goal.

8. Vision

A leader must be able to articulate a compelling vision that is imaginable, desirable, feasible, focused, flexible, and communicable.

9. Communication

A leader's most obvious job is communicating the mission and vision of the organization both internally and externally, day in, day out, without fail. They lead in a consensus-building style. Real communication involves listening.

10. Openness

Leaders walk around a lot. They make themselves accessible. They harbor no hidden agendas.

11. Balance

Leaders have balance in their lives. They recognize their various roles and are able to separate them and keep them in balance.

12. Empowerment

Only by delegating authority and sharing power can a leader develop people who will be the organization's future. Leaders give others real responsibility and allow others to take real risk. They remove formal structures and systems that make it difficult to act. Leaders provide training; without the right skills and attitudes, people feel disempowered. When people make mistakes and things go wrong, leaders provide support and use the situation as a growth opportunity. They are mentors.

13. Credibilty

A leader needs trust, which is only developed over time by displays of professional competence, fairness, honesty, and follow-through (walking the talk).

14. Conflict Management

Change creates tension, and leaders must be able to mediate and know how to diffuse anger. As organizations and hierarchies flatten, dialog is the glue that holds the organization together. Leaders need to control themselves and help those who cannot communicate easily. The way people talk to each other is key to the way they work together. Leadership requires an increased awareness of and sensitivity to solving people issues.

15. Business Acumen

Leaders have to be good businesspeople. To effectively lead an organization, leaders must have an understanding of legal, financial, and other issues that affect the business side of our practice. Understanding business issues makes our leaders more credible with our clients. Leaders understand the client's bottom line as well as our own.

When asked about the list, Setter Leach and Lindstrom CEO George Theodore explained, "We use it to develop our leadership, to evaluate the performance of our leaders, and we used it as the basis for our management team's "360 Assessment," assisted by consultant Appel Associates. Each of our leaders was assessed by four people above them, four below them, and four peers. The results of the 360 were, and are, used as development tools for each individual."

Figure 1-14
Source: "Stasiowski On..." *PSMJ Resources,* March 2, 2000.

reasons that may seem right but feel wrong. Follow your instincts and rate leadership candidates in the following 11 areas:

1. Years of service with the firm
2. Management responsibility
3. Marketing ability
4. Client relations
5. Staff management skills
6. Integrity
7. Overall people skills
8. Technical skills
9. Financial commitment to the firm
10. Professional registration
11. Professional or civic activities

Prioritize and weight this list according to your firm's needs and culture. In addition, you should create a list of behaviors you expect leaders to exhibit. Figure 1-14 contains a list of 15 traits you might look for when evaluating who among your employees could be the next CEO. Many firms still pick future leaders solely on the basis of subjective opinion. A few, however, have established published criteria for "moving up" in the firm. Figure 1-15 is a case study of how one firm encourages leadership growth. Figure 1-16 lists sample criteria for becoming an associate.

Unfortunately, many firm owners start thinking of leadership transition about five years before they hope to retire. This puts them in the position of having to choose an existing employee to fill the captain's chair. Owners with true vision for the future of their firms continually seek out stars they can hire and groom to take over.

Accounting Plan The accounting plan details the legal and financial transactions needed to bring future owners into the firm. Usually referred to as an *ownership transition plan* or *buy-sell agreement*, it attempts to address the issue of leadership. This is discussed in further detail in Chapter 10. A sample buy-sell agreement is featured in Appendix A.

Leadership Wants The company should consider its future and describe the *and Needs* type of leader it needs. Ask: Should we bring in an outside managing partner? Are there people in the second generation we want to target? Should we pick a future chief from the third generation? Or should we decide to focus on company growth or profits instead of leadership transition?

Helping Employees Become Leaders

Firm:	*Tsoi/Kobus & Associates (TKA)*
Staff:	*105*
Specialty:	*Multinational A/I firm*
Address:	*One Brattle Square*
	P.O. Box 9114
	Cambridge, Mass. 02238-9114
	www.tka-architects.com

When Ed Tsoi and partner Richard Kobus began to internally transfer ownership of their firm, they decided to do it right. "We set a target of eight to ten years," says Ed. As a result, they practically created another occupation for themselves. "We call it our second day job," Ed remarks, two years into the process. "It is one of mentoring, of cultivating new ways brought to us by the empowered new leadership."

This leadership has emerged as a result of Tsoi/Kobus's deliberate approach to professional development. Everyone at the firm gets a copy of the "Leadership Transition Guidelines," which is a confidential document—no one outside the firm is permitted to see it—containing TKA's leadership criteria. This list was created during periodic meetings with a facilitator and retreats with firm associates.

The leadership criteria are telescoping, meaning each new level retains the requirements of the previous level and adds more criteria on top of those, and divided into four levels:

1. Team Leader (not an official business-card title; created to recognize employees with many years of experience who are not interested in climbing up the management hierarchy)
2. Associates
3. Associate Principals
4. Principals

The criteria are both objective and subjective. For example, an objective criterion for Associate Principals: The individual must have given at least one speech, workshop, or presentation during the year. A subjective criterion: The individual must possess a broad outlook about the office and the profession. "This is difficult to measure," explains Ed Tsoi, "but some people have it and some people don't."

The firm also uses a 360-degree review process, where each person sits with a superior, a peer, and an employee to be reviewed against the firm's published leadership guidelines. "There's literally a checklist," says Ed. "We used to not be so diligent about going through every criterion, but now we go through everything. It helps our employees understand the firm's expectations."

In addition to this review, every employee has his own professional development plan, which is his description of how he will improve his skills. This factors into the 360 review as well.

Ed Tsoi believes one of the biggest benefits of this process to his firm is that "there's no longer a sense of a glass ceiling." Staff members know the guidelines for success and are able to rise to the top and become new principals by meeting publicly acknowledged requirements.

"This type of approach may apply to small firms more critically than any other," believes Ed. "When should people start thinking about identifying new leaders? Certainly not a year before they want to retire or sell stock. It takes a long time to think through what the founders want to see accomplished with a transition to new owners. After this is determined, it takes time to make it successful. New leaders have to be trained. I know we want the outside world to develop as much trust and rapport with the new principals as they have with the founders."

Figure 1-15

Source: Tsoi/Kobus & Associates. Used with permission.

Rules of Eligibility for Becoming an Associate

1. You must exhibit a willingness to accept responsibility.
2. You must exhibit an attitude of professionalism in the conduct of your responsibilities.
3. You must exhibit exemplary character, integrity, honesty, fairness, loyalty, dependability, and professional ethics in your working relationships with both those inside as well as outside the company.
4. You must be deemed by the Board of Directors as having gained and maintained the respect of fellow employees.
5. You must exhibit continued competence in your particular area of expertise. Due to the technical nature of the engineering profession, it is likely that most Associates will be technical employees; however, secretarial, accounting, marketing, business, and other supportive disciplines are not excluded from eligibility.
6. You must be capable of successfully meeting quality, budget, time of completion, and client satisfaction goals on projects in which you are involved.
7. You must be actively involved in working full time in the engineering/surveying/land planning profession for a minimum of five years.
8. You must exhibit the ability to be accepted by our clients, as those elected to carry the title and exposure that come with being an Associate are recognized by our clients to be representative of the quality and character of our organization.
9. You must initiate discussion about your intent to become an Associate.
10. Preference will be given to those who have been employees of the company for a minimum of three years.
11. You must be elected by two-thirds of the Board of Directors.

Figure 1-16

Include All the Elements   Your strategic plan must include all six elements. Figure 1-17 is a summary of the six elements of the strategic plan.

CONDUCTING A PLANNING MEETING

The essence of all successful strategic plans is that they are *simple*, *realistic*, and *easily communicated*. The following simple 11-step process is designed to show you how to conduct a strategic planning meeting, put a plan in writing, and communicate it to the rest of the firm.

1. Start with Yourself
Make a list of things you want to happen over the next few years. Do you want more income? more challenging projects? a sabbatical? a different role? Write down a descrip-

Summary of the Six Elements of the Strategic Plan

1. Purpose
   Mission statement
   Culture statement
2. Marketing plan and direction
   Measurable goals
   Focus
   Cost and organization
3. Delivery system
   Market-focused teams (studio)
   Departmental organizations
   Matrix organizations
4. Financial plan
   Standardization
   Employee involvement
   Profit

5. Human resources plan
   Staffing and recruitment
   Position planning
   Performance appraisal
   Career planning and training
   Compensation/rewards/benefits
   Flexibility
   Recordkeeping
6. Leadership and Ownership Transition
   Leadership selection criteria
   Accounting plan
   Leadership wants and needs

Figure 1-17

tion of your personal vision of what the firm and you will look like three, four, or five years from now if all goes as you wish.

2. Establish a Time Span
Long-range planning does not mean 20 years. Think in terms of a three- to five-year planning span. This will help make your plan realistic and keep it simple.

3. Involve Others Early
Identify those in your firm with the most potential impact on its future and ask each to write down his or her personal ambitions and desires. Then have each describe the firm three to five years from now. No need to ask that these written statements be turned in; they are simply to force individuals to think about the issues in anticipation of a group planning session.

4. Pick a Planning Leader
Identify an individual in your firm who is good at conducting brainstorming sessions. Ask this person to coordinate and conduct a planning session among the senior employees in your office with the goal of synthesizing their personal goals and desires into a concise long-range plan. If no such person is available in-house, bring in a consultant as a catalyst to help you lead the meeting.

5. Set a Date

Schedule a full-day planning session for all those involved in Step 3 above. The session must take place outside your facility to avoid interruptions and to underscore your commitment to the planning process. The room should be comfortable and provision made for a flip chart, markers, and masking tape. No more than 10 to 12 individuals should be invited to the session.

6. Don't Do Extensive Research

The purpose of the planning session is to clarify goals and direction. Subsequent to the session, assignments can be made to verify specific aspects of the plan through research. Your experience, however, and that of your colleagues should discourage extensive advance research.

7. Establish Your Own Yardstick

Using flip chart and markers, begin your planning session by asking all individuals to describe orally what the firm will look like in three, four, or five years. Pick a number of years in the future (we suggest three) and list specific items, such as 150 projects, 32 employees, $4 million in gross fees, two new markets, and so on. Be certain to discuss all aspects of the firm—production, marketing, human resources, finance, technology, and management—in terms of goals and targets. Be realistic, yet stretch your expectations a bit.

Also, don't be trapped into clichés such as "growth." If you bought this book, you may actually desire not to grow.

The importance of this step is to actively seek and draw out from those who will get it there the most realistic three- to five-year picture of what the firm will be.

8. Set One-Year Expectations

After agreeing on three- to five-year goals, ask each individual where the firm will be in one year so as to be on track for the three-year goals. Use the flip chart again and list in more specific terms exactly where the practice should be in a single year.

9. Give Individual Six-Month Assignments

Identify individuals within the session who agree and commit to the group to carry out specific assignments in order to begin working toward the goals. Set target calendar dates, not elapsed time dates, and establish specifically what is to be done, by whom, and who else will assure that it is done. For example, one possible three-year goal is to be a recognized expert in a new (for your firm) building type; in one year, you intend to have three projects in that building type, and by 1 January 2002 (30 days), John Smith will have developed a written marketing plan to get the three projects.

10. Communicate All You've Written

At the end of your session, summarize in outline form on your flip chart your three-year, one-year, and six-month plans. Using the flip chart forces you to be concise and clarify decisions. Take the newsprint sheets back to the firm and have your long-range plan typed directly from them. Using this method assures that your written plan will be no more than three to six pages long. It will be simple, clear, and easily understood.

Assign each group session participant the responsibility to talk with two to four staff people about your planning session and to personally hand out copies of your plan to them. Do not bind the plan in fancy covers or permanent binders. Instead, mark it "DRAFT: To Be Updated in June 2002" (six months from now). Doing so tells the staff that their input can still have an impact on the firm's direction. When discussing the plan with the staff, the primary objective is to get feedback, not to lay down dogma.

11. Schedule Your Next Planning Session

Before leaving your one-day meeting, pick a calendar date six months ahead, a location, and specific people for another all-day planning session; repeat the entire process six months later. Following this rule means that you will be devoting two days (16 hours) of your staff time per year to planning, which is a price you can afford. It also means that you will respond to the input you receive over the next six months from others on your staff.

REPEAT THE PROCESS PERIODICALLY

By following the planning process, you will see that strategic planning is nothing more than setting goals, establishing one-year objectives, and assigning six-month strategies and action plans for achieving your goals. Instead of reacting to events, you will be able to take the initiative with a six-month planning period. You will determine where your firm is going and when it will get there.

More significant than documentation of the goals is the process itself, which enhances communication of the firm's direction and helps you and your associates measure where you are in relation to your plan. Each person in the firm knows where to go and is aware that his actions support or hinder it.

What is true about your plan today may not be true several years from now. Key areas of the plan and the forces that act on them are in a state of constant change. Periodic reassessment is the only way to ensure that the components of your strategic plan are relevant and respond to your organization's environment. Figure 1-18 is a typical strategic plan.

Sample Strategic Plan for the ABC Group

The ABC Group offers planning, design, and management services for the built environment.

Was founded in 1971 by the CEO of the A Group, Inc.; was incorporated in 1979; and is now part of the ABC Group.

The 60 employees include architects, construction project managers, engineers, interior designers, landscape architects and support staff. The ABC Group offers the following services:

Bank planning and design	*Hospital renovation and design*
Campus planning and design	*Library planning and design*
Church planning and design	*Mental health facility planning and design*
Construction project management	*Downtown redevelopment*
Office building planning and design	*Retirement facility planning and design*
Educational facility planning and design	*Parks and recreation planning*
Energy management	*Historic preservation*

Memorandum to: *The ABC Group Staff*

About: *Strategy Plan*

From: *CEO*

Date: *29 August 2001*

This is a follow-up to our 16 February 2001 annual business meeting and the work of the strategic planning session.

We are submitting this first draft for review, comment, discussion, and revision.

OVERVIEW

We want to and are committed to provide outstanding professional services in keeping with our shared values based upon the continuing work of the Step Beyond group.

The strategic statements/goals cover the following eight areas:

1. Quality service
2. Finance
3. Design
4. Growth
5. Business development
6. Human resources
7. Facilities
8. Operations

Figure 1-18

1. Quality Services

A. To provide service of outstanding quality to our clients.

B. To provide outstanding technical product.

- Do an annual client survey to measure performance of our service including projects one year after occupancy.
- By 1 October 2004, the results of the survey place us above 80 on a scale of 1 to 100.

2. Finance

A. Reduce long-term debt by completing payment of our current consolidated loan.

B. Eliminate personal financial guarantees for the ABC Group Inc., on or before 1 October 2005.

C. Provide financial strength required to grow while meeting B above.

D. Have a 15 percent operating income (before allocations), which means to be in or above the 75 percent of design firms operating by the end of FY2003 and beyond.

E. Provide salaries and benefits within or above 75 percent of similar firms in our region by 1 October 2004.

3. Design

A. To meet the needs of our clients as a team (form, function, time, cost).

B. To respect the local project environment (contextuality) and our Shared Value #9.

C. To provide alternatives. Every issue should be presented in alternatives. We should state our preference, but the client must have choices to decide.

- Do an annual planned review, starting in 1990, of the various specialties/disciplines with appropriate realistic practical peers to evaluate and measure the above.

4. Growth

A. To devote 50 percent of current discipline efforts to prime client service by 1 October 2004.

B. To have an additional specialty team operational by 1 October 2004.

C. To have a second new specialty team operational by 2005.

D. To achieve an average growth of 12 percent per year in the next five years (85–90 people).

OPTION:

1. Golf course design
2.
3.
4.
5.
6.

- Special organizational emphasis will be devoted to Engineering, Interiors, and Civil to accomplish the above.
- The two new specialty teams are expected to grow out of services/subspecialties currently provided.

Figure 1-18 (continued)

5. Business Development

A. To have a minimum backlog of nine months of signed contracts at all times based on the annual budget.

B. To have a minimum of nine months of weighted leads based on the annual budget by 1 June 2001.

C. To have a minimum of a 12-month value of weighted leads at all times based on the annual budget by 1 October 2003.

D. Be recognized as experts as follows:

Nationally: In two specialty areas
Options: 1. Retirement and mental health
                2. Retirement and churches
                3.
                4.
                5.
                6.
Options: 7.
                8.
                9.
                10.

Regionally: In two specialty areas and two disciplines
Options: 1. Engineering/architectural
                2. Architectural
                3. Mental health
                4. Engineering
                5.
                6.
                7.
                8.

Locally: The entire firm
Options: 1.
                2.
                3.
                4.
                5.
                6.
                7.
                8.
                9.
                10.

E. That each Discipline Director have a systematic marketing plan implemented by October 2001, including a family of documents for public relations.

Figure 1-18 (continued)

6. Human Resources

A. To recruit outstanding talent.

B. To train the staff.

C. To enable personal growth by maintaining an effective organization.

D. To have staff satisfaction be equal to or greater than client satisfaction identified in #1A.

- Use a yearly survey administered by an external individual to measure the organization's performance in B and C.
- Use outside recruiting assistance as necessary.
- Pay special attention to "travelers."
- Pay special attention to individuals who find themselves required to provide significant extra effort.

7. Facilities

A. With respect to our facilities, it was decided at the Board Meeting on 11 May 2001 that we would proceed to expand the 425 building. This will allow us space for the next two to three years.

B. It is our plan that, in two to three years, the main office will be at a new location in a new facility, either constructed or purchased. This is, of course, contingent on the firm's financial strength and a positive economy.

- Address image long term.
- Provide statement on long term of branch office.
- Address the concept of Pennsylvania expansion. Make a go/no-go decision.

8. Operations

A. Provide personal computer support to each specialty, discipline, and project team by 2004.

B. Adapt spec system to the ABC Group, Inc.

C. Expand and organize the library.

D. Complete building technical standards system.

E. Complete building project management systems.

F. Develop specific standards for design and technical items for each discipline/specialty.

Figure 1-18 (continued)

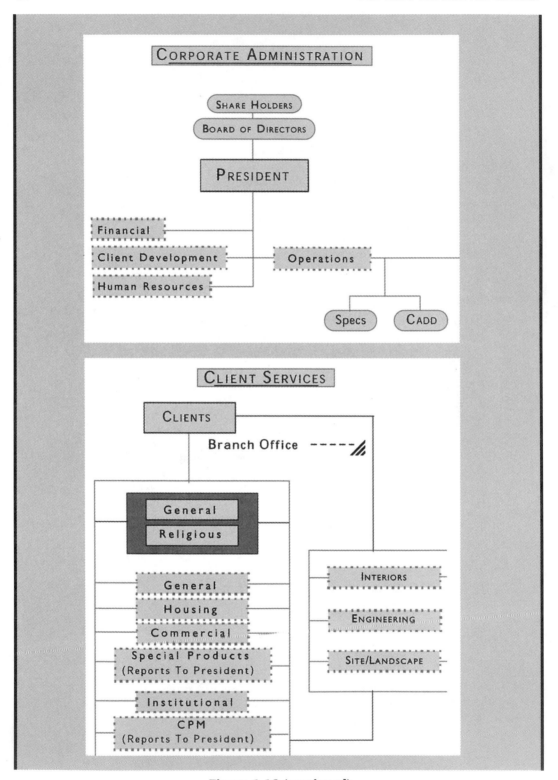

Figure 1-18 (continued)

SUCCESS CHALLENGES

1. Have you really focused on your own personal vision of what you want your company to be? If so, write it down now.
2. Are you communicating your vision to your staff, and do they really believe it?
3. Evaluate your marketing plan. Does it directly relate to fulfilling your vision?
4. Look at your financial plan. Are your ratio goals conservative? If so, raise them.
5. Draw a market-focused organizational plan for your company.
6. Does your human resources plan actually draw in high-caliber candidates? If not, why not?
7. Divide your staff into thirds—top, middle, and bottom. Of the top third, which individuals have leadership qualities?
8. Set a date for your annual strategic planning meeting and for the subsequent meeting.

REFERENCES

1. Tom Peters. Nightingale/Conant Sount Management Report, Vol.1. Chicago, Ill.
2. Information for this section taken from *PSMJ's Strategic Planning Manual*, ©1997.
3. *2000 A/E Financial Performance Survey,* PSMJ Resources, Inc., Newton, MA, ©2000, p. 44.
3. As reported in *PSMJ Best Practices*, July 2000, p. 5.

Chapter 2

Focusing
Your Practice

Professionals often hang out their shingle without clearly defining their purpose. Usually, their broad purpose is "to be an architect" or "to be an interior designer." Whether or not there is a need for the service in their community is not even considered. Expressing that need in terms of a specific market for a type of service is far from the minds of most architects and engineers starting a business. As a result, there is a pattern of small firms made up of design professionals who will perform any type of service for any client.

Yet, small firms that are consistently successful focus their practice on a few elemental services unique to their staff members, and they sell that focused service in the marketplace.

Consider why you are in business. To serve clients? To create monuments? To make money? To provide security for your family? All of these are significant and realistic goals for some design professionals—but they do not necessarily focus the practice.

The two ways to focus your practice are by project market or type and by service type. By and large, focusing on providing a service is the more profitable option. Firms marketing an element of their service (facilities planning, selecting art for hotel interiors, providing construction management services) tend to be significantly more profitable than those that sell design services for project types (hospitals, education facilities, etc.). According to historical data in PSMJ Resources' annual *A/E Financial Performance* surveys, specialty firms that focus on one client and project type are significantly more profitable.

The service focus is more profitable because your organization is able to learn much more effectively the language of a single type (or, at most, two or three types) of client. Every client group has jargon of its own. For example, in the health care marketplace, one encounters terms such as certificate of need (CON). If you are providing services in this market, you must be familiar with this document. Small

45

firms that provide a multitude of services to various markets are severely handicapped in communicating with the various types of clients in their own language, compared to the firm that lives, eats, and breathes in one or two markets.

By focusing on a service, you become an expert—for example, as a facilities management consulting firm to hospitals. Chapter 4 further explains the idea of focusing on a service.

ADVANTAGES OF FOCUSING THE PRACTICE

Many small-firm principals fear focusing, believing that if they focus on one client type their client base may shrink in a recession. (Review Figure 2-1 for insight on the benefits of focusing.) But firms that focus narrowly on a particular service are able to anticipate a recession better than other firms and, as a result, are able to move into new specialties faster, thereby avoiding economic downturn.

An example of a focus firm that has been in business for many years is Thomas Wirth Landscape Architects. Wirth focuses on the kinds of projects he most enjoys—small signatory gardens—and has become renowned at providing this service. A profile of this firm appears in Figure 2-2.

Some firms are able to focus in several areas by dividing into specialized teams. Companies of 30 or 40 can divide their resources into two or three teams, each focusing on a particular small market niche.

STEPS TO FOCUSING

Focus your practice by choosing a service at which you excel. Look not only at your skill but also at your credibility with clients. Compile the past accomplishments of all staff members in your service area; you may have everything you need in-house. Learn everything you possibly can about that service so that you can become an expert.

By focusing, you learn much more than your competitors about a particular market's needs, wants, and desires and, therefore, are perceived to be more valuable to the clients within that marketplace. By being perceived as the expert, you can charge higher fees, employ a much more directed staff, and more easily refuse to take on projects that do not fit the focus of your firm. The steps to focusing are:

The Basic Brilliance of Branding

"What's a brand? A singular idea or concept that you own inside the mind of the prospect. It's as simple and as difficult as that." Thus ends the 172 pages of wisdom contained in an excellent book, *The 22 Immutable Laws of Branding,* by Al and Laura Ries (HarperCollins, 1998).

The hundreds and thousands of hours you spend on marketing are completely wasted if a dedication to your brand isn't driving the process. Seeding the mind of clients and the marketplace at large with your brand identity must be the thrust of your marketing and business development activities. Consider these three examples of brand reinforcement:

1. A design firm known for excellent hospital design hires a former nurse to work full time reviewing all building plans and meeting with clients from the proposal stage through to completion.

2. A resort design firm sends a monthly newsletter to clients and potential clients that discusses not current projects but philosophies, tactics, and advice for running a great resort.

3. A Latin American architect imbues every world-class building he designs with the colors, spirit, and functional harmonies of his homeland.

These are all true cases of excellent branding being practiced by real people in our field. What are you doing today to focus your service and build your brand?

In response to this question, A/E/C principals often end up speaking about diversification. "We've diversified services to expand our presence in the marketplace, meet the needs of clients, and match the expanded offerings of competitors." If there is one thing that's proven to be true—and it's echoed in *The 22 Immutable Laws of Branding*—it's that diversification is always risky and usually disastrous. Here's why: Diversification dilutes your brand. If yours is the firm of choice for hospital design in your area, why venture into school design? This will no doubt cloud your name in the mind of clients and eventually erode market share.

Ask yourself, "What is my firm's brand?" Whatever the answer, hammer it home in everything you do and every decision you make. Grow your business not by service diversification but by geographical expansion. Take advantage of your brand in ways that support its long-term health and power.

Figure 2-1

Source: "The Basic Brilliance of Branding" by Frank Stasiowski, *PSMJ Best Practices,* August 2000.

1. Targeting clients, not projects
2. Networking
3. Exploding a niche
4. Employing usefulness selling
5. Learning to say *no*
6. Conducting meaningful marketing.

Each step is addressed in the sections that follow.

Profile of a Focused Firm

Firm: *Thomas Wirth Associates, Inc.*

Staff: *6–8*

Specialty: *Signatory residential and specialty gardens*

Address: *20 North Main Street*
                 Sherborn, Mass. 01770

Thomas Wirth's primary niche in the field of landscape architecture is custom residential site and landscape projects on which he works closely with owners, architects, and contractors. His firm also designs signatory specialty gardens—for example, a garden inside a school courtyard, a memorial garden, or a theme garden at a resort—forays into the commercial and institutional realm.

A boon to his success, he says, has been his appearance as the landscape architect for public television's "This Old House" and "The Victory Garden," and the writing of a book, *The Victory Garden Landscape Guide* (Little, Brown & Company, 1984). Wirth says the connection with the do-it-yourself home programs has given good exposure to the profession and the firm.

Wirth contends that, although he promotes limited commercial and institutional work, he is content with his own residential niche and considers it a fine art. Now two children have joined him and will move the firm into the next generation with the expectation of expanded opportunities.

Figure 2-2
Source: Thomas Wirth Associates. Used with permission.

Targeting Clients, Not Projects

Retaining a consistent workload means retaining repeat clients. Therefore, target clients, not projects. Many small firms move from project to project, never taking the time to get to know the client well. Instead, work hard to build client relationships. Identify clients' personal preferences and get to know each member of their staff. In working closely with a client, you should come to understand them so intimately that they end up telling you subconsciously what their needs are, thereby helping you to better market a new project.

Success in a small firm depends on repeat work from satisfied clients. Your ability to create ways to assure happy repeat clients of your choosing is crucial to your future success.

Repeat clients can be retained in several ways, three of which are illustrated below:

- One small firm in Hartford, Connecticut, returns to every project six months after construction completion to perform a postconstruction design critique free of charge to the client.

  ■ An engineering firm in the Midwest offers one day of free consulting to its top ten clients each year.
  ■ A West Coast architecture firm runs ads in San Francisco newspapers highlighting clients' projects and companies.

Any firm can afford to run ads, especially successful firms. For other suggestions on retaining clients, see Figure 2-3.

ADD, Inc., in Cambridge, Massachusetts, is a national architecture, interiors, and planning firm. Although it is not a small firm, the small-firm principal can learn from it. Most of ADD's business results from maintaining constant client contact. "There's no substitute for face-to-face networking," claims ADD president Wilson Pollock. "They'll never hire you if they don't see you."

One way Pollock maintains contact with clients is by sending them direct mail pieces three or four times a year. The mail piece might be a brochure or an announcement of an award. This serves to keep the firm's name in front of the client. "You've got to get in and nurse them and talk with their people," Pollock says. When clients recognize your name because you repeatedly have sent them information, your chances for a meeting are dramatically enhanced.

Suggestions for Retaining Clients

1. Always arrive at meetings ten minutes early.
2. Always call to confirm meetings.
3. Call current clients at a prescribed time each week (instead of waiting for them to call you).
4. Issue meeting minutes on the day of the meeting.
5. Never switch project managers on a client.
6. Anticipate problems and do the unexpected—such as introducing a client to a new lender when you know the client needs financing, even though you don't really provide such a service.
7. Be prepared with answers for all possible objections or questions.
8. Admit mistakes quickly and take decisive corrective action.
9. Follow up on all details of the project.
10. Take charge of key routine tasks, such as writing the agenda for your weekly client meeting and making the reservation for your client's flight to the job site.
11. Communicate consistently and regularly on project progress as related to client expectations.
12. Make your client representative look good in the eyes of his or her superiors.

Figure 2-3

Leverage Your Marketing into Strong Financial Results

Firm: *Tishman Construction Corporation*

Specialty: *Preconstruction, construction management, program management,*
                 consulting services

Address: *666 Fifth Avenue*
                 New York, NY 10103-0256
                 www.tishmanconstruction.com

Tishman Construction *isn't* a small operation, but its New England office director of business development, Scott Bates, takes ingenious, affordable approaches to networking that win him big jobs. The same techniques work well for small-firm practitioners.

Just five years out of his MBA program, Scott Bates, director of business development at Tishman Construction of New England, won the title of Marketing Executive of the Year (2000) from the Boston Chapter of the Society for Marketing Professional Services. How did he do it? For one thing, he manages $1 billion worth of projects, assisted only by his marketing coordinator. It also helps that Scott's found a way to sniff out opportunities sooner than his competitors and seal the deal.

Scott reports that construction work helped form the backbone of his marketing skill. "On my first internship, the principal told me, 'The best way to learn this industry is to work construction.' He helped me get a position in a large design/build firm. I was put in the field with laborers from all different backgrounds, doing all the grunt work. But in those six months, I learned how clients, architects, superintendents, project managers, and laborers all work together," Scott explains.

This insider's look has helped Scott hit the right buttons with business prospects and existing clients. He has parlayed his industry knowledge into big business opportunities for Tishman: "We like to get in early on a project, so I network with architects, engineers, geotech consultants, you name it. Even furniture suppliers. They know who is moving to another building. I know the brokers. They know who wants to buy a new piece of land. I stay aware of opportunities in my five areas.

"Say a hotel is thinking about adding a third floor. For me to get that knowledge early is critical. Then I can call and say, 'I understand you're contemplating a third-floor addition.' But once it gets in the news, everybody is calling. And, as the hotel owner, you don't know where to start. Getting in early is crucial because I can gain your trust and help you formulate your strategy."

A key element in this equation is the emotional one. Scott points out the importance of helping the owner without being threatening. You need to let the owner have the say. "A lot of it comes down to ego and personality. In business development, I have to find a client's motivations."

With projects like the Boston Convention and Exhibition Center, Terminal A at Logan Airport, and Foxwoods Casino and Resort under his belt, it's pretty clear Scott has a knack for doing that. His approach is to make the prospect feel comfortable and to communicate with the person in a comfortable way. Scott: "If I am meeting with a construction person, I will wear jeans, dress the way he does. And I will come with a superintendent, a guy who can share war stories with that person. If I am meeting with a CFO, I will match principal to principal. I will bring my boss."

Knowing who to go after is a crucial factor in the likelihood of Scott converting a business call into a contract. Tishman has created a strong brand image as an industry expert in five specific sectors, and Scott is always mindful of reinforcing that image.

"If you are working on a fabulous job, *now* is the time to market it, whether it's through advertising, PR, direct mail, or the Web," Scott told us. "At the Wang Center [in Boston], we had to replace the roof without damaging the ornamental ceiling just feet below. Nobody in the community would have known that unless we had done PR. I sent postcards, brought editors to the site.

"Also, in our brochure, you can see the markets we go after: public sector, hotels, historic preservation, college and university, and telecommunications. When I target companies, I call on these five markets only—where we have a track record. The key thing is that we don't take everything. We try to keep to our strengths, in our five markets, where we have people who can do the right work."

Aligning marketing efforts with the firm's strategic plans for business development and profitability has made it possible for Scott to make more strategic contacts of his own. "It's not about chasing projects but chasing clients," Scott says, when asked about how his role as marketer helps support Tishman's financial success, "Clients are long term."

"Recently, I met a facilities planner from Fidelity, got to know him at association events. We're on the same panels. These people know me as a colleague. I actually had them review my brochure. I'm not asking them for a job. It was nonthreatening. But I've formed a bond. And if there is a job tomorrow, I can call and say, 'Hey, John, I heard Fidelity will be putting up a new building in the suburbs.' And I already have the relationship."

Figure 2-4

Source: "Leverage Your Marketing into Strong Financial Results" *PSMJ Best Practices*, April 2000, p. 8.

Persistence is a virtue. Pollock cites a colleague who visited the Corps of Engineers' offices in Washington every three months for three years until he finally was given a design project.

Networking Small firms often do not command enough dollars of revenue to do marketing on the scale that a big firm can. What they know about is getting work from friends and contacts. Developing your networking skills replaces the need for big dollars spent on marketing. For a look at small-dollar networking tactics available to every firm, see Figure 2-4. Find out what resources are available to you in your locale and make contacts today.

1. *Community activities*—Small firms should become involved in community activities, specifically those that meet the needs of their clients. In addition to joining the local architects' society, become an associate member of a local association of clients, such as

developers, school officials, building managers, cler-
gymen, and garden clubs.

2. *Volunteer*—Don't simply join an association. Volunteer to work on a project unrelated to design services. Join a committee. Volunteer to run a program
for the group. Become visible.

3. *Teach*—Become an adjunct professor at a local college, serve as a speaker at various business functions, or hold your own seminars. Whatever the scenario, placing yourself in a teaching position gives
you instant credibility, a nonthreatening demeanor,
and ready accessibility to potential clients.

4. *Get published*—Cultivate your image to local newspaper staff and suggest or develop stories on issues
useful to your client group. If you are an expert and
you appear to speak that client group's language, you
will be more readily published. If you lack writing
skills, retain a writer to prepare the material. Do not
ignore journals that are read by your clients, as
opposed to architectural, interior design, or engineering professional magazines, which are more
commonly read by your peers.

Here are additional suggestions. Always be visible. Make
sure that whatever you do in the community makes you visible. For instance, if you volunteer to be a Cub Scout master,
make sure that newspaper announcements of your activities
not only mention that you are the scoutmaster but also that
you are the managing partner of ABC Associates, engineers
for the city's new wastewater treatment plant.

Network in the circles where your service is bought and
get to know as many clients as you can within that circle. This
technique will help you build a solid client base on which to
build working relationships. For example, a design firm specializing in hospital ancillary units in upstate New York
sought to open a branch office in Boston. It built a network by
assembling several administrators from area hospitals for a
roundtable discussion focusing on the needs of the hospital
community in the Boston area at that time. The firm's role
was to facilitate the discussion within a nonconfrontational,
nonsales environment. The objectives were to get to know the
Boston clients and to acquaint them with the firm, and the
effort was successful.

Successful entrepreneurs are classic networkers. They
enjoy meeting people in every social and economic circle.
They have the skill to introduce themselves in a way that is
nonthreatening and to be remembered as a valuable person
in the client's own marketplace.

Networkers are liked, and they like networking.

Exploding In the 2000s and beyond, thousands of small businesses will
a Niche develop by dealing with a specific portion of a larger project
or entity. An example is mission-critical work for the high-
tech industry. Rapid production of call centers of one million square feet requires a highly specialized team. Firms
providing such service have exploded a niche.

Find a narrow service sector in the architecture/engi-
neering marketplace, define it well, and explode that niche.
For example, you might narrow your service to selecting art
for resort properties. "How many resort properties are there
in Sioux City, Iowa, these days?" you may ask. Not many.
Becoming and billing yourself as the expert, however, will
attract developers building resorts in all parts of the country
and abroad.

The driving force behind entrepreneurship is the ability
to control your destiny. One aspect of this is to have one's
own business. People want to reduce their overhead, control
a much smaller amount of work, and do work that nobody
else is doing. In essence, they want to become experts serving a small niche. Today, with the introduction of strategic
alliances in the A/E/C marketplace, this specialization can
be more profitable than you imagined. Teaming with a firm
in another location or with a firm that provides complementary services to yours can open doors once closed to narrowly
focused small-firm practitioners.

Strategic alliances also offer the benefit of access to a
large workforce when necessary—taking the concept of
smaller full-time staffs and access to plentiful, skilled part-
time workers and independent contractors further than it's
ever been taken. Keeping a small number of full-time staffers and relying on part-timers or contractors to fill in the
gaps has economic benefits. See Figure 2-5 for a simple
profit–loss statement showing the difference between
having more versus fewer people on staff.

Steps to Selecting To select a niche, look for places where there is either a lack
a Niche of service or service that is being provided free. Here is a list
of recent and promising niches:

- Mission-critical facilities for high-tech firms
- Bridge renovation
- Environmental waste cleanup
- Power engineering
- Trophy houses

An example of how zoning and other municipal-related
activities became a niche for one West Coast firm involved
virtual operation of a municipality's entire zoning depart
ment. This relieved the community of a tax burden, because
there was less staff, and the zoning function was performed

Independent Contractors versus Full-Time Staff

	Annual Full-Time Costs, 10 People Full Time	Annual Costs (5 People Full Time, 5 on Call @ 50% Utilization)
Direct salary	$400,000	$200,000
Fringe benefits @ 30%	120,000	60,000
Lost time, 10%*	40,000	20,000
Total Cost	$560,000	$480,000
Savings		$ 80,000

*Due to social interaction of lunch, coffee breaks, office parties, and so on.

Figure 2-5

more expeditiously, because this arrangement eliminated the political bureaucracy that surrounded previous zoning department operations.

Areas of Service Today, a consumer can walk into any computer superstore and buy a CD that helps her design her dream home. The plans can be used by a contractor to construct the house. What's the big sales pitch for these products? Don't waste your money on a designer—we've got everything you need for just $69.99.

If you're a small residential design practitioner who has traditionally made money drawing plans for custom-designed homes, such CDs don't conjure up good feelings. Like it or not, this technology is the competition for the services you've been providing. Similarly, if you serve commercial customers, you now face formidable opposition from CADD shops in low-price labor corners of the world like India and Mexico.

Dwindling Design Budgets In the diagram labeled "Four Phases of a Project" in Figure 2-6, the second project phase is Design—and it's a revenue stream that is decreasing extremely fast relative to the length of time the A/E/C industry has been in existence. Technology is taking over drawing production. Clients know this. They aren't willing to pay top dollar—or wait around—for drawings. Good, fast, error-free design is expected of every firm. If this is the main service you provide, look

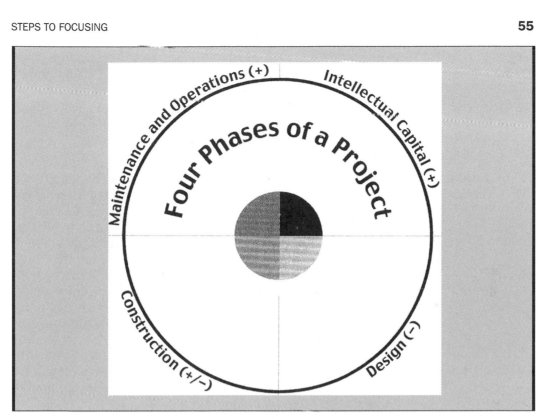

Figure 2-6

around. You're smack dab in the middle of a commodity marketplace.

Have you considered shifting your focus to the two more promising and profitable phases of a project: provision of intellectual capital and maintenance and operations?

Intellectual Capital for Sale It's time to start charging for the project analysis, feasibility studies, and scope of services work you perform free for the opportunity to do drawings for a client. Your clients have selected you precisely because of the smarts and skills you bring to the table. Your keen up-front work relates directly to low life-cycle building costs and reasonable maintenance and operations budgets. Get paid for this intelligence! Some A/E/C firms have created consulting branches and planning departments that provide these services and make money billing clients for them.

Maintenance and Operations Means Money The same thing that's putting your design services to rest is opening up huge opportunities in maintenance and operations. Thank technology for thrusting maintenance and operations (M&O) into the hands of the highly educated knowledge workers needed to run complex building systems. These are systems that you design and know how to operate. Why aren't you providing M&O services for the life cycle of the very buildings you've helped create? Clients are begging for this service. Translation: Go to M&O to find the money.

Construction Holds Steady The only project phase relatively unchanged despite the evolution of the A/E/C marketplace is construction. It still takes building crews, machines, and materials to create a structure. Barring robotic construction workers, profitability and costs of construction will remain relatively stable.

The most successful firm—small or large—in the 2000s is the one that provides all four project phase services to its clients and makes sure clients know that these four phases are available. The provision of these services may be achieved through partnerships or alliances, but a one-stop provider gains the competitive edge. And the savvy provider—milking its intellectual capital and seizing opportunities to supply M&O services—cashes in on the business.

Figure 2-7 gives a detailed list of services design professionals can offer clients.

Usefulness Selling Meeting in a nonpressure environment, or usefulness selling, is a valuable way to target and retain repeat clients. One means to do this is to use newsletters and magazines to promote recognition of your firm's name (see Figure 2-8). An example newsletter used to attract business is featured in Figure 2-9.

Another method is to develop dictionaries for your client. The dictionaries can contain architectural, electrical, mechanical, plumbing, and other terms, with your firm's name and logo on the cover. This is a form of promotion developed by Stanley Engineers.

Yet another method is to produce a textbook or history book containing examples of how your firm helped in your community. For example, a Bloomington, Minnesota, architectural firm published a town history. The book, which also happens to span the company's 100 years of existence, actually captures the history of the whole area and has become a popular history text in the community.

Two decades ago, Howard, Needles, Tammend & Bergendoff (HNTB), located in Kansas City, Missouri, introduced itself to the hospital marketplace by starting a newsletter, *Facilities Decisions,* on how to run a hospital more effectively. The newsletter provided useful information—tips, techniques, processes—valuable to hospital administrators. Prompted by then–marketing director Frank Zilm,

List of Services to Provide

Upfront Services

■ Preproject approval processes: zoning, permits, conceptualizing, traffic studies, feasibility studies, marketing studies, cost studies
■ Health care planning
■ Program planning
■ Environmental impact studies
■ Market analyses
■ Construction cost studies
■ Circulation/traffic studies

Project Services

■ Facilities management
■ Financial planning
■ Securing finances
■ Construction management
■ Drafting services

Postproject Services

■ Construction administration
■ Materials handling and processing
■ Scheduling
■ Budgeting
■ Quality control on the job site
■ Value engineering programs

Figure 2-7

HNTB started mailing the newsletter to hospital administrators, none of whom knew the firm but many of whom liked the newsletter. It was produced for two years. The firm laid the groundwork for making contacts in the hospital market with a usefulness selling technique—the newsletter—making the firm appear as informed about the hospital marketplace as any of its competitors.

Zilm created a demand for HNTB through the newsletter. As a result of publishing it, the company was able to attract clients and create its own niche in the market. The concept is *pull-through marketing,* which means you create demand and you pull the market through to you. Usefulness selling and pull-through demand techniques are not expensive. Such techniques allow the small firm to enter a market without spending a great deal of money on elaborate programs and media. Usefulness selling—in particular, the newsletter—is a cost-effective way to spread market awareness of your talent.

Usefulness Selling with a Newsletter

Firm Name: **Jack Johnson Company**

Staff: **70–75**

Specialty: **Resort design for all seasons**

Address: **1777 Sun Peak Drive**
                    Park City, Utah 84098

With the advent of the year 2000 and Jack Johnson Company's 25th anniversary, the firm reintroduced a monthly newsletter. Unlike in years past, this newsletter included trends and issues that affect the resort and recreational environments. Rather than highlight their company's projects and successes, the newsletter focused on issues that would affect and benefit their clients.

Resort Design Oracle was chosen as the name because it represented Jack Johnson Company's specialty the significance of an oracle—a counsel or authority that foresees the future. The newsletter circulates monthly and has positioned the firm as an expert in resort design. The company expected to see results in a year after its first publication; however, the feedback and response was immediate and the newsletter has proven one of the most effective methods of marketing.

The *Oracle* is sent out free to recreational, community, and resort developers as well as consultants. It is mailed first class and is packaged unfolded in a large envelope; this differentiates the *Oracle* from other forms of mail. The layout is a simple four-page news-letter, which includes a table of contents, the *Oracle*'s mission, two main articles, and three sidebars with articles. (See Figure 2-9.)

Figure 2-8

Source: The Jack Johnson Company. Used with permission.

In other words, provide something useful to your clients that also gives you marketing credibility.

To build a usefulness selling campaign in a small firm, consider what your clients do both during and outside working hours. Hospital administrators do not think so much about hiring architects or engineers as they do about how to manage a facility, pay doctors, run the parking lot, and compensate the nursing staff. Here, then, is how you can develop a usefulness selling campaign for your company:

1. After two hours of brainstorming, compile a list of the facts your clients might be interested in learning.
2. Rank that list. Organize the items from top to bottom in terms of what is important to your clients.
3. Collect data from the library and other sources.
4. Communicate those data. Create a newsletter, or simply copy an article and send it with your business card to a group of clients in your marketplace. Limit the group to 50; it would be hard to keep track of more.

(text continues on page 63)

Figure 2-9. The Jack Johnson Company newsletter.
Source: The Jack Johnson Company. Used with permission

resort design

ORACLE

A RECIPE FOR THE
FUTURE

- **Broaden demographics**: listen to the needs and wants of the youth (10-20) and women.
- **Integrate with nature**: environmental sensitivity is key.
- **Challenge the lure of the armchair**: the North American culture is a vicarious culture. It is imperative to understand the mystique of the couch potato and then challenge the phenomenon.
- **Be ADD rich**: the American advertisers embrace ADD (Attention Deficit Disorder). The average person is bombarded by so many competing, attention-grabbing alternatives that the natural response is to filter and block.
- **Ease of use**: implement simplicity of layout and options.
- We are all in the entertainment business.
- **Traditions**: adhere to existing ones; formulate new ones.
- **Romance**: make it intimate, warm and amenity rich.
- **Reduce the hassle factor**: make circulation free flowing and have great signage!
- Build facilities that complement the experience.
- Build-in the long-term right to exist.
- Imbed the feeling and ambiance into the "corporate"/ vacationer and/or community culture.
- Align with other businesses.
- **Find/train leaders** who are agents of change and innovation.
- Recognize the importance of long-term profitability and how to maintain a steady upward curve.
- **Silence is deadly**: hearing nothing from the visitor, employee or owner is more frightening than receiving complaints...silence = indifference.

TAKE THE PLUNGE Looking at the list, it makes sense. What is stopping those who aren't making it? The next step is to take the idea and transform it into tangibles. Throughout 2001, the *Oracle* will closely inspect, research and try to explain the process of implementation for the above thoughts. The ideas are abundant but the next step is crucial. Who will wear the shoes and who will stumble over the shoelaces? ☐

What is the Competition?
THE LAST ARTICLE IN A FOUR-PART SERIES

August's headline read "Skiing: Is it withering away?;" September offered a glimpse into the mind of a new skier in "Welcome to Never-Ever Land"; and October brought skiing and golf into the ring with →

MOUNTAINS OF DISTINCTION
An impressive example of an alliance in the ski industry is "Mountains of Distinction." The "Oracle" recently spoke with Brian Fairbank of Jiminy Peak to learn more about this resort collaborative:

What is Mountains of Distinction?
Mountains of Distinction is a group of 8 Northeastern ski operators that meet to put their ideas, strategies and information about their areas and the ski industry on the table. We collaborate, share information, look for ways to create marketing synergies and buying power.

Why did you begin Mountains of Distinction?
We created this group to assist in cost savings and to share information. Four years ago ASC (American Skiing Company) and Intrawest came to the east and began to acquire several resorts. We realized that for a small to medium sized ski area to survive it might need to work with others.

What do bigger corporations have that small/ medium size areas don't?
First of all, ASC and Intrawest have buying power. This implies that they have the ability to get sponsorship dollars to defray the marketing costs. Coca Cola or other corporations sponsor their area to increase their market share, thus cushioning the marketing costs that would be necessary to run a large-scale ski area. Secondly, large areas can afford to have value added discount packages. Because they have 5-10 resorts, they can share the dollars across the board. Another aspect is that they have management synergies. What is meant by this is, for example, they can create complex software packages for rentals or ticketing and share the cost among the resorts. Basically, the development costs are spread across the board.

Figure 2-9 (continued)

"Let's get ready to rumble…" It is difficult to summarize in four articles the ideas, thoughts, examples and ways to increase annual visits, retain skiers and basically transform a stagnant industry. Therefore, this last article, by no means, is meant as the entire solution. It is yet another way to think outside of the box, to begin to change old and fixated habits, and to possibly see things in a different light.

THE WORDS | In a recent article the following was suggested: "While the [NSAA] Model was developed initially to be used at the national level, it works best when applied to a region or individual resort. If the ski industry is to break out of the past and reinvigorate itself, *our best hope lies in the capacity of individual resorts to work in their own self interest,* concentrating their efforts to introduce a slightly higher number of people to snow each year and, more importantly, to ensure that beginners' initial experiences are the best the resort can provide."[1] (Emphasis ours)

THE ISSUE | As stated in the above quote: *Our best hope lies in the capacity of individual resorts to work in their own self interest.* This statement is wherein the problem lies. What happens is that the resorts are pitting themselves against one another instead of against other tourist attractions. The demise of the industry will be individual resorts looking out for number one. ASC, Vail Associates and Intrawest could possibly look out for themselves and do fine. However, small resorts will be impacted the most from this type of mind-set.

MODEL GOALS | The main objectives are: introduce more people to the sport and improve the beginners' initial experience. How can each resort only think on a micro-level without considering the impact that other areas may have?

DAY'S DEMAND | Let's say Joe Skier and Sally Snowboarder visit a local area. Neither have ever skied or boarded. They arrive at a small resort and are shuffled through the process. The day has its moments of enjoyment but all in all it is a day to forget rather than remember. This experience has impacted the industry as a whole. No matter how miniscule it may be, this experience took away another potential skier from the market and could affect other potential never-evers because of the impact that "word-of-mouth" marketing has upon the consumer.

BRAND LOYALTY? | Brand loyalty does exist in the skier market, but as far as vacation visits go, the loyalty tends to dissipate. One skiing family may go to Aspen one season, Killington the next and Tahoe the year after. If one resort experience leaves a sour taste the family may look to other entertainment/recreational markets to spend their vacation dollars. Another aspect to consider is the rise of timeshares in ski resorts. This market promotes trading. The brand loyalty resides in the product not the destination. →

MOUNTAINS OF DISTINCTION *CONTINUED*

What is the biggest frustration in creating an alliance?
The biggest frustration we have encountered is actually the toughest for our coordinator. She schedules our meetings and organizes the information. The issue she faces is how do you get independent areas to respond when they are not bound to her or each other?

What benefits are you reaping from this alliance?
Let me say that Mountains of Distinction is not paying the bills, but we have positioned ourselves as the "good guys" of the industry. One of our members who recently joined the group is a mid-west operator. He already has expressed that the information shared regarding their skiing programs has revamped and improved his program 10-fold.

Mountains of Distinction is an excellent example of the latest in business trends: CEO Networking. This forum of minds and battle scars provides the opportunity to share and discover new ideas for companies and products. It's similar to a peer group, but with a strategic business flair. Alliances are not the final answer, but they are a beginning, especially for small to mid-size businesses trying to survive in the age of the mega-merging corporation.

A Special Thanks to Brian Fairbank for interviewing with the *Oracle.* Brian is the CEO of Jiminy Peak located in Massachusetts. He is Chairman of NSAA and was a driving force in creating Mountains of Distinction.

Figure 2-9 (continued)

resort design
ORACLE

A MARRIAGE During the 1999-2000 ski season, Brighton ski area used the following slogan for one of their ad campaigns: "This is Utah. Why be wedded to one resort?" This campaign verbalizes brand loyalty issues beautifully - why only visit one resort? Every other facet of entertainment and recreation offers a plethora of options. Why should a skier be committed to just one ski area?

BRAND LOYALTY? It should be realized that unless lifestyle or real estate is involved, most people and families will tend to try different areas. The concern is that the ski industry and the Model are both trying to gain a market share of a constant population rather than spending effort to attract new people away from other forms of recreation. Cruise lines, overseas vacations, Las Vegas, pro athletics, amusement parks, golf, national park visits, movies...this is the competition. Resorts compete, not just with other resorts, but with other industries.

WHAT IS AN ALLIANCE? An alliance is joining together to get more visits, to share successes and failures, to understand the needs of the customer and to increase the bottom line. Of course, the competitive spirit cannot be erased, but the focus can't be on each other. An alliance is a bond or connection between families, states, parties, or individuals and this association is utilized to further the common interests of its members.

PRO-ALLIANCE An alliance does not imply that every resort has to share skier visit dollars. What could be shared is the cost of marketing, training, business strategies and ideas. It can be regional, national or international. The point is: why knock heads when several areas can come together and step up the quality of service, the initial experience of the beginner and the development of incentives that retain the current population of skiers.

HEALTHY COMPETITION Of course resorts will continue to compete to attract the skier; that is the nature of business. But the main race to win is the competition for vacation dollars. Strategize, join forces, adapt to and change the market needs and push the industry back up to the top rung of the recreation ladder. ▯

[1] Rosall, Nolan. "NSAA Model for Growth: The Next Steps." *NSAA Journal.* Oct/Nov 2000. 7.

JACK'S AUGURY

The designer and developer are very similar creatures. Both want the project to be beautiful, flow, complement the environment and be timeless. However, the initial crush often turns to a passionate affair of love and hate. Meaning that money becomes the focus and future envisioning fades.

Money is an issue in all projects and in every type of business. The bottom line provides a gateway to the next venture. However, visions of dollars can take away from the sustainability of a project. Will the business still thrive in ten, twenty or possibly 100 years? The right-to-last is difficult in a culture that is constantly changing. Thus, timeless design is essential for a project to live past a decade without showing telltale signs of a soon to be forgotten destination.

Can we vision for success and cause change with design? The objective of the developer and designer is to please their customer. But as deadlines approach and the business is personalized the future outlook can diminish. The goal of any business is profit. With this as a constant factor, the future's framework shrinks to achieve financial milestones. When the focus shifts to numbers the longevity of a project diminishes.

The industry that we are in is amazing. We create incredible products that enrich people's lives and we design lifestyles. Understanding the place in which we work, it is imperative to look past the numbers, simply go with our intuition, and ensure our legacy.

Jack Johnson, President & Founder
JACK JOHNSON COMPANY

The monthly advisor for the resort industry

Figure 2-9 (continued)

WEB WISE

A company Web site is a relatively inexpensive market-ing tool. The word *relatively* is used for this reason: The image and information a site can convey about your company are much larger than the cost of developing it. Here are eight undeniable benefits of a Web site:

1. Establish a presence
You want to be part of the high-demographic, multi-million-member online community. You know that your competitors are out there; you should be, too.

2. Network
A huge part of doing business is simply connecting with other people. On the Web, you do this 24 hours a day, every day. It's inexpensive and effortless.

3. Answer frequently asked questions
Post customer questions and your answers on the Web site, and you will remove another barrier to doing busi-ness with your firm.

4. Break into international markets
You can open an international business dialog as easily as you can meet with a company across the street.

5. Create 24-hour service
Your Web site serves visitors at all hours, seven days a week. You can collect their requests and give responses at the start of your business day.

6. Change information lightning fast
You can change your Web site information as frequently as necessary. In fact, you can even use a database to customize a page's output as many times a day as desired.

7. Encourage feedback from your clients
If your direct marketing isn't paying off, find out why. Use your Web site to solicit feedback from current and future customers by using an e-mail response mecha-nism.

8. Reach the media
The media is a wired profession. Online press kits are common, and you should have one. Here's why it makes sense: Digital images can be posted without traditional stripping and shooting, and digital text can be edited and output on tight deadlines.

---

5. Do this about every two months. Then, when you decide to call a client prospect, he or she will already be familiar with you and your services.

Learning to Say No   Another aspect of focusing your practice is knowing when to reject an opportunity. Many design firms accept any work. While often done out of a need to be practical, this ten-dency will dilute the focus of your company and your ability to achieve your vision. By designing too many different pro-jects for too many varied markets, you spend your most valuable resources, especially time, in areas where you prob-ably should not be. Concentrate instead on areas where you will be most productive. Learn to say no so you can focus on what will get you the biggest return for your input.

Figure 2-10 presents the philosophy used by the firm of Backen, Arrigoni, and Ross, which never became really suc-cessful or distinctive until it began to discriminate between projects it would do and those it rejected.

Positive Ways to Say No   You must discipline yourself and your firm into saying *no* to clients that either do not appreciate your efforts or fail to match your firm's profile of desired clients. But there is a right way and a wrong way to do this, and you want to choose the right way because a client may have a project in the future that is appropriate for your company. Remember,

Being Selective

Firm: **BAR Architects**

Address: **1660 Bush Street**
                 San Francisco, Calif. 94109
                 www.bararch.com

When a client requests a price quote for architectural services, BAR applies a go/no-go policy to determine whether or not to do the project. The principals of the firm analyze the project carefully and base decisions on tangible reasons and criteria. Does the project have financing? Is the project in our niche market? Does the client have a history of paying on time? Does the firm have the people available to do the work?

For reasons of economics, design focus, and lack of potential for repeat work, some projects are not worth accepting, says managing principal James Mitchell, and, if the firm agrees to do such projects, heavy restrictions are built into the contract. For example, the firm decided to plan for an orderly retreat from the condominium market due to its high liability. When the firm takes on a condominium project now, the client must meet the following criteria:

1. The client must be substantial enough to pay for the project.
2. The client must be familiar with the condominium development process.
3. The client must understand the risks involved with developing condominiums.
4. The client must pay a fee sufficient to produce a first-quality design as well as quality construction documents.
5. The client must grant the firm veto power over the contractor.

Another way of controlling the project is to set added limitations on liability. In some cases, BAR produces only the design for a project, not the working drawings.

Size is another criterion. For example, unless a small project has some interesting characteristics—that is, it is a challenging architectural problem, or the client may provide more, larger projects in the future—it may be turned down.

When possible, it is preferable to go for fewer larger projects than many small ones. Small projects generate too many bills, invoices, and subcontracts for their size. It costs almost as much in overhead to do a small project as a medium-sized one.

BAR investigates a client by talking with previously retained architects, asking about past payment practices, working relationships during a project, change order frequency, and possibility for future work. If the principals of BAR decide to say no they give a diplomatic "We're too busy."

Selectiveness helps in getting good projects, good clients, and good fees, as the following experience demonstrates. BAR once spent three weeks negotiating with a repeat client, a local university. In negotiating a $600,000 contract, the firm and the university had a $20,000 difference. When the client's negotiator said the client was not willing to pay the $20,000 difference, the firm suggested handing the job to another architect. (BAR had already started work on a fee basis.) The university backed down and agreed to the difference. As Mitchell says, "That was the amount we needed to do the good job they wanted, and we weren't willing to do a not-so good job."

Many firms concede that the least successful jobs are the ones taken at too low a fee. In such cases, the client is often inexperienced at construction and does not realize that the money he pays now will save money later.

Figure 2-10
Source: BAR Architects. Used with permission

cater to clients, not projects. Here are three ways to say *no* positively:

1. *Referrals*—Refer clients to other firms, then follow up to find out if a good job was done. The client will be surprised by your care in following up on a referral. You may give away a project, but you will keep the client.
2. *Increase the fee*—Say *yes*, but raise your price. By raising your price, you either price yourself out of the market for a particular client or, if you do get the job, at least you will make a good profit. This also establishes a higher price scale if the client comes back to you later.
3. *Delay the project*—Quote a higher price and say you won't start it until six months from now, or until you have enough staff free to perform the job.

In the three suggestions above, you are not saying *no*; you are saying *yes, but....* This is much more positive than just saying *no*. Remember, your primary goal is to target clients, not projects, and this is a way to keep the clients.

Saying *no* will:

■ Give you confidence that you have the ability to survive without having to accept every project.
■ Show your staff that you have the ability to be strong and that you are committed to your vision.
■ Save you from wasting your time and energies on work you probably shouldn't be doing.
■ Provide a more structured setting in which to plan moves needed to stay successful.

Think of the positive impact that saying *no* to a few clients will have on your best clients, your staff, and your own well-being. If you feel you must take a project because you have no work, then you are not successful. Revise your planning, marketing, and networking efforts so you will never be in this position. Figure 2-11 contains questions involved in a go/no-go decision, as well as a go/no-go criteria worksheet.

Meaningful Marketing Small firms often have neither the time nor the resources to do extensive market research, which includes researching a market, defining its boundaries, assessing the competition, and developing a strategic plan of attack. Most small firms have primitive marketing plans that emphasize networking. Yet the arguments for a structured marketing effort are powerful:

Questions to Ask When Facing a Go/No-Go Decision

1. How deep is the client's commitment?
2. What are the client's perceived as well as actual needs?
3. Does the client's available budget match its needs?
4. How much personal contact have you had with this client?
5. Who are the real decision makers?
6. Who are your competitors?
7. Do you have the commitment to win?
8. Are key members of your team available?
9. Will all efforts be enough?
10. Do you have relevant experience?
11. Do you have a sales plan?
12. Could you hire a consultant to do joint ventures?
13. Do you believe you are the logical winner of this project?

Go/No-Go Criteria

	CRITERIA	YES/NO	COMMENT
1.	Requirement — is it real?	Y / N	
2.	Funds — are they available?	Y / N	
3.	Is client using a consultant?	Y / N	
4.	Do we have enough technical know-how?	Y / N	
5.	Have we had prior contact with client?	Y / N	
6.	Can we commit maximum effort to the job?	Y / N	
7.	Do we have the staffpower to do the job?	Y / N	
8.	Do we believe we are the logical winner?	Y / N	

Figure 2-11

1. Marketing forces your firm to stay aware of developing client expectations. No market is constant or static. You need to anticipate and adapt to changes.
2. Marketing can create a higher demand for services, which allows you to charge higher prices for the same effort. The result is higher profits on the same work.
3. New opportunities appear when you are in touch with the marketplace. (*Example:* One architectural firm developed a profitable graphics service department after identifying the needs of developers during a marketing campaign.)
4. Marketing moves you close to the client community and allows you to become more intimate with the language of the client. It positions you in the client prospect's mind whenever that client needs help.

Consider the statistics in Figure 2-12 from PSMJ Resources' *2000 A/E Financial Performance Survey* on what percentage of gross and net revenues firms spent on marketing. The chart shows statistics for firms with and without full-time marketers.

Seminars, Publications, Surveys Once you have identified a niche, you need meaningful marketing tools. As a small firm, you need imaginative ideas rather than traditional expensive tools. Do something different to show that you have knowledge in the niche. For instance, hold a seminar for potential clients and charge for attendance.

Publish a book on the subject. Gather your notes, supplement them with real-life project examples, and type or dictate into a cassette tape recorder. Contact a publisher for guidelines on submitting a viable book proposal. Send your proposal around to well-known technical book publishers. (Obtain a list of design and construction publishers from *Books in Print* or *Literary Marketplace*, available at most local libraries.) Then hire a writer to transform this information into a manuscript. Chances are you will not make a lot of money from the book sales, but the approach is a way to become known as the authority in your niche area.

Perform client surveys. Focus on your client group and perform surveys on information that other professionals in their field want to know about each other. One Texas firm surveyed 130 branch banks to uncover energy-efficient methods that save on air-conditioning costs. A St. Louis interior designer annually assesses capital spending plans of the top 100 corporations in Missouri. Client prospects will

(text continues on page 71)

Marketing Costs Comparison (Gross Revenues)

	Total Marketing Costs as a Percentage of Gross Revenues (with Marketers)		Total Marketing Costs as a Percentage of Gross Revenues (without Marketers)	
	Median	Mean	Median	Mean
Overall	4.3%	4.8%	1.0%	2.0%
Staff Size 1 to 10	4.3	4.3	1.0	3.0
Staff Size 11 to 15	NR	NR	0.3	1.5
Staff Size 16 to 25	5.2	5.2	0.5	0.5
Staff Size 26 to 50	3.3	5.3	1.3	2.1
Staff Size 51 to 100	3.8	5.6	1.6	2.2
Staff Size 101 to 200	4.3	3.9	4.8	4.8
Staff Size 201 to 350	4.5	4.7	0.5	0.5
Staff Size 351 to 500	6.0	5.6	NR	NR
Staff Size over 500	5.0	4.2	3.7	3.7
Architectural	3.6	7.3	1.0	1.8
Architectural/Interiors	4.3	4.2	6.1	6.1
Engineering (Prime)	5.0	4.6	0.8	2.1
Engineering (Subconsultant)	3.9	4.8	1.2	1.5
Engineering (Survey)	1.7	1.8	NR	NR
A/E	5.9	5.5	0.9	0.9
A/E/P/I	3.9	4.3	1.6	1.6
All U. S.	5.3	5.4	1.0	1.7
Northeast	3.9	4.4	1.0	0.8
South	4.2	4.1	0.8	0.8
Midwest	3.3	5.6	0.6	0.8
Southwest	1.7	1.7	0.0	0.0
Mountain	4.6	5.0	0.7	0.7
West	3.9	4.0	1.6	3.1
Canada	2.5	2.9	NR	NR
Private	4.3	5.7	0.7	1.5
Government	3.9	4.2	1.3	2.0
Mixed	4.5	4.1	1.1	3.7
Transportation	5.0	4.6	2.4	2.4
Government (Buildings)	3.6	8.5	1.3	2.0
Environmental	6.8	6.8	3.7	5.5
Commercial (Users)	5.7	6.7	3.8	3.8
Commercial (Developers)	2.7	2.6	0.5	0.7
Housing	3.0	3.0	0.6	1.8
Health Care	2.6	2.8	3.8	3.8
No Specialty	4.4	4.4	0.7	1.3

Figure 2-12

Marketing Costs Comparison (Net Revenues)

	Total Marketing Costs as a Percentage of Net Revenues (with Marketers)		Total Marketing Costs as a Percentage of Net Revenues (without Marketers)	
	Median	Mean	Median	Mean
Overall	6.1%	6.3%	1.2%	2.6%
Staff Size 1 to 10	5.7	5.7	1.6	3.9
Staff Size 11 to 15	NR	NR	0.4	2.2
Staff Size 16 to 25	6.8	6.8	0.5	0.6
Staff Size 26 to 50	5.2	6.5	1.4	2.8
Staff Size 51 to 100	6.2	7.6	2.0	2.6
Staff Size 101 to 200	5.8	5.1	5.4	5.4
Staff Size 201 to 350	5.2	6.0	0.6	0.6
Staff Size 351 to 500	7.3	6.9	NR	NR
Staff Size over 500	6.4	5.8	5.8	5.8
Architectural	6.2	10.7	1.5	2.9
Architectural/Interiors	6.1	6.4	8.1	8.1
Engineering (Prime)	6.1	5.8	0.8	2.6
Engineering (Subconsultant)	4.8	5.5	1.2	1.7
Engineering (Survey)	1.8	1.9	NR	NR
A/E	6.7	7.0	1.1	1.1
A/E/P/I	5.8	5.7	2.0	2.0
All U. S.	7.4	7.5	1.1	2.2
Northeast	6.2	5.8	1.5	1.2
South	5.3	5.0	1.0	1.0
Midwest	5.2	7.4	0.7	1.0
Southwest	2.1	2.1	0.0	0.0
Mountain	5.5	6.4	0.7	0.7
West	4.8	5.4	2.3	4.5
Canada	3.1	3.3	NR	NR
Private	6.1	7.4	0.8	1.9
Government	6.0	5.8	1.8	2.9
Mixed	6.2	5.3	1.1	4.2
Transportation	6.2	5.7	2.7	2.7
Government (Buildings)	5.6	11.9	2.0	2.9
Environmental	10.3	9.1	5.8	6.8
Commercial (Users)	6.4	7.5	4.9	4.9
Commercial (Developers)	3.3	3.0	0.8	0.8
Housing	3.5	3.5	1.1	2.5
Health Care	2.9	4.1	5.9	5.9
No Specialty	6.2	5.7	1.0	1.5

Figure 2-12 (continued)

Labor as a Percentage of Total Marketing Costs

	Labor as a Percentage of Total Marketing Costs (with Marketers)		Labor as a Percentage of Total Marketing Costs (without Marketers)	
	Median	Mean	Median	Mean
Overall	68.4%	63.6%	0.0%	26.2%
Staff Size 1 to 10	71.4	71.4	0.0	12.9
Staff Size 11 to 15	NR	NR	0.0	18.7
Staff Size 16 to 25	83.8	83.8	0.0	4.4
Staff Size 26 to 50	69.2	58.8	0.0	27.6
Staff Size 51 to 100	62.1	58.7	68.0	49.6
Staff Size 101 to 200	71.1	67.6	81.3	81.3
Staff Size 201 to 350	71.1	70.2	0.0	0.0
Staff Size 351 to 500	72.8	74.0	NR	NR
Staff Size over 500	63.6	61.9	100.0	100.0
Architectural	69.9	65.1	0.0	21.8
Architectural/Interiors	60.9	59.5	25.6	23.1
Engineering (Prime)	72.9	65.5	0.0	25.7
Engineering (Subconsultant)	77.5	71.1	26.7	35.1
Engineering (Survey)	38.3	41.5	NR	NR
A/E	65.1	64.1	0.0	17.9
A/E/P/I	61.9	58.6	56.9	56.9
All U. S.	62.3	64.0	71.4	57.5
Northeast	80.2	80.1	0.0	0.0
South	71.1	63.8	0.0	0.0
Midwest	57.7	54.2	0.0	5.0
Southwest	32.2	32.2	0.0	0.0
Mountain	83.3	81.1	13.3	13.3
West	73.5	66.1	13.0	32.1
Canada	66.4	69.3	NR	NR
Private	68.3	66.7	0.0	20.3
Government	66.9	61.2	0.0	31.7
Mixed	70.6	61.8	0.0	31.0
Transportation	25.4	38.3	40.6	40.6
Government (Buildings)	68.3	59.5	25.2	36.5
Environmental	71.0	72.2	77.8	59.3
Commercial (Users)	63.7	56.9	21.8	21.8
Commercial (Developers)	77.6	62.6	26.7	38.1
Housing	70.4	70.4	0.0	6.4
Health Care	51.3	61.4	24.7	24.7
No Specialty	68.8	68.1	0.0	13.5

Figure 2-12 (continued)

begin to call you for advice on how to interpret the data, which establishes you as the expert and, when the time comes, the firm of first choice.

Publish a newsletter. Develop a focused newsletter with informational data. Although you are a design professional and not a publisher, you can hire publishing or marketing consultants to produce a professional-looking product. The newsletter is a good way to establish credibility, and expert information is usually readily available at your local library or from other sources such as client periodicals, consultants, actual project histories, past clients, and so forth. See also the section called "Usefulness Selling" (earlier in this chapter) for advice and examples on how publishing a newsletter can enhance your image. Figure 2-13 lists the features of an effective newsletter.

When to Hire a Small firms generally hire their first full-time marketer *Marketer* when they have grown to between 20 and 30 staff members, and that person is usually a marketing coordinator. Beyond that, design firms hire one marketing staff person per 35 employees, for firms of up to 150 people.

Characteristics of Effective Newsletters

■ Short words and short sentences make for easy readability. There are a number of ways to determine readability, including FOG index, FORECAST, Easy Listening Formula, Empathy Index, and Grazian Verb Power Index. A search of the Web or a visit to your local library should turn up resource information about these methods.
■ The smallest recommended type size is 9-point.
■ You lose 30 to 50 percent of your readers when stories continue onto a second page.
■ Serif typeface is easier to read than sans serif.
■ Text should be aligned ragged right—it's easier on the eyes than full justification.
■ The most frequently used paper colors are white, light tan, gray, and ivory.
■ A two-column format is confirmed more readable than one- or three-column layouts: 38 percent of newsletters are two-column, 7 percent one-column, 25 percent three-column, and all other formats comprise the remaining 30 percent.
■ Most newsletters are printed on 50-pound paper.
■ Successful newsletters present information in terms of what it means to the reader.

Don't forget, electronic newsletters are also a great option. You can avoid all printing and postage charges by emailing your newsletter to clients and potential clients. The most effective way to retain formatting and guarantee a high-quality end product is to create a PDF file of the newsletter document you create. For more information about creating PDF files, visit www.adobe.com.

Figure 2-13

Marketing Hints

- Place a one-line advertisement in the local Yellow Pages for clients' convenience in finding your telephone number.
- Design your Web site so that search engines detect your firm name as well as a brief description of your services.
- Research to develop a unique market niche.
- Develop a one-page direct mail piece that emphasizes the value of your service.
- Target markets for existing facilities surveys.
- Follow up finished projects with a final meeting; send a questionnaire to client to leave job on an up note.
- Update your Web site frequently so that visitors will want to return again and again.
- Plan appearances in the media that focus on the client rather than your profession. Consider books, articles, television appearances, and lectures to public groups.
- State your mission up front in your brochure or marketing package.
- Consider changing the name of your service to avoid being pigeonholed. For example, take out the words *architects* or *engineers* from your firm's name and substitute *interiors planners, correctional facilities planners,* etc.
- Talk with large out-of-state firms to make contact for small job referrals.
- Use present clients to expand your future client base.
- Utilize the uniqueness of your firm (e.g., minority- or woman-owned) to target clients, especially those who prefer to aim for such participation.
- Identify unique services needed by new clients (i.e., clients with new project types).

Figure 2-14

Note that *marketing staff person* refers only to employees engaged full time in direct or support marketing functions. It does not include technical professionals, principals (unless full time in marketing), or the marketing director. It does include outside prospectors, the marketing coordinator, in-house public relations/graphics, and clerical support.

Use your own judgment in applying these figures to your situation. For example, marketing staff per employee is greater in firms that are just venturing into marketing, that have an aggressive program, or that compete in the municipal market. On the other hand, the marketing staff ratio is lower in firms where the technical staff does the selling, or where the firm receives large projects or significant repeat work from the same clients. Figure 2-14 summarizes some marketing hints.

Creating a Marketing Plan Before your small firm even thinks of developing a formal marketing plan, here are five steps to take:

1. *Create professional-looking materials*—Although brochures alone should not represent the bulk of your marketing effort, a brochure can project the image of having your act together, even if you're not totally organized. If you already have a brochure, refer to Figure 2-15 for tips on how to improve it.

2. *Improve your mailing list*—Use your miscellaneous holiday cards, gift cards, and reception invitations to compile a comprehensive computerized mailing list of clients, prospects, and friends of the firm.

3. *Start with inexpensive public relations*—Send brief, one-page, double-spaced press releases on new personnel, new contracts, or design awards to local media and associations. Send announcements on senior personnel and major awards to your entire mailing list. The Fuessler Group, out of Boston, Massachusetts, publishes a directory of press information for the A/E/C industry called *The Publicity Directory*. For more information, visit www.fuessler.com.

4. *Set out a one-year action plan*—Once you have these basic elements in place, you can objectively review where you came from, where you want to go, and how to get there. (See Fig. 2-16.)

Brochure Usefulness

Ninety percent of all design firm brochures are made for other design professionals instead of for clients. Do clients really want to see tabloid pictures of hundreds of your projects? This is misusing your valuable time and money. Ask yourself if your brochure really works for your clients by considering the following questions:

- What use will your client have for your brochure?
- When your brochure reaches your client's desk, specifically what will he or she do with it?
- What specific items are contained in your brochure that provide continual benefit to your client in his or her business?
- Do you think that your client's brochure files are similar to those kept by your specification department for building products?
- Is your brochure longer than ten pages? If so, does your client ever read it?
- Do the pictures in your brochure have captions?
- Does your brochure feature dated headshots of principals who have left your firm?
- Is there any useful information in your brochure that would prompt your client to keep it as a reference tool?

Figure 2-15

One-Year Action Plan

Goal: *To secure three projects in the restaurant industry within 12 months.*

Tactics	Measurement
1. Call 100 clients in each of three building project types to determine anticipated restaurant projects now planned.	1a. Develop lists by 2/1. 1b. Assign 50 calls each to 6 people by 2/15. 1c. Make calls by 3/1.
2. Assemble list of real projects in each area.	2. Measure potential fee dollars of each project.
3. Assign each PM a contact list of 15–20 real contacts.	3. Do on 4/1.
4. Contact five clients per week.	4. Measure on 6/15.
5. Make a total of 10–20 presentations on real projects.	5. Between 6/1 and 9/1, meet weekly on Mondays to assess.
6. Have a first project.	6. Achieve no later than 7/1.
7. Assess overall plan.	7. Do on 9/1.

Figure 2-16

■ *Establish measurable goals*—Don't plan to contact 20 developers if you haven't contacted even one in the past year. Review and correct your plan every three months. Consider addressing major image problems (name change, substantial growth where you are still seen as small, etc.) with a direct mail piece.

Only now should you consider creating a formal one- and three-year marketing plan.

Writing the Although planning the marketing effort was discussed in
Marketing Plan Chapter 1, the specifics of the plan are now discussed in more detail. The marketing plan is the final step toward putting your vision into action. This is where you write down exactly how you are going to reach that vision, and this strategy should be broken into tangible yearly goals.

The purposes of the marketing function are to:

1. Decide what services to offer which clients.
2. Prepare the marketing plan.
3. Perform public relations, possibly including advertising.

4. Review and create sales tools such as brochures, newsletters, an effective Web site, and so forth.
5. Outline cold prospecting.
6. Find project leads.
7. Sell particular projects.
8. Perform client follow-up.

The marketing plan is a written plan outlining target markets and projected yield for a specified period, usually one year. It should address the marketing effort and define responsibilities for its implementation.

The elements of a marketing plan are:

1. A goals statement
2. An overall marketing program
3. Identification of specific markets
4. Overall administration or marketing control
5. Budget

Goals statement. Before setting your goal, perform a preliminary analysis to ensure that the goals are both realistic and specific. Without a framework, blue-sky goals creep in, such as "attain excellence in the sports facilities market" and "grow 50 percent this year."

To perform such an analysis, look at your internal strengths and weaknesses. Be brutally honest. Also, research (e.g., telephone calls to a few past clients) your image among present and potential clients. If you are a new firm with a short track record, this may be all you have to do.

If your firm has a marketing history, analyze the results of past efforts. Areas to consider include:

- Practice mix by type of project, client, and geographic area
- Profitability for each of these markets
- Proportion of repeat work and clients
- Number of proposals submitted and interviews attended, and the resulting success ratio
- Marketing costs compared to annual revenues and bookings
- Effectiveness of supporting functions such as public relations, marketing tools such as brochures and the Web, and written presentation materials as well as oral presentations.

Next, look at your external environment:

- What external factors will affect your market? Consider, for instance, the economy in general, the bankruptcy of a client, new government regulations, or the opening of new branch office by a major national firm.

- What government actions will affect client activities or regulate their operations?
- What economic or social factors will create or eliminate markets?
- What actions are the clients themselves taking to expand business and become more competitive?
- What factors are affecting clients in their selection of planning and design firms?

Some firms hire an outside consultant to perform this marketing research but, for the small firm, the most effective market research is by your technical experts in the particular field. For example, your chief mechanical engineer is in the best position to research the solar energy market.

Having analyzed the market, to some extent, you are ready to set goals. Be realistic, clear, and specific: "Increase revenues to $850,000," "Achieve a pretax return on sales of 15 percent," "Enter the Southwest market," and the like.

Overall marketing program. Most important for the small firm developing a marketing plan is time management; in other words, determine what effort will best achieve the results you want. To translate overall marketing goals into specific marketing tasks, list objectives that will get you to your goals. Note that a market is defined as project type plus client plus geographic location.

Sample objectives include:

- Elderly housing work for nonprofit clients in Iowa and Minnesota; increase fees in this area to $575,000, achieve a 20 percent return on sales (ROS), and limit marketing costs to $44,000.
- Spend $35,000 in direct labor responding to Corps of Engineers and Navfac RFPs announced on *Commerce Business Daily*'s (*CBD*) Web site. (*CBD* is a digest, updated daily, of government contract procurements and contract award notices. You can customize it to meet your specific needs. All records are arranged by Federal Supply Classification Codes. See www.cbd. cos.com.)
- Have three projects published in national design magazines.
- Set a quota for making cold calls. Make four prospecting calls a week.

As a small practitioner, also remember to delegate everything you can to your employees, even if you only employ part-timers or a limited number of people.

Identification of specific markets. Included in this section are a statement of each market (who, what, why), geographic particulars, the markets' size and potential for growth, expected share and edge in those markets, and how each market will be pursued. The latter section should include employee responsibility, intensity, methods, schedule, and fees.

Overall administration or marketing control. Plan how often you will hold meetings and who will attend. Appoint a leader of marketing, either yourself or another key individual in the firm. Update the plan regularly, perhaps every six months and at least once a year. Make economic projections based on the marketing program.

Budget. As a small firm, your bottom line on marketing spending may be "What do I have available from the overhead?" Consider principal's prorated time, marketing support salaries, materials, postage, telephone, travel, and entertainment. One way to estimate how much money you have for marketing is to allocate 8 percent of your gross billings for the past year to marketing. (See Fig. 2-12 for percentages of money spent on marketing.)

As a small firm, allocate funds prudently. To ensure that you are not overspending, create an accounting program to track your time and expenses.

Focus the Employees on Selling Members of the firm need to develop the skills needed to procure and maintain clients, to put the marketing plan into action, and to sustain the success of the company. Although not everyone is good at face-to face sales efforts, each employee plays a part in the success of your small firm. Your whole company should develop sales skills in case your current client base shrinks.

Before explaining selling techniques for the small firm, we first clarify the terms *marketing* and *selling,* about which there is considerable confusion. Small firms often use the term *marketing* when in fact they mean *sales.* Here is the distinction: Marketing is oriented to client needs, whereas sales is oriented to project commitment.

Marketing is the activities associated with planning, organizing, directing, and controlling the marketing effort to secure clients. Marketing is focused on the needs of the client. It involves market research strategy and direction. Sales, in contrast, involves the face-to-face work of securing a project. This is done by the project manager, the principal, or whoever will actually convince the client to choose the firm for a given project.

Marketing, in the truest sense, is the analysis of client needs in order to determine a strategy for pursuing the contract to meet those needs with services and professional talent.

The principal. The principal is often among the best salespeople in the firm. Here's how to use your principal(s) as a resource:

- Contrary to popular wisdom, encourage the principal to say *I* often. Only he or she can say to the prospect, "I have people who can commit to your project."
- Position the principal as an expert who comments in the media on design issues that matter to your firm. Principals have extra credibility by virtue of their position.
- Value tough questions by the principal to you about your marketing effectiveness. Such confrontational behavior reminds staff of the obligation to justify their actions.

Technical people. Technical professionals, on occasion, talk with the client and are in a good position to sell your firm's services. It makes sense to expose them also to the advice of experienced salespeople. As an introduction to sales techniques, begin with one or two selections from books on the subject. Consider:

- *The New Strategic Selling: The Unique Sales System Proven Successful by the World's Best Companies,* by Stephen E. Heiman, Diane Sanchez, Tad Tuleja, and Robert B. St. Miller (Warner Books, 1998)
- *Spin Selling,* by Neil Rackham (McGraw-Hill, 1998)
- *How to Master the Art of Selling,* by Tom Hopkins (Warner Books, 1994)

These books provide tools to help you train technical people to sell. Read them and remember that, as a small-firm entrepreneur, you must always be selling. Even while you are drafting, formulate plans for your next client meeting, brainstorm your next presentation, or mentally envision yourself winning your next presentation.

Project manager as salesperson.[1] A recent PSMJ Resources survey[2] asked what percentage of project managers (PMs) are responsible for the following marketing tasks:

Project proposal	75.0 percent
Project contract	62.5
Project presentation	58.3
Fee negotiations	58.3
Subconsultant selection	50.0

Asking project managers to participate in sales-related activities is a necessity for many small firms. They simply can't afford the number of full-time salespeople necessary to build the long-term, trusting relationships essential to success. Many of your seasoned project professionals can bring business to your firm. These are the seller-doers of your firm. Some employees may do excellent project work but not bring in new business. These are the doers. Your first desire may be to transform everyone into seller-doers, but some employees will never make the switch. Focus your efforts on those doers who have a bent toward selling.

When questioning employees who are not successful in bringing in new work, you are likely to receive answers such as "It's not my job," "I don't know what to say," and "I don't like to do it." If you probe further, you will find that reluctance to sell boils down to two real reasons: fear and not knowing how.

Fear comes in several forms:

- Fear of being rejected
- Fear of showing ignorance in an unfamiliar subject (losing the aura of being the expert)
- Fear of bringing in a colleague who might not measure up (risking the loss of my client)
- Fear of bringing in a colleague who will do a better job (causing me to lose control of my client)

The not-knowing-how attitude stems from the assumption that people instinctively know what to do and how to do it. Sometimes this is true, but for most people, selling is a learned skill.

You can provide an empowering environment and sales training to your doers with a bent toward selling, but first, you must answer their question: "Why should I also be responsible for selling? I'm already doing my job." Make sure team members understand that the selling function is an important part of every assignment for every employee. Your staff should understand what the firm's marketing objectives are and make client contacts aware of other valuable services you offer. Remind employees that telephone calls are wonderful opportunities to obtain high-quality referrals to potential new clients and to others in the client's organization at the same or other locations.

Additionally, provide training in the following areas:

- Planning
- Positioning
- Procurement
- Proposals
- Presentations
- Project execution
- Follow-up

With support from you and the seller-doers of your firm, employees who would like to sell but just don't know how can become significant assets as you strive to promote your firm.

Areas of Sales Concentration for Project Managers. Your project managers should have distinct responsibilities to help ensure a continuing supply of work. The following is a list of sales activities for the project manager:

- *Extras*—Be aware of actual and potential extras and charges on a project. There is a definite opportunity to sell these to a client.
- *Additional services*—Offer services outside of those for which the client has contracted. The project manager should make sure the client is aware of all services the firm offers.
- *Other projects*—Actively seek other projects from clients. Ask about other activities of the client firm to find out about possible projects.
- *Client maintenance*—Establish a program for regular client contact after a project is complete. Call the client once a month; make sure she receives your holiday cards; send regular announcements; put her on your monthly newsletter list. Make sure that the project manager personally calls at least once a year and takes out a member of the client firm for lunch at least once a year. Invite the client to occasions such as your firm's annual party or company softball games, or obtain hard-to-get sporting event tickets for them. Encourage the project manager to keep the client aware that you exist.
- *Other likely clients*—Ask clients if they know of other potential clients and projects. Direct referrals are excellent sources of work.
- *Network building*—Develop a reputation and awareness about the firm among project managers' acquaintances. When they have a project, they should think of your firm. Encourage project managers to make liberal use of their business cards.

Nevertheless, Don't Let Everyone Sell. As mentioned earlier, not everyone should have a chance to be involved in face-to-face sales efforts. Identify those who are especially good at it and use them often. But because even star performers will bomb with some clients, this group should be diverse so your prospects will have a better chance of being matched with an appropriate person in your firm.

Your best bets are those individuals who:

- Like to meet people and have many contacts and acquaintances.
- Are prepared to champion new ideas within your firm.
- Recruit well.
- Are enthusiastic about their work.
- Run good meetings.
- Are politically smart.

Save these special sellers for situations requiring persuasion: presentations, interviews, and selected meetings. Assign marketing functions to less sales-oriented individuals who can prepare photographs and slides of past projects, write project histories, or fill out government forms.

Managing Your Client To best manage current and prospective clients using your workforce, consider breaking up your staff into in-house marketing and marketing-sales client managers:

- *In-house marketing*—In-house staff perform marketing support such as proposal response writing, brochure generation, development of marketing materials, research and development, and creation and maintenance of information systems. For very small firms, such support may be among the duties of your administrative assistant.
- *Client managers*—Field marketing staff make direct contact with potential clients; that is, they sell. Unlike typical salespeople, however, their participation does not stop once the job is secured. As an added bonus to the client, the client manager should continue to be involved in the job by visiting the site regularly and attending major job meetings with the project manager.

Here are additional sales hints:

- Make face-to-face contacts.
- Hire project managers (engineering and architecture) who will be responsible for acquiring a given level of revenue.
- Put sales expectations in writing.

■ Review performance expectations at predetermined stages.

■ Use direct contact with project managers and principals.

Client managers actually manage clients by leading client meetings, establishing contractual relations with consultants, anticipating changes in work for clients, and meeting unexpected client demands. The client manager should develop and nurture each client's trust from the signing of the agreement all the way through to occupancy of the completed project. Developing secure, long-term relationships will result in contracts. This is a powerful concept in the design professions; using client managers effectively will distinguish your firm from the competition.

Honing Telephone Skills   Sales efforts for the small firm must be lean and efficient. The small practitioner can achieve real sustained success by the judicious honing of telephone skills.

Compare the management and growth of a practice with portfolio investments. You do not react to every hot tip or attempt to manage a portfolio so large as to be out of control. To be small and stay small, one must be selective and focus on connecting with a limited number of potential clients at any given time.

Call directly the person you want to reach. If you are a structural engineering or interior design firm, for example, locate a listing of architectural firms and seek to be considered when they accept multidiscipline assignments. Determine if there are particular architects whose design approach or style meshes with yours and put them on your prospect list.

A reasonable effort should be restricted to 4 calls a day and no more than 20 a week. This allows you adequate time for long telephone conversations in which you and the prospect can take each other's measure and begin to relate to one another. If the chemistry is wrong, you can tell early on, and both you and the prospect will save a lot of time and expense.

Plan the calls with a checklist and write out answers to possible queries or objections. Why are you the better mouse trap? If you cannot answer most questions positively, don't make the call. Figure 2-17 contains typical client objections and possible answers. Figure 2-18 is a sample marketing call report form, and Figure 2-19 a client contact memorandum.

Client Objections/Answers

1. "Your price is too high." This is a common objection. Do not become defensive and start to justify your price. Instead, focus on the scope of work that's being provided for the price. Tell the client they are getting better quality and better service than the competition provides for the same price. Give the client the choice of reducing the price by reducing the scope of services. Tell them the price quoted reflects the highest standard. This is a positive defense when the client objects to price.

2. "The schedule is too long." A client will often say this when the firm has built into the schedule expected delays or client changes. To defend this, ask the client what their preferences are for the schedule. Given their restrictions, advise them that it is possible with less reviews or an increased intensity in the reviews, which may cost more money. Another alternative is to suggest that you will work overtime to shorten the schedule and that you will have to charge more money to cover the associated costs.

3. "You're putting too much emphasis on quality." Again, do not become defensive. Suggest to the client that they help define the quality level so that you can understand the client's quality expectations.

4. "You're putting the wrong people on the project." This can be difficult to overcome, especially if you have committed people to the project in the proposal and presentation stages. A firm can win or lose a project based on the people they put on the job. You can overcome this objection by guaranteeing to the client that a certain principal or the firm president will oversee the day-to day project progress. Most clients, especially when dealing with small firms, want the principal to be involved in the project. One of the key advantages that a small firm has over a large one is that it can allocate the principal's time to a project much more readily than a large firm can.

Figure 2-17

Here are ways you can prepare for the call:

- Know your purpose.
- Research telephone techniques.
- Embrace an attitude of enthusiasm.
- Communicate that you'd like to help solve problems, not just find projects.
- Make observations, then listen.
- Ask open-ended questions, not ones that can be answered with only a *yes* or a *no.*
- Use positives, not negatives.

MARKETING CALL REPORT

Date ____ / ____ / ____

PLACE BUSINESS CARD HERE

Brochure ■

Referred by _____

Related _____

Mailing List ■

By _____

Organization: _____

Web Address: _____

Name: _____

Title: _____

Address: _____

_____

Phone: _____ Fax: _____

Email: _____

Potential Project: _____

INFORMATION	ACTION TO BE TAKEN

Figure 2-18. Marketing call report.

CLIENT CONTACT MEMORANDUM

Date: Division: Contact By:

Type of Visit: Office ☐   Telephone ☐   Other ☐

1.	Company:			
2.	Address:			
3.	Division or Department Contacted:			
4.	Person(s) Contacted	Position/Title	Telephone Number	Add to Mailing List?
	a			
	b			
	c			

5. Objective of Visit:

6. Project or Prospect Identified:

7. Who is Decision Maker?

8. Summary of Discussion:

9. Is Proposal to be Prepared?   **Date:**   **Est. Dollar Value:** $

10. Commitments to Client:

11. Literature Left:

12. Action to Follow (What? By Whom? When?):

Distribution (Attention): ☐ CORPORATE MARKETING

☐ Houston	☐ Const. mat.	☐ New Orleans
☐ Little Rock	☐ St. Louis	☐ Ventura
☐ San Francisco	☐ TERA	☐ London
☐ Saudi Arabia	☐ Singapore	☐ Other

Signature:

Figure 2-19. Client contact memorandum.

SUCCESS CHALLENGES

1. Are you really working on securing clients, or are you working on securing projects? The key indicator is whether, after you complete a project, you keep in touch with a client.
2. Are you developing networking activities that routinely allow you to meet more and more people?
3. Are you developing usefulness marketing tools, such as a client newsletter, to provide a backbone to your marketing effort, or are you simply providing selling tools, such as project photographs and advertising brochures, to your staff?
4. Are you learning to say *no* to clients in a way that helps focus your marketing response by eliminating clients you should not be courting?
5. How does the focus of your practice reinforce your vision of where your firm should be?
6. Examine the services you now provide. List three that could be expanded into focused niches in which you can be perceived to be a real expert.

REFERENCES

1. Information in the section entitled "Project Manager as Salesperson" is taken from the article "Get Those PM's Selling!" by Robert Hirsch in *PSMJ Best Practices*, January 2000, p.5.
2. *PSMJ A/E Pulse,* November 2000.

Chapter 3

Strategic Alliances

For the small-firm practitioner hoping to expand his or her horizons and generate more fees without adding staff or branch offices, strategic alliances are an excellent option. Technological advances that are now part of everyday life—cell phones, email, laptop computers, and so on—make keeping in touch with geographically remote partners not only possible but simple.

Successful strategic alliances are typically forged between noncompeting firms. Competition may be removed because of distance—a civil engineering firm with a stronghold on the Texas market does not feel competition from a civil engineering firm that works primarily in Washington—or discipline. Firms that form strategic alliances have done so to win projects they otherwise never would have landed, either because of location or specialty.

The exciting aspect of strategic alliances is how many benefits—with virtually zero risks—firms can realize from being in them. Allied firms can market jointly and share costs. They can pursue jobs in sectors previously impenetrable to them. They can combat labor shortages with ease. The risk is extremely low because the firms are competing neither geographically nor with respect to discipline.

A PSMJ Resources November 2000 poll showed that for those firms that have established strategic alliances, the results have been highly favorable. Among the firms that have formed strategic alliances, 88 percent have been awarded work, and almost 70 percent indicate that their efforts have already been profitable. Participants in strategic alliances also appear to be satisfied with their arrangements, with 50 percent looking to expand their participation in such partnerships.

Perhaps equally as important, no firms report they will discontinue their existing alliances. The most popular type of strategic alliance is one that pursues particular project types, followed by alliances for either select clients or individual projects. Least common are strategic alliances aimed at serving geographic markets.

About half of those participating in strategic alliances indicate they have prepared unique marketing materials or agreements, either for clients or for the alliance partners. Less than one-third of the participants give the alliance its own name. The firms that are participating in alliances appear to be well satisfied with them. Given the success of existing alliances, it is somewhat surprising that more firms are not pursuing arrangements of this type. For detailed results of the poll, see Figure 3-1.

Because of the nature of the A/E marketplace in the 2000s, firms planning to rely on the traditional subcontracting model will see decreased proposal success and fewer

Detail of Survey Results from Firms Involved in Strategic Alliances

	% Yes
1. Firms that currently have strategic alliances:	14
For those firms that answered yes to having strategic alliances:	
2. Types of work the strategic alliances are pursuing:	
Specific project types	81
Specific clients	63
Specific geographic regions	56
Selected individual projects	63
3. The strategic alliances have:	
Prepared marketing information and materials	56
Standard contracts between alliance partners	56
Established fee-sharing policies for alliance partners	50
Marketing cost-sharing agreements between alliance partners	38
Defined responsibilities for marketing the alliance	56
A separate name for the alliance	31
4. The strategic alliances have been:	
Awarded work	88
Profitable	69
5. Firm's satisfaction with strategic alliances:	
Very satisfied, looking to expand	50
It's okay, could be better	56
We will finish current work and not continue	0
Not satisfactory, we disbanded the alliance	0
It is too early to judge success	19
6. Firms that don't have strategic alliances currently:	
And are not planning to form any alliances	6
But are exploring alliance opportunities	13

Figure 3-1
Source: PSMJ A/E Pulse, November 2000.

contractor-originated requests for proposal (RFPs). In this environment, strategic alliances will be a true boon to profitability—especially for small firms.

With their emphasis on joint marketing and shared project responsibility, strategic alliances will drive much of the A/E/C marketplace's future. As business gets deeper and deeper into the e-commerce model, strategic alliances enable firms to go virtual—supplying services beyond their immediate locale and traditional service sectors. Typically, a strategic alliance requires an exchange of one or two key firm personnel, with the rest of the project communication carried out online.

At the industry level, strategic alliances can smooth the ever-fluctuating ebb and flow of work that constantly challenges the stability of the A/E/C workforce. The hire/fire shops of the 1960s, 1970s, and 1980s will be replaced by strategic alliance networks that allow firms to say *yes* to jobs, knowing they can do the work.

THE UNIQUE REWARDS OF STRATEGIC ALLIANCES[1]

"If a business merger is like a marriage, then a strategic alliance is like living together for a while," says Charles Nelson, AIA, FRAIA, the managing director of the Melbourne, Australia–based Building Technology Systems. Nelson has participated in half a dozen strategic alliances between U.S. and Australian firms as well as between Australian and Chinese firms.

For A/E firms, what might be the payoffs of living together? Here are three:

1. *Expand your sense of self*—By allying with a firm that can do something you can't, you add to your market and building specialties and create a perception among prospective clients that your firm is bigger in size and scope (in both capability and geography) than it really is. When the bigger projects come in, you'll be able not only to handle them but also to focus on what you do best, and thus deliver more value.

2. *Move the project along*—Especially in a transnational alliance, you can speed the project by dedicating more hours to it. If one partner is in Australia and the other in New York, your alliance can work on the project 16 hours a day and, through the Internet, communicate in real time. This benefit could pay off plenty in today's business climate, where owners want their projects done last week.

"WHERE DO I FIND SOMEONE TO LEAD A STRATEGIC ALLIANCE?"

Someone in your firm can probably help.

American firms have historically seen little need to undertake strategic alliances. As Wayne Baker of the University of Michigan Business School describes the situation, "In their heart of hearts, traditional U.S. managers would rather fight than cooperate." But our economy now finds itself in a paradox where, says management guru Tom Peters, "More competition requires more cooperation."

Unfortunately, A/E firms have developed few effective ways to engage in such cooperation. Indeed, they have overlooked one of their most potent resources—those strange social extroverts on their staffs who, by connecting with outside, far-ranging firms, could lead them to wider practices through alliances.

Who are these resources? They are the natural networkers who know everyone at conferences and seem to spend too many hours on the phone with colleagues and professional contacts. They are boundary spanners—constantly drawn into relationships with folks in other industries and business cultures. They may be better at managing laterally than in the traditional hierarchical mode. They hail from backgrounds that seem at odds with those of others in your firm. They have a different kind of knowledge. And often, you don't know what to do with them.

But if you are ready to undertake a strategic alliance and move to a new level of success, these are the people to do it for you. The question is, how do you identify them?

Beyond having first-rate project management skills, these alliance makers need to know how to communicate in ways not typical of the rest of your staff.

Those most likely to best shape alliances scan for new opportunities and potential sources of synergy and value. By inclination, they think of ways to cobrand, comarket, or codesign. Notes Baker, "By definition, these [opportunities] are ill-defined, incomplete, and hidden. They don't turn up in formal searches. You find them by networking. The best alliance partners are always on the lookout for new ways to create mutual benefits and invest in the relationship."

Thus, for alliance shapers, building relationships is more important than anything. The emerging position of Relationship Manager will likely be held by people who demonstrate the following traits:

1. **They invest time and energy in personal contact.** Building trust takes time. An alliance shaper must continuously nurture relationships and tend to their health. Says Baker, "How do you know what

your partner's intentions are? How do you know if [he or she is] ready for commitment—or that the commitment is changing? How do you know about [his or her] frustrations, problems, or grievances? The only way is by constant meeting, talking, and interacting....Continual dialog, mutual visits, informal socializing—at all levels—are essential to build the groundwork for mutual understanding and to find mutual benefits."

2. **They are more transformational than transactional.** The cult of the deal died in the 1980s. Marketers, accountants, and lawyers do not catalyze or craft the best strategic alliances. Strategic alliance leaders are not overly legalistic; they don't try to capture everything in the contract or adhere to the contract at the cost of critical relationships.

3. **They are sensitive to language differences.** These include vernacular usage, idioms, nuances in spoken and body language, and professional terminology. Language barriers can mask cultural differences that could bring technical differences. A good alliance shaper must be able to read between the lines—even in his or her own tongue.

4. **They communicate across different operating levels.** An effective alliance shaper must resolve differences with a multilevel approach and build and sustain firm-to-firm peer links, both vertically and horizontally. He or she must become involved and communicate easily with all levels of personnel.

5. **They manage by remote control.** The alliance shaper can create a clear enough vision to direct and motivate team members of two or more firm cultures with a constant presence. In this context, he or she must be able to detect unresolved, hidden, or brushed-aside issues—such as those around work practices—with an early warning system.

Michigan's Baker stresses, "Building strong alliances has a lot in common with building strong personal relationships. Both person-to-person and company-to-company relationships depend on the same secret formula: mutual understanding plus mutual benefit. When there's true mutual understanding, each party understands why the other acts in a particular way and accepts the behavior as legitimate and authentic despite the tensions or inconvenience it might cause." The good news is that while "different cultures *do* make mutual understanding more difficult, ... opposites attract when you are looking for mutual benefits."

"Where Do I Find Someone To Lead A Strategic Alliance?" *PSMJ Best Practices*, November 2000, p. 10.

3. *Do more work with less staff*—If two can live as cheaply as one, then partnering offers economic benefits. "In Australia," says Nelson, "a 100-person firm is a very large one. So it is common for A/E firms to get together for huge projects." You can also find cheaper labor in other countries. Says Nelson, " If you normally spend 40 percent of your fee locally on documents, you might be able to buy the same work offshore for 22 percent. That means an 18 percent profit."

As attractive as the payoffs are, though, strategic alliances work best when the partners establish ground rules. Nelson has identified four:

1. *Common goals*—If one firm wants to make money or a name and the other wants only to turn out good design, then basic value differences could sabotage the project. Make sure *going in* that you and your partner want the same things. Find a point of agreement in your firm cultures. It's best, for example, that you share the same work ethic. If one firm routinely puts in 60-hour weeks and the other clocks out at 5:00 every day, tensions could surface.

2. *Complementary skills*—Allying with someone who can do something you can't means you both have a bigger tool kit of building types and competencies— as well as the marketing contacts to go with it. You can learn from one another and grow as individual firms. On the other hand, an alliance where both partners share the same strengths and weaknesses could prove unprofitable.

3. *Comprehensive agreement*—Both legal and operational. It is essential that you agree with your partner—in advance—on who is responsible for what and on what methods and protocols you will use. Who will do the marketing? How will you handle project management? What type of payment system do you want? What about drawing abbreviations and CAD protocol? You want no gray areas of joint responsibility; if no one partner signs on for a task, no one is likely to do it.

4. *Cross-team representation*—You can nip all cross-cultural communication problems in the bud by stationing a member of each firm in the other firm's office *for the duration of the project.* These people become translators; they resolve communication problems before the communications go out on the wire. By checking documents prior to transmittal, these representatives can help ensure quality control.

MEMPHIS FIRM TURNS TO STRATEGIC ALLIANCE TO STAFF MAJOR PROJECTS

In 1998, Hnedak Bobo Group (HBG) of Memphis had a big year; they landed over $500 million in project contracts for clients including Harrah's, Federal Express, and the new Opryland Hotel and Convention Center in Orlando, Florida. The 135-person firm was ready and eager to tackle these major hospitality and corporate jobs.

But there was a hitch. In addition to its already sizable staff, HBG needed extra manpower to make the projects deliverable. "We did a lot to attract additional people," says Greg Hnedak, cofounder and principal, "But talking with fellow architects all over the United States, I found firms everywhere were having problems finding experienced workforce." With the robust, employee-driven economy, HBG was not alone in seeking talent.

Finding New Talent Through an Alliance

It was time to try something new. "I had heard that, to solve their personnel problems, some U.S. firms had already set up strategic alliances with firms overseas," Hnedak says. So he started looking at potential partners in countries including Canada, Australia, and Malaysia. "We needed to target countries that could offer experienced people and a good rate of currency exchange–at least equal. Ideally, we wanted to be where the US dollar would give us the support we needed while allowing us to maintain our profit goals."

Hnedak eventually met with a consultant who recommended Gazzard Sheldon Architects (GSA) of Sydney, Australia, saying that GSA had a strong work ethic and that the two firms were culturally similar.

Finding the Right Partner Is Key

"They had worked extensively in metric and imperial, and used they AutoCad" says Hnedak. "Their size and project types were similar." GSA met the currency criteria, too. "It's one thing to get work done efficiently. But with GSA, we could meet our financial goals, while they would receive full retail price for their man-hours on our project. It was an exceptional win-win for both firms. We began to realize the consultant was right."

But Hnedak wanted to see if his firm and GSA could work together. "So we had them send folks over here for three to six months each," he says. "We put them to work on an hourly basis on smaller projects. Seeing them in action, we realized they were technically strong and shared our mission for producing quality work. Without a doubt, we wanted to pursue this." Four months into the alliance, the partners started working on a major project assignment together.

Sharing Goals Can Keep Costs Low

Hnedak wanted an alliance that would last for more than just one project. For this, a loose-fitting arrangement worked best. "Mark Sheldon, GSA's owner, and I wanted the same thing: an agreement to share each other's strengths for the benefit of both companies. To this day, we work from a memorandum of understanding—a single three-page letter." For each project, the partners make a more detailed agreement. "We do a contract, with schedules, responsibilities, scope of services, payments, and everything else."

To make such an easy arrangement work, Hnedak feels it was important that the partners shared common goals. "We both were committed to quality architecture and client service, wanted to expand our firm's capabilities, and believed that the alliance had to be financially viable. I was not going to subsidize another firm, and neither were they."

With that common understanding, the alliance kept costs low. "If we had started with a lot of legalese from attorneys, we might have spent too much just to find out later that we didn't like each other or were uncomfortable with each other's work."

Alliances Can Bring Business

Has it worked? Says Hnedak, "We were able to complement the talented staff we already had with equally talented personnel we could not have acquired through any other means. The arrangement allows us to go after larger projects, too. GSA has a great reputation for world-class architecture. We both know what would be attractive to the other. We each have a partner, should we need one."

Hnedak says the alliance also helps the partners handle the ups and downs in workload. "At the end of a project, if we don't have another immediate assignment, I have no responsibility to keep their people working. They are someone else's financial responsibility."

The arrangement has juiced up HBG's marketing, too. "Our day ends at 5:00 P.M. CST," says Hnedak. "In Australia, that is 7:00 A.M. the next day. We transmit data at the end of the day over the Internet. We go to bed; they continue working all night. Ideally, we put in a 16-hour day on every project. This could mean significant time savings—second only to cost control in every client's mind. Each time I mention this to prospective clients, it intrigues them."

"How to Staff Major Projects Through Alliances," *PSMJ Best Practices*, November 2000, p. 4.

Also, partnering firms must communicate with each other *on all peer levels:* principal to principal, designer to designer, PM to PM. This way, everybody will talk about everything that needs to be talked about.

COMMUNICATION IS THE KEY

If you can discuss and agree on every facet of your working relationship before you begin it, you will be starting well. In an alliance, you must think through and document all aspects of your methodology and technology. And you must spell out—in advance—how you will report and resolve problems. Planning is essential—much more so than when working on your own.

FRAMING A STRATEGIC ALLIANCE

There are two approaches to a strategic alliance agreement: loosely defined and tightly defined. The approach that fits will likely depend on your firm's size, how long you've been in business, and the type of product or service offered through the alliance. Whichever type of agreement fits your business, all agreements should include:

- Your common goal
- A strategy defining each partner's role in reaching the goal
- The parameters of working toward the goal.

Loosely Defined Agreements Young or small businesses may prefer a broad, loosely defined agreement so as to allow the partnership to grow in new directions as their business evolves.

Tightly Defined Agreements Larger or older businesses, or those in technology fields, may fare better with an agreement that spells out the precise scope of the alliance and the details of how it will be accomplished. A tightly defined agreement may also:

- Identify key steps that each partner will take to meet the agreement's requirements.
- Include a time frame for achieving those key steps.
- Define each partner's accountability by including consequences for worst-case scenarios, such as missed deadlines, budget overruns, or products not delivered as promised or in the format expected.
- Provide a framework for resolving conflicts if they occur.

SUCCESS CHALLENGES

1. Have you considered forming a strategic alliance with a like-minded noncompeting firm?
2. What benefits would you realize from entering a strategic alliance?
3. Are you and other firm leaders prepared to open your books and adjust operating procedures in order to participate in a strategic alliance?

REFERENCE

1. Information in this section taken from "Strategic Alliances Offer Unique Rewards," *PSMJ Best Practices*, November 2000, p. 3.

Chapter 4

Servicing the Client

Students go to architecture or engineering school hoping to become renowned for great design. From day one, graduates want their names associated with the world's greatest designs, whether a bridge design to span the widest river, a wastewater treatment design for the newest technology, or the design of the most brilliant high-rise facility. The ego-driven design orientation is part of every design professional's background.

Design, however, from the client's perspective, is a feature, not a benefit. All clients expect the firm they select to produce high-quality design. Unfortunately, to the client, good design is like a spark plug in a Porsche. Spark plugs do not sell Porsches. Glamour, sex, and life style sell Porsches, as do speediness, color, and image.

In design, it is the *service* element of the business that will keep the small firm in successful practice over the long run. The most successful design firms in the marketplace become known for the service they provide—their ability to anticipate client needs and go above and beyond the standard of care delivered in the industry at large—while also providing a high level of quality in design. See Figure 4-1 for a report on the expectations of clients in today's marketplace.

It is easy to distinguish good service from bad. When you drive up to a gas station, the attendant either washes your windshield and checks your oil, or he doesn't. It's a black-and-white issue. But there is more: Perception becomes reality. You must not only provide good service; you must be perceived as doing so.

In design, the quality of service can be measured by the following eight components:

1. **Knowledge**

   Does the firm seem to know the client's core business as well as the client himself does? Try this definition of quality on for size: A project manager or principal who walks into a client's office offering solutions to business challenges as well as promising to deliver top-notch, accurate, on-schedule, and on-budget design.

Faster, Better, Cheaper—Those Crazy Clients Want It All!

A radical change is occurring in buyer behavior in the A/E/C industry. Clients are no longer willing to sacrifice price and speed for high quality. Or vice versa. Today, they're sitting in their meetings looking for the provider who can do it all: faster, better, and cheaper.

From the 1960s to the mid-1980s, most firms could do a professional (read: better) job on any type of project; they were master designers and builders. As a consciousness about marketing arose in the late-1980s and early 1990s, many firms fell into promoting cheaper, faster, *or* better. If they could build a solid reputation for any one of these, they were consistent winners.

Today, pushed by a more demanding marketplace, 60 percent of decision makers believe they can get at least two of the three: cheaper, faster, *and* better.

Faster is the quality that has most often been responsible for success in design/build arrangements. This is mostly because another major benefit—avoiding litigation with multiple parties—appears to have almost faded away, a victim of partnering.

Cheaper is often a major benefit of faster. However, more than 50 percent of decision makers responding to a recent survey sponsored by I3 Intelli-Sys Info, Inc., said that they would move from one very satisfactory firm to a new one if they could save just 3 percent on the total project cost. How loyal would your clients be if they were offered a potential 3 percent in savings on a project by a respectable competitor?

Better has been the Achilles heel of many marketers. Better service, more flexibility, responsiveness, and commitment have all, for the most part, become outdated benefits. Most decision makers (82 percent) rate their current providers very well (8 plus on a 10-point scale), so the claim that you do it better will fail if used to differentiate yourself from others.

To be meaningful to decision makers, *better* must have results that translate to the bottom line. If you can:

- reduce operations and maintenance cost,
- bring back features that were eliminated in the original wish list budget,
- or use software that helps clients avoid a history of documented costly surprises or controls surprises better,

your claim to *better* is legitimate.

It's important to understand the levels of consciousness in the market today. The American business public is, among other things, finally reaping the rewards of computerization and downsizing. In this environment, design/build teams are now faced with the challenge to, at a minimum, add *better* or *cheaper* to their appeal.

This be especially difficult for the ad hoc or often inexperienced teams put together for short periods or for a project or two. It takes market-driven, highly specialized and experienced teams to deliver cheaper, faster, and better.

The immediate challenge for most design or construction firms will be to accurately measure what percentages constitute the departure threshold, or when buyers in a particular targeted market will move from one firm to another. This will become the basis for all internal goals, strategic plans, training, and bonuses in the future.

Figure 4-1

Source: Roger Pikar, "Faster, Better, Cheaper—Those Crazy Clients Want It All!"
PSMJ Best Practices, February 2000, p. 8.

2. Schedule
- Does the firm set up a realistic initial schedule?
- Does the firm perform according to the schedule?
- When it cannot adhere to the schedule, is the firm honest, up-front, and swift in notifying the client?

3. Budget
Is the firm meeting its design budget and its projected construction cost budget? Budget and schedule go hand in hand. If the firm is meeting its schedule but exceeding its budget, it is spending too much just to meet the schedule.

Set a realistic budget and suggest to the client contingencies within the budget. Consider a 3 to 5 percent construction contingency to make up for changes in the budget later in the project.

4. Performance
- Is the firm technically qualified?
- Is the firm selling its qualifications realistically?
- Does the firm go beyond its technical capabilities?
- Does the firm fulfill its budget and schedule promises?

5. Meeting Management
- Does the firm set up meetings, or is it simply reacting by attending already scheduled meetings?
- Does the firm arrive to meetings on time?
- Does the firm cancel meetings?
- What is the firm's active role in serving the client? Clients want leaders who will take charge of a project and set up job meetings with contractors.
- Does the firm take control of meetings by arranging them, setting the agenda, and leading them?
- Does the firm follow up with action after the meetings? (See the sidebar on page 115 for information on better, more efficient meetings.)

6. Satisfactory Working Drawings
- Are the drawings realistic?
- Are the drawings clear to the contractor?
- Is the contractor pricing the jobs appropriately based on the quality of the drawings?

7. Bidding
- Provide more than enough drawings to the contractors.
- Telephone contractors to inquire about questions/problems with the plans. (Be careful—legally, you must communicate equally with all bidders.)
- Involve the owner/client in the bidding process, within an interview scheme. Allow each bidder to interview the owner to better ascertain mutual understanding of project scope.

In general, all of the above point to reinforcing communication during bidding.

8. Construction
- Document daily project activities.
- Appoint a project site representative to be on site and to document performance on the job. This includes monitoring the schedule, material delivery, and daily activities.
- Keep the client aware of the project's progress.
- Photograph the site several times from the same angles, producing a photographic history of the entire project. Pick five, six, or seven key points on the site and photograph them every day. This record can be invaluable during any liability disputes later on. Photographs are invaluable to understanding covered up materials such as concrete, reinforcing bars, and so on.
- Hold regular on-site job meetings with owner's representatives to review aspects of construction.

Successful design firms have an ability to perform on schedule and stay within the budget to a degree that may exceed their own targeted projections. They are realistic when they:

- Target project performance.
- Establish project schedules and budgets with enough leeway to achieve their goals.
- Are able to convince their staff that schedules and budgets can be met.

This chapter explains how your small firm can be profitable if it focuses on providing a good service rather than on design; ways to be responsive to your client to provide better service; how to establish a quality control program to ensure quality as part of providing that service (and to avoid liability); and suggests ways to innovate your activities so the client perceives your firm as providing exemplary service.

SERVICE VERSUS DESIGN

Small firms often try to be a little of everything. They want to have some outstanding element of each arena—that is, of design and service. According to studies by the Coxe Group, it is far better to make a choice as to what type of firm you want to be: an ideas firm (design-focused), a strong-service firm (gray-hair firm), or a strong-delivery firm (referred to as a *service firm* in this text). The Coxe Group has researched and identified these three types of firm technologies and also two types of value systems. The choice of technology and values will affect every aspect of organization and project delivery—and, ultimately, your firm's profitability.

Figure 4-2 contains a description of these classifications and explains the Coxe Group's test results showing that successful firms make a choice on one focus or another. Firms that don't make choices cannot possibly succeed in all areas and therefore are not among the most profitable. Develop a clear notion of what your firm does best and plan your organization accordingly. Make a choice. For the very small firm, establishing a design reputation may be difficult; you first need to develop a good reputation. The easiest and fastest way to do this is to deliver. Provide good service and you will become well known. Whether or not you can grow from there to provide good service and win design awards depends on many variables, some of them out of your control. For the small firm, it is far better to begin by focusing on providing good service. A firm that can promise to finish a job on schedule and within budget will stand out in an industry where these criteria are not often met.

LITTLE THINGS THAT COUNT BIG

Providing good service begins with the little details, which actually convey the spirit of the firm's focus to the client. The following list may contain some items you think you are doing—but do you stand out from the competition in each of these areas? If you do not differ from your competitors in each element, review and change your procedures. For information about how technology can enhance the service you provide, see Figure 4-3. Here are little things you can do to upgrade bad or mediocre service to good service:

1. Provide good telephone service—that is, answer calls to the company in a pleasant and unique manner. For instance, employees of one firm answer the telephone with "Good morning, it's a great day. This is ABC Associates." You may think this is trite or cute, but the concept is to instill a positive feeling in listeners before they even speak. In so doing, you can short-circuit angry people and perhaps change their present frame of mind and intentions.

2. Respond quickly to letters, email, and other materials. Things to consider: What is the time frame implied by "a quick response"? When you instruct an employee to send a letter "immediately," does he or

Categories of Design Firms

The Coxe Group Management Consultants (Seattle) delineates three types of technologies and two types of value systems within design firms. By technologies, they refer to the focus in which projects are delivered. The three types are:

1. *Strong-idea (brains) firms*, organized to deliver singular expertise or innovation to unique projects. Project technology for this type of firm flexibly accommodates the nature of any assignment and often depends on a few outstanding experts or stars to give final approval.

2. *Strong-service (gray-hair) firms*, organized to deliver experience and reliability, especially on complex projects. Their focus is to provide comprehensive service to a client that is closely involved in the process.

3. *Strong-delivery (procedure) firms*, which provide efficient service on similar or routine assignments to clients who seek a product rather than a service. This firm repeats previous solutions over and over again with highly reliable technical, cost, and schedule compliance. (Referred to as *service firms* in this text.)

A company's technical emphasis may shift during the following process:

1. New ideas come from strong-idea firms.

2. As they become understood and accepted in the marketplace, the ideas are then applied widely by strong-service firms.

3. When the idea becomes routinized and is in demand by many clients, strong-delivery firms will start to provide the service, where repetitive projects and efficiency are stressed.

Thus, firms should periodically review their status on this continuum to ensure that they are keeping the focus where they want it to be. The technology of a firm affects:

- Project progress
- Project decisions
- Staffing (middle and lower)
- Marketing (choice of market)
- Products being sold
- Prices
- Management style

The choice of technology shapes the design process, and it is becoming recognized that all really successful firms have a clear, consistent project delivery process that fits into one of the above three categories.

The other area that shapes a firm's service delivery system is its values. Do you run your business as a practice or as a business? This can make a difference in

- Organizational structure
- Decision-making process
- Staffing (top level)
- Marketing strategies

■ Identifying clients
■ Organization of marketing
■ Rewards
■ Management style

To determine what type your firm is, look at your bottom line:

■ *Practice-centered business*—Your major goal is the opportunity to serve others and produce examples of the discipline you represent. Your bottom line is qualitative: How do we like what we're doing? How does the job serve the client's needs? Our needs?
■ *Business-centered practice*—Your major goal is a quantitative bottom line, focusing on the tangible rewards of your efforts. How did we do? How much money did we make?

Many firms succeed in any combination of these technologies and values, but the objective is that you should have a focus. You should choose yours based on your individual preferences and goals. The Coxe Group surveyed 100 firms of different sizes, markets, and organizational formats. The results of that survey showed that firms that have a clear notion of what they do best (technology) and a common set of goals (values) succeed—for themselves and their clients.

Figure 4-2

Source: *Success Strategies for Design Professionals: SuperPositioning for Architecture and Engineering Firms.*
Authors: Weld Coxe, Nina F. Hartung, Hugh Hochberg, Brian J. Lewis, David H. Maister, Robert F. Mattox,
Peter A. Piven. The Coxe Group Management Consultants. Used with permission.

she think three days is a quick response, or does the letter go out in that day's mail?

3. Follow up on details. You will be remembered for the small details, such as recalling the name of a client's spouse or the birthday of a client's child (see the next section, "Responsiveness"). But details also include remembering that the bathroom is to be done in chrome, not brass.

4. Be open and warm to all clients. Make them feel they come first even though you may have 14 other clients.

5. Thoroughly document meeting minutes, telephone calls, meetings with product suppliers, mistakes and/or changes on the job, and contractor questions.

6. Never hide from a problem. Be up-front. There is no use in pretending a problem doesn't exist merely to avoid client conflict.

7. Make sure your office telephone number, cell phone, and pager numbers are on all correspondence to encourage contacts and queries from the client.

Boost Your Sales Voltage—Go Electronic

Keeping life in your A/E/C sales and marketing machine comes down to one word: *relation-ships*. If you could just stay current with every client and prospect—remember what's important to each of them, stay on top of every deal, track your priorities, and make certain you keep every commitment—you'd be flying high.

But with hundreds of personal encounters in your business week, how do you do keep all those people blinking on your radar screen, and how can you put your hands on the information you need about them the moment you need it?

Fortunately, a family of new Web-based sales automation tools can help you with this staggering task. These services manage your accounts and contacts so you can quickly find and act on critical information. Because they originate from the Internet, there's no software to buy, install, or maintain. Anyone in your firm involved with sales and marketing can get into the system immediately by just clicking onto the Web—from the office, from home, from Tahiti, 24 hours a day, 7 days a week. Problem solved.

What Do the Programs Have in Common?

Most of these services offer baseline features including:

- A personal home page where the user can find at-a-glance lists of today's tasks, appointments, opportunities, important contacts, hot prospects, and more. Hyperlinks connect you with other site pages giving more in-depth information. For example, click on a contact to get a complete dossier of his or her firm.
- An accounts page quick-listing of all current clients or prospects, their industries, locations, status, links to their Web sites, and drill-down links to more complete information.
- A contacts page showing full demographics of the contact's company, including current stock quotes, annual sales and income, partners, open activity, and presenting opportunities.
- An opportunities page where you can track the progress of every deal in the making.
- Web-based design allowing access from any point of entry in your firm. If two departments are working on a prospect for different possible projects, each can work off the same information. This strengthens collaboration and eliminates duplication.

Figure 4-3
Source: "Boost Your Sales Volume—Go Electronic," *PSMJ Best Practices*, August 2000.

8. Make sure every piece of paper that crosses your desk is dated so you can provide an accurate time/dated record of all activities if called on by your client to do so.

9. If you have an important telephone conversation, record it, with permission, so you can later recall its key elements. (See Figure 4-4 for a sample phone call record form.)

Record of Phone Conversation

Email has become a predominant form of communication among design firms, their clients, subconsultants, and project team members. The project manager emails periodic project reports and status updates. The design team provides the latest revisions to drawings and specifications over the Internet. Schedule and budget status is exchanged via intranets or project Web sites. Project reports are delivered electronically, sometimes followed by a printed copy sent by regular mail. In each of these situations, documentation exists to show that the communication took place, and each contains the essence of what was discussed. Emails, letters, and transmittals are marked with date, time, sender, addresses, key points, and so on. Each indicates clearly the distribution of the information, including the names and addresses of the sending and receiving parties. There remains one type of communication that continues to lack effective documentation—the phone call!

Phone calls have always been poorly documented, even when most people talked on the phone while sitting at their desk. At least paper and pencil were readily available to take notes, which allowed for completing a telephone record at some future time (obviously, the sooner the better, if completeness was critical!). Now, with the extensive use of cell phones, many conversations are conducted at job sites, in airports, and so on, where the ability to take notes is severely hampered by the inability to write legibly. Nevertheless, a permanent record of these conversations remains just as important, especially if follow-up actions are required or commitments are made. The sample Record of Telephone Conversation form captures the key facts about a conversation (date, time, company, name, actions, etc.). Copy and modify it to create a custom form for your firm. Make it available in electronic format (for emailing) as well as in pad form by each phone. In addition, create a smaller version that can fit into a shirt pocket or business planner to use when away from a desk.

Make both the large and small versions of the form a bright color that is different from your firm's standard phone message pads (usually pink). Use the smaller version to record basic information during or immediately after each cell phone call. Transfer this information to a full-size standard form (either electronic or paper, see the next page for an example) and transmit it to the parties needing the information. Keeping track of telephone conversations (especially action items and commitments) has never been easy or done effectively. Unfortunately, with the pace of business today and all the new communication gadgets, it becomes more and more difficult to keep up with phone calls. This makes recordkeeping all the more vital, and the implementation of a standard system to record phone conversations an absolute necessity!

Figure 4-4

Source: PSMJ's *The Ultimate Project Management Manual,* ©1999.

10. Be certain to record telephone, fax, cell phone, and pager numbers, as well as email addresses, of all key people on a project so that they can be reached.

11. Outfit project managers with a cell phone or pager so they are accessible in a crisis.

RECORD OF TELEPHONE CONVERSATION

Date ____ / ____ / ____   Time _____ ( ) AM ( ) PM

( ) Call to   ( ) Call from   Name _____

Company _____ Phone No. _____

Project _____ Project No. _____

Regarding _____

_____

This memorandum confirms the conversation of _____ between

_____ and _____ in which it was said:

_____

_____

_____

_____

_____

_____

_____

_____

_____

_____

Action to be taken / decisions made:

_____

_____

_____

_____

_____

_____

_____

_____

Signed _____

_____

Distribution:

( ) Owner   ( ) Contractor

( ) PIC   ( ) File

( ) Project Manager   ( ) _____

Figure 4-4 (continued)

12. Learn how to send faxes and email messages so you don't depend on others in your office in an emergency or crisis.

13. Develop a key contact list of pertinent building departments so you can call the right person in a crisis.

RESPONSIVENESS

Responsiveness is critical to being perceived as providing outstanding service. The small design firm must know its clients intimately in order to court long-term relationships, which are important to success (as explained in Chapter 2 under "Targeting Clients, Not Projects"). There is nothing more embarrassing and detrimental to client perception of responsiveness than getting into a conversation with a client, who has mentioned his or her spouse previously (in detail), only to forget that spouse's first name when it comes time to ask, "How is (blank) anyway?"

To show your clients how much they are valued, set up a filing system to record personal facts. One way to do this is suggested in Harvey Mackay's *Swim with the Sharks Without Being Eaten Alive.*[1] Mackay, who owns an envelope corporation, has a 66-question customer profile for each customer that his employees come into contact with. Because it is impossible to answer every question in one telephone call or visit, the questionnaire is kept in the file and filled in as the firm gets to know the client. The list includes such items as the spouse's name; birthdays of the client, spouse, and children; nickname; and college fraternity. (See Fig. 4-5 for a CEO customer profile form based on Mackay's questionnaire.) These days, such client information can also be stored in a personal digital assistant (PDA) such as a PalmPilot for easy updating and access. Developing such a list for your organization will make you appear more concerned, more responsive, and more service-oriented. Responsiveness helps retain repeat clients.

PROJECT MANAGEMENT[2]

The backbone of excellent client service is effective project management. (See Chapter 5, Figure 5-2 "21 Traits of a Powerhouse PM.") Once you've won a project, is it important to select a project manager and get that person involved immediately in the process.

Getting Off to a Good Start Project planning begins when the project manager is selected. A principal (or another appropriate director) should inform the PM of the assignment and provide all available documentation relevant to the project. Usually, this meeting also includes at least one senior technical person and potential senior team members.

The initial briefing's goal is for the PM to leave with:

1. A general knowledge of the project and the client

CEO Customer Profile

CUSTOMER

1. Name ....
    Nickname ....
    Title ....

2. Company Name ....
    Address ....
    City, State, Zip ....

3. Home Address ....
    ....

4. Telephone: (Work) .... (Home) ....
    Cell: .... Pager: ....
    Email: .... Fax: ....

5. Birth date and place ....
    Hometown ....

6. Professional Licenses In ....

7. Assistant's Name   Tel Ext _____
    ....

EDUCATION

8. College ....
    Graduation Date .... Degree ....

9. College Honors ....
    Advanced degrees .... School ....

10. College fraternity/sorority ....
    Sports ....

11. Extracurricular college activities ....
    Noteworthy sports awards ....

12. If customer didn't attend college. Is he or she sensitive about it? ......
    What did they do instead? ....

13. Military service ....
    Discharge rank ....
    Attitude towards being in the service ....
    Veteran: Yes ▮   No ▮

Figure 4-5. CEO customer profile.

CEO CUSTOMER PROFILE continued

FAMILY

14. Marital status .... Spouse's name ....
Previously Married: Yes ☐ No ☐   # of Times _____

15. Spouse's education ....
Spouse's Job/Career ....

16. Spouses Interests/activities/affiliations ....
....

17. Wedding anniversary .... Year Married ....

18. Children, if any, names and ages ....
....

19. Children's education ....

20. Children's interests (hobbies, problems. etc.) ....
....
Special Notes About Family ....
....

BUSINESS BACKGROUND

21. Previous employment: (most recent first)
Company ....
Location ....
Dates   .... Title_____

Company ....
Location ....
Dates   .... Title_____

22. Previous position at present company: Title_____
Dates ....

23. Any "status" symbols in office? ....

24. Professional or trade associations ....
Office or honors in them ....

25. Any mentors? ....
....

26. What business relationship does client have with others in our company? ......

27. Is it a good relationship? Yes ☐ No ☐   Why? ....
....

28. What other people in our company know the customer? ....
....

29. Type of connection ....
Nature of relationship ....

30. What is client's attitude toward his or her firm? ....

31. What is his or her long-range business objective? ....
....

32. What is his or her immediate business objective? ....
....

33. What is of greatest concern to customer at this time;
a.) ☐ the welfare of the company   - or-   b.) ☐ his or her own personal welfare?

Figure 4-5 (continued)

CEO CUSTOMER PROFILE continued

	BUSINESS BACKGROUND cont.	

34.	Does the customer think of the present or the future? ··
	Why? ···

SPECIAL INTERESTS:

35.	Clubs or service clubs ··
36.	Politically active? Yes ☐ No ☐ Party importance to customer ·························
37.	Active in community? Yes ☐ No ☐ How? ··
	Religion? ····················· Active ···
38.	Highly sensitive items not to be discussed with customer (e.g. divorce, member of AA)
	···
39.	On what subjects (outside of business) does customer have strong feelings? ······················
	···

LIFESTYLE:

40.	Medical history (current condition of health) ··
41.	Does customer drink? Yes ☐ No ☐ If yes, what and how much? ················
42.	If no, offended by others drinking? Yes ☐ No ☐
43.	Does customer smoke? Yes ☐ No ☐ If no, object to others? ·····················
44.	Favorite place for lunch ···
	Favorite place for dinner ···
45.	Favorite type of cuisine ···
46.	Does customer object to having anyone buy his or her meal? Yes ☐ No ☐
47.	Hobbies and recreational interests ···
	What does customer like to read? ··
	What type(s) of books? ··
48.	Vacation habits - Airline Preference: ··
	First Class ············· Coach ····················
	Hotel Preference Room Type ···
	Rental Car Preference ···
	Does family travel with customer? Yes ☐ No ☐ ··
49.	Spectator-sports interest: sports and teams ··
50.	Kind of car(s) ································ Color ····························
51.	Conversational interests ···
	···
52.	Whom does customer seem anxious to impress? ··
	···

Figure 4-5 (continued)

CEO Customer Profile continued

Lifestyle: cont.

53. How does he or she want to be seen by those people? ....
....

54. What adjectives would you use to describe customer? ....
....

55. What is he or she most proud of having achieved? ....
....

56. What do you feel is customer's long-range personal objective? ....
....

57. What do you feel is customer's immediate personal objective? ....
....
....

The Customer and You:

58. Has customer or firm had any bad experiences with our service? Yes ☐ No ☐ ....
....

59. What moral or ethical considerations are involved when you work with the customer? ....
....

60. Does customer feel any obligation to you, our company or to our company's competition? Yes ☐ No ☐
If so, what? ....

61. What are the key problems as our customer sees them? ....
....

62. What are the priorities of the customer's management? ....
....
Any conflicts between customer and management? Yes ☐ No ☐ ....
....

63. Can you help with these problems? Yes ☐ No ☐ ....
How? ....

64. Does our competitor have better answers to the above questions than we have? Yes ☐ No ☐
If so, what are some of these?
....

Additional Notes:

....
....
....
....
....
....
....
....
....
....
....

Figure 4-5 (continued)

2. A planning work assignment
3. A planning budget
4. A project file containing all relevant documents

Prior to the meeting, the project manager must review all project documentation and be prepared to raise any questions he or she might have. Such project documentation includes:

- Copy of the RFP
- Copy of the firm's proposal
- Copy of the contract
- A project notebook
- Project initiation form
- Other documents as appropriate

The meeting should focus on:

- The project background
- Technical and managerial requirements

Initial topics for discussion should include:

- The nature of the project
- Pertinent marketing history
- Proposal philosophy
- Contract negotiations
- Special contract requirements
- Agreements with subcontractors, joint venture partners, or others

NINE ELEMENTS OF A STRONG PROJECT MANAGEMENT PLAN FOR A MAJOR PROJECT

1. Goals and objectives

2. Scope (what is to be done; include a copy of key contract terms)

3. Schedule (when is it to be done; interim and final milestones, etc.)

4. Financial plan (what it will cost in hours and dollars)

5. Team organization, resources, and responsibilities (who will do it)

6. Quality definition (how quality will be assured; quality assurance/quality control, or QA/QC, plan)

7. Change order process

8. Client management/communications plan (how to keep the client satisfied)

9. Risk management and contingency plan (what must be done to reduce potential risk)

Regardless of project size and complexity, a good project management plan is as short as possible and easy for the team to access and use.

Many project managers prepare project management plans as if they were writing a novel. A good project management plan is not a thick book with a great deal of description. It is a compilation of charts, tables, and figures (with little or no text) that will serve as a summary master plan throughout the project and will be used by the project manager, the client, all the other project team members, and the firm's management.

PSMJ's Advanced Project Management Manual, ©1999.

Anyone who attends the meeting should also be prepared to discuss:

- Project documentation
- Possible alternative technical approaches
- Research possibilities and other long-term payoffs
- Comparisons with related past projects
- Anticipated technical and management problem areas
- Skills required to perform project tasks
- Availability of personnel for assignment to the project
- Special in-house talents that might be applicable
- Overall project scheduling and time frame
- Client relationships to be established and past experiences with the client
- General nature of the project work products
- Scope and budget of the remaining planning effort
- Selection of the project planning team
- Review of remaining project planning tasks

See Figure 4-6 for a copy of a project manager's briefing checklist.

No Plan? Mission Impossible! Without proper planning, it's impossible to deliver a quality project on time and within budget. A lack of planning inevitably will result in an unprofitable project. Even good luck can't save an unplanned project.

The major purpose of a plan is to clearly define the scope of work, the schedule, and the resources by subdividing broad contractual goals into succinct, manageable tasks that can be understood by all involved. Proper planning provides a PM with an accurate means of measuring a project's progress, helping him or her anticipate possible problems, allowing time for corrective actions, and avoiding crises.

The larger the project, the more time the project manager should plan to allocate to the initial planning process. Although the percentage of the fee required for initial project planning is often lower for a large project than for a small project, remember that the time needed to plan a project's execution is in direct proportion to its complexity.

Identifying and Delivering on Your Client's Priorities After a contract has been signed and the scope of work identified, a project manager must look beyond the standard project goals (such as the purpose of the facility, the cost, when it will be completed, etc.) to determine the client's other priorities. Such priorities are often subtle, and a failure to understand them can lead to disastrous client relation problems down the road.

Project Manager's Briefing Checklist

Project Number: _____   Start Date: ___ / ___ / ___

Job Name: _____

Client: _____

1. Set the meeting: Date:_____   Time:_____

   Place: _____

2. Contact meeting attendees:
   ❑ Project Manager: _____
   ❑ Program Assistance:_____
   ❑ Technical Development:_____
   ❑ Contract Administrator: _____

3. Contact Division Vice President and Program Assistance regarding set up of project review board.
   ❑ Yes   ❑ No

4. Gather data and materials to be given to Project Manager at meeting.
   ❑ Copy of RFP
   ❑ Copy of proposal
   ❑ Copy of contract documents
   ❑ Project notebook
   ❑ Other needed documents _____

5. Prepare to bring Project Manager up to date on:
   ❑ Nature of project
   ❑ Marketing history
   ❑ Proposal philosophy
   ❑ Contract negotiations
   ❑ Special contract requirements
   ❑ Teaming, other agreements
      (This may require discussions with Contracts, Program Assistance, Technical Development, Proposal Manager, others.)

6. Prepare to provide Project Manager guidance on:
   ❑ Possible technical approaches
   ❑ Potential problem areas
   ❑ Client relationships
   ❑ Availability of personnel in-house contacts
   ❑ Overall scheduling
   ❑ Nature of project products
   ❑ Remaining planning steps

7. Schedule the project kickoff meeting.
   Date: ___ / ___ / ___   Time: _____
   Place: _____

Figure 4-6

Source: PSMJ's *Advanced Project Management Manual,* ©1999.

For example, a client may be a government manager whose first priority is to maintain a spotless set of project files in which every report is submitted on time, every invoice is in the proper format, and every decision is thoroughly documented. These may be the criteria that his manager uses to evaluate his performance.

If, in a zealous attempt to meet an ambitious schedule, the PM is perpetually delinquent in maintaining his or her progress reporting, the client may be dissatisfied even when the firm successfully meets the project's goals! No matter what one might think, design and construction firms are not in business to perform projects. They exist to serve clients.

Identifying the client's other priorities must be done at a project's outset, when the relationship between client and project manager is fresh and open. The best way to do this is through a series of probing questions. Consider the following dialog between project manager and client for a new wastewater treatment plant.

PM: I want to assure you that I'll do everything possible to meet each of your goals. But it would help me if I could understand what would happen if one of these goals can't be met. Let's say we get halfway through the design and the state issues new wastewater discharge requirements resulting in a total redesign. Suppose this caused the design schedule to slip by two months?

CLIENT: Well, I guess we could get a two-month extension if there were a good reason for the delay.

PM: What if the construction cost increased by 10 percent as a result of these new regulations?

CLIENT: That would be tougher. I suppose we would tap into the city's capital revenue fund if the increase were not more than 10 percent.

PM: What if we accelerated the redesign in order to minimize schedule delays, but this introduced a number of conflicts that had to be sorted out by construction change orders?

CLIENT: To tell you the truth, the mayor and council really blasted me about all the change orders on the last project. If that happened again, I'd probably be fired!

After asking just a few more probing questions, the PM has a clearer idea of the client's other priorities as well as his or her goals. This information should be shared with the entire project team and reinforced by the PM's actions and directions.

Turn Your Project Goals into SMART Objectives Be sure to transform the major goals you identify with the client into project objectives. This is especially important when you're managing a large, complex project. Doing so will ensure that you and your project team understand all that will be required to achieve them.

Each project objective should be:

Specific
Measurable
Actionable
Realistic
Time-based

You should examine your objectives against the SMART criteria to ensure that your planning is effective and worthwhile. Objectives that don't meet all five criteria will cause you major headaches when you attempt to measure performance.

A project objective is usually defined as a task (or group of tasks) or a result to be achieved by a certain time and within defined parameters. To keep the team effort focused, the project manager must clearly define the project's objectives.

Here are two examples of smart objectives:

1. Complete the design of a 40-mgd wastewater treatment plant within 180 days. The plant must meet effluent requirements established by the state and have sludge-drying facilities. The plant must be constructed for under $80 million and for a design fee of $6 million.
2. Develop highway design plans and specifications to complete Segment E of the Grand Parkway within nine months. The project must be constructed for a cost of under $20 million.

Attack Meetings, Save Time On a large project, meetings are a vital and necessary part of running the project smoothly and effectively. They are the primary mechanism you have to communicate with the team.

Establish Why You Are Having the Meeting The most important step in making meetings effective is to answer the question, "Why are we having this meeting?" If you can't answer the question, cancel the meeting!

Here's a basic list of reasons to have a meeting:

1. You (team) tell me (PM) something
2. I (PM) tell you (team) something
3. You (team) tell each other something
4. Brainstorming for a solution

5. Decision-making

6. The client requests a meeting

Each meeting should attempt to satisfy one of these goals. If you try to mix types, you usually fail at achieving your goal. You should start each meeting with a clear statement of the type of meeting you're convening and establish expectations. In addition, make the first type of meeting a one-on-one so you don't waste the other attendees' time.

Reduce the Number of Meetings The best way to avoid wasting time at meetings is to reduce the number of meetings you call or attend. Eliminate all unproductive meetings that have no agenda. Such meetings tend to ramble on and are totally unproductive. Use email, telephone, or write a memo instead.

The Next Best Thing to Reducing the Number of Meetings If a meeting cannot be eliminated entirely, the next best thing is to reduce the number of attendees. The rule here is that only active participants be invited. Observers should not be invited.

Reducing the list of invitees is not easy. Many people invite everyone they can think of to a meeting because:

- They are afraid that someone might be offended if not invited.
- They want everyone to hear the discussions.

BETTER, MORE EFFICIENT MEETINGS

A few thoughts to consider:

1. Schedule meetings to be 1 to 1½ hours long. This limit has been found as the ideal time span for highest productivity.

2. Schedule meetings to take place during late morning hours. The participants will be fresh, and lengthy discussions will be discouraged by the desire to end in time for lunch.

3. Schedule meetings to begin at odd hours—for example, 10:53 or 4:07. People will tend to come on time because the odd time implies punctuality.

4. Distribute a clear, succinct agenda ahead of time. If required, assign tasks ahead of time so that people are prepared.

5. Have stand-up meetings. Meetings can be kept short by removing all chairs from the room or telling people not to sit down.

6. Start meetings on time, even if everyone hasn't arrived, and don't repeat things for those who come in late (even if it's your boss). If someone is late for a meeting, look at him or her, then look at your watch. The latecomers will probably be on time for the next meeting.

7. Include a facilitator and limit the time for each discussion item. Be sure to create action items and distribute copies before ending the meeting.

8. Put clocks in your meeting rooms; if there's no clock, put your watch on the table to indicate that you intend to maintain schedules.

9. Combine subjects for your one-on-one meetings. Five subjects can be addressed at one meeting in less than half the time it would take to hold a separate meeting for each one with the same person.

10. Summarize at the end of the meeting to ensure that you have met the expectations you set at the start.

11. Take your own meeting minutes; if you control the minutes, you control what happened and the actions that follow.

PSMJ's Advanced Project Management Manual, ©1999.

Let everyone know the new rules for efficient meetings so that they will not become upset if not invited. Meeting minutes should be prepared and distributed to those who might use the information from the meeting but were not invited to participate.

Eliminate Wasted Time Despite your best efforts to avoid them, a number of meetings will (and should) be held on a scheduled basis. The next secret is to cut the time they consume. A meeting agenda can be a useful tool in reducing time. Consider the following suggestions to eliminate wasted time:

1. *Always* prepare an agenda.
2. The agenda should be sent to all meeting participants at least one day ahead to let them organize their thoughts and prepare material.
3. If any handouts are needed for preparation, they should be sent with the agenda. This improves focus and avoids disruptions while everyone at the meeting reads the handouts.
4. The agenda items should be ranked, with the most important items first. This tends to avoid lengthy discussions on unimportant issues and ensures that priorities are covered.
5. A specific time should be identified for beginning each item on the agenda.
6. The individuals responsible for each item should be identified in the agenda. People whose names are not listed need not attend. People whose names appear on only one or two items may only be brought in during discussion of those items.
7. The hourly cost of the meeting (based on billing rates) should be shown on the agenda. (This is especially useful to control clients who love to have long meetings and don't want to acknowledge how much they cost.)
8. The last agenda item should identify the time when the meeting is scheduled to end. (See Figure 4-7 for a sample agenda.)

Forming a Successful Client Relationship The following five goals, when achieved, contribute to a successful client relationship.

1. **Treat the client as a person**
   The most effective way to establish a strong relationship with a client is to relate to him or her on a personal level. Treating the client as a person rather than as an agency

Sample Agenda

DATE:	5 March 2001
LOCATION:	Fourth Floor Conference Room
ATTENDANCE.	Maris Perlman Amy Mirtallo Gene Bridgeford
SUBJECT:	Improving Schedule Performance

8:57	Reasons for Schedule Problems
9:10	Techniques for Monitoring Schedule Status
9:45	Alternative Ways to Improve Schedule Performance
10:15	Ways of Measuring Results
10:30	Adjournment

MEETING COST:	$185/hour

Figure 4-7

Source: PSMJ's *Advanced Project Management Manual,* ©1999.

or an organization will make the client want to work with you again. Clients are people, too.

2. Focus on the client's interest

Seeing the world from the client's perspective is the key to putting the client's interests first. By understanding and even empathizing with a client's problems, you indicate your concern for his or her needs. Using these methods to convince the client that you always think of his interests first builds mutual trust and confidence.

For instance, being too formal or distant in a presentation can make the client uncomfortable and less willing to select you for the project. The client also may be concerned about your ability to relate to the city council, planning commission, citizen's groups, or others that may be involved with the project. Try to make the client feel comfortable, even in naturally uncomfortable situations such as contract negotiations.

During the project, you should consider yourself and your team as a part of the client's staff and promote this concept with the client. The best projects occur when you are considered as an extension of the client's organization. One of the most powerful things you can do to impress your client and to secure repeat business is to exceed their expectations—to wow them!

3. Exhibit professionalism and technical competence

If providing service is the driving force in the success of a relationship, then the backbone of service is professionalism and technical competence. Professionalism is manifested in many ways.

One way is to deal in an honest, straightforward manner with the client at all times. This is done by:

- Showing your respect for the client by being on time for appointments.
- Conducting efficient meetings.
- Presenting advantages and disadvantages for each alternative or recommendation.
- Admitting when you do not know the answer and explaining how you intend to find out.
- Admitting mistakes as soon as they occur.
- Providing thorough follow-up on every detail of the project.
- Spending the client's money so that he or she gets the best value for the services required by the scope of work.

4. Demonstrate project control

One of the most effective ways to solidify a good relationship with your client is to demonstrate that you have thoroughly considered everything needed to complete the project and that you have a plan to meet those needs. The strongest manifestation of this is a detailed schedule that is easy for the client to understand.

5. Develop effective communications

Client relationships are based on good communication. Effective communication is not a random occurrence but rather must be developed consciously.

Establish effective communication channels and maintain them before, during, and after completion of the project. This sometimes means adjusting your style of communication to that of your client.

For example, when first meeting a potential client, it is important to determine his or her preferred style of communication. Some clients respond better to written communication while others prefer face-to-face discussions.

In the first case, it is desirable to provide the client with a written report on a topic in advance, then meet with him or her to discuss the report and to answer questions. In the latter case, the client probably would prefer that you meet first, then present the report as an oral summary of the issues and recommendations.

The emphasis is on flexibility. Always be prepared to adjust your style to match that of the client in order to make him or her feel more comfortable with you.

QUALITY CONTROL

In the minds of today's clients, quality equals exceeding promises made. To design firms, quality still means meeting technical requirements. This section is a discussion of the importance of meeting technical requirements. As you read it, however, don't forget that clients assume you will be technically competent. Good *quality control* will not make your firm stand head and shoulders above the rest. Good *quality*—going above and beyond what your clients expect of you—will.

Along with establishing education standards for your staff and encouraging continuing education, you should set up an organized quality control program. A comprehensive quality control system is a foundation for providing top quality service to clients. It also helps limit liability. The following pages are based on David Kent Ballast's *Guide to Quality Control for Design Professionals.*[3] They are a good introduction to quality control for the small design firm.

Overview Due to the booming economy of the early 2000s, liability is a secondary issue to speed of project delivery, but it is always a concern. Insurance costs are a substantial part of firm budgets and are predicted to begin rising soon. Everyone is sensitive to practice methods and liability exposure. Reduce your errors and you have gone a long way toward solving a potential liability crisis for your firm. Setting up a rigorous quality control program is the best way to reduce errors and thereby reduce litigation.

Quality control revolves around good project management, which involves four key issues. These can be applied to every area of the project, from predesign through postoccupancy evaluation:

1. *Budget Control*—Well-run firms clarify the difference between client expectations and reality for each expenditure to be made during both design and construction. Misconceptions often lead clients to seek legal counsel when costs exceed anticipated expenditures.

2. *Scheduling*—Honesty about elements of a project that are within a firm's control and those that are not is critical. Many delays caused by outside agencies have been blamed on design firms, and many mistakes have been made by design professionals trying to make up time in fear of a client's wrath.

3. *Coordination*—Regular communication with all project team members is probably the single most important element of a good quality control program. Good communication assures that little problems don't grow large and that big problems are handled quickly.

4. *Records management*—Maintaining a well-documented trail of written communication about all aspects of a project assures that each liability claim can be properly defended. Creating such documentation also helps each person to understand a project better.

Holding your firm to standards of quality must be a part of providing good service. A quality control program can help to:

- Prevent errors and resulting claims and litigation.
- Satisfy owner requirements (insurance and quality control).
- Help you practice better and offer the most competitive service possible.

What Is Quality Control? The level of performance implied with good quality is established by tradition, standard practices, and legal precedent. Quality control attempts to assure that the normal, correct project delivery tasks and the management of those tasks and supporting office activities proceed according to plan, as free of error as possible. Quality control can be thought of as management of management. For a profile of a firm that infuses every aspect of its firm activities with quality, see Figure 4-8.

Checking and approval systems differ for each type of design business. Whatever type of business you run, however, there are guidelines to setting up a quality control program:

1. Top management must support and encourage a quality control program. You cannot assign the task to someone and then forget about it.

2. One person or a small committee should be given the responsibility to guide the daily efforts of the program.

3. Everyone in the office must be involved. This is especially true when the firm is first being formed; solicit suggestions from all employees concerning problem areas and how procedures can be modified to improve things. A quality control program thrust upon employees will not work. Quality circles are especially useful in motivating and involving employees.

4. Review past problem areas. Start with a list of those problems that cause your firm the greatest difficulties or that have the potential to do it the most damage.

5. Once you understand your office's unique problem areas, set up priorities and a schedule for action. Only you can do this, as every office is slightly different and as you won't be able to solve everything at once. Use the past-problem list as a starting point. You may find that improving your standard agreements is the most needed action or that documentation needs to be improved.

6. Finally, stick with your program. Monitor it continuously, eliminating what doesn't seem to be working and keeping what helps the most.

An effective quality control program takes time and money to set up and maintain. Even for the smallest of firms, it may mean the inclusion of checklists for each phase. As the small firm grows, the quality control system grows too, and the payoff will be fewer errors, reduced liability exposure, efficiency, and improved service to your clients.

How to Set Up a Quality Control Program for the Small Design Office

Predesign Stage

The first step in a quality control program is to look at a client and the feasibility of the project and make a go/no-go decision. Does the client want too much? Has the client come to you with unreasonable expectations or demands? Answering such questions is the first step in your quality control program because even if you need the work, a project could end up costing you more money than you might earn.

In reviewing the client's expectations and budget, consider also whether your firm can complete the proposed project. Look at:

- Number of personnel
- Experience in the proposed project type
- Current workload

Be sure you are not presenting your firm as a specialist in an area if it is not. Specialty firms are held accountable for a higher standard of practice than general design firms

Infusing Quality Throughout the Firm

Firm:	*Talbot & Associates Consulting Engineers*
Staff:	*20*
Specialty:	*MEP/fire protection firm*
Address:	*119 East 8th Street*
	Charlotte, N.C. 28202

It is no accident that Talbot & Associates Consulting Engineers has recently made *Inc.* magazine's "Inner City 100" list, which ranks the fastest-growing privately held companies in America's inner cities. With a staff of just 20, this Charlotte, North Carolina, firm has been logging a growth rate of 25 percent per year since 1990 and, according to firm founder Mike Talbot, intends to keep that going for the foreseeable future.

The problem is, what happens when the seams start to burst? Talbot decided to let them out. In June, the firm put in place a strategic plan that allowed it to continue this 25 percent growth rate while maintaining high-level service.

Planning Cuts Your Time and Improves Your Quality

The plan is no seat-of-the-pants decision. Over the past ten years, Talbot has built its practice around tested and effective methodology. So why not take the same approach with growth? The new strategic plan stems from Talbot's long tradition of planning. "Most of our clients are architectural firms, and we have been able to keep every one of them," says Talbot. "We have a process for every function in our office—for construction documents, shop drawing review, construction review—everything. The processes reduce the typical time for doing the work, but they also increase the quality." The firm has developed automated procedures that help each person work more productively.

"Our engineers use personal CAD routines," says Talbot. "By letting someone do his or her own design input instead of redlining and giving it to a CAD operator, we save time, get a better quality drawing, and eliminate drafting errors."

Talbot also sets design criteria early in each project via a written report, complete with cut sheets of plumbing and electrical fixtures, "so clients get a clear understanding of what specifics we are proposing," says Talbot. "That saves a lot of going back and forth once we have started the actual design."

Strategic Planning Helps You Grow

With its reputation for good service and high value, the firm started to have growing pains. "We couldn't handle our workload with our current way of doing things," says Talbot. "And we wanted to see how we could maintain the 25 percent growth rate as a larger company. We needed additional process for doing that."

Enter the strategic plan, which does more than merely set forth goals; it creates a design for reaching them. "We want to maintain our growth and double in size by 2003," Talbot says. "The strategic plan maps out our path. It helps us see what a 40-person firm must look like to maintain high service—as opposed to a 20-person firm."

Talbot & Associates opted for a studio strategy. They also used an outside facilitator to help get everyone behind the plan.

"All I did was to create a vision of what Talbot & Associates will look like in 2003, with regard to staff size and breakdown, client and project types, project delivery, company organization, and technology utilization," Talbot noted. "We threw it out on the floor, got everybody's input, then incorporated it into the strategic plan. The facilitator helped a lot, too. He got people involved."

Has the plan worked out? Although it is still too early to tell, the firm has gained three new clients since June. Says Talbot, "Before, we could not have handled the additional work."

TALBOT'S NINE OPERATING PRINCIPLES FOR A WELL-TAILORED FIRM

1. Deliver on time.
2. Deliver good quality.
3. Don't borrow money. Instead, pay for everything from operating income so you can negotiate the best cash prices.
4. Keep your staff efficient and productive by staying as high-tech as possible.
5. Eliminate clients who don't pay or who shop price on every project.
6. Create time- and cost-saving methodology in all departments.
7. At critical growth points, write a strategic plan describing ways to reach your goals.
8. Enlist everyone's support for the plan.
9. Keep your staff happy, motivated, and rewarded.

Figure 4-8
Source: "Planning to Stay on the Street," *PSMJ Best Practices*, September 2000, p. 5.

Review the client's proposal carefully. Does he or she want you to use existing plans? If so, review possible pitfalls with the client and protect yourself in the agreement or contract. In submitting your proposal, include a detailed list of services included in the cost. Do not attach previous cost estimates or preliminary estimates to the contract. These may bind you to design a facility within a certain cost limit.

Also consider scheduling. In addition to normal scheduling activities, identify special requirements or possible delays. List these in writing and submit them to the client, explaining that this is not all-inclusive. Items causing delay might include:

- Elevators
- Hardware
- Special finishes
- Mechanical equipment
- Construction strikes
- Seasonal weather factors

ONE GOOD WAY TO AVOID GETTING SUED

Take note: Negligence claims filed by clients often do not arise from design errors or omissions. Instead, many such claims are actually counterclaims filed against a design firm after the firm has first sued a client *for failure to pay its bills on time.*

Nonpayment Lawsuits: A Can of Worms

According to research from the Professional Liability Agents Network (PLAN), a select group of insurance agencies specializing in risk management and loss prevention programs for architects, engineers, environmental consultants, accountants, and lawyers, clients sued for fees are likely to respond in kind, suing the design firm for negligence. Nor are these countersuits always meritless in the client's eyes. Few architects or engineers deliver perfect plans, specifications, or projects. While imperfections may not rise to the level of negligence, a disgruntled client will likely have little trouble finding a lawyer with a hired-gun expert who will testify that the design firm performed below the standard of care. They will contend that this inadequate performance caused damage to the client and presented a valid reason for nonpayment.

It's likely that defending a negligence claim would cost you a lot more than the fees you might net from a nonpayment claim. So, in this situation, your client holds the cards. This is why many design firms often settle a dispute by accepting only a fraction of the fees they have earned.

Contractual Prevention: The Best Cure

With today's complicated project delivery methods and contractual relationships, it is more critical than ever to use strong billing and statement language to avoid a countersuit. Develop contractual clauses that specify methods and terms of payment. Leave nothing open to interpretation.

Billing and Payment Clauses

Try these sample billing and payment clauses, adapting them to your situation:

■ CLIENT recognizes that prompt payment of CONSULTANT's invoices is an essential aspect of the overall consideration CONSULTANT requires for providing services to CLIENT. Accordingly, CLIENT agrees to advise CONSULTANT as to the preferred billing cycle, invoice format, person to whom invoices should be addressed, and such other pertinent details CONSULTANT should observe to help CLIENT expedite payment.

■ The CLIENT shall make an initial payment of _____ dollars ($____) (retainer) upon execution of this Agreement. This retainer shall be held by the DESIGN PROFESSIONAL and applied against the final invoice. Invoices shall be submitted by the DESIGN PROFESSIONAL (monthly, bimonthly, etc.), are due upon presentation, and shall be considered past due if not paid within _____ (____) calendar days of the invoice date.

Satisfaction with Services

Another option to consider is a provision stating that your client's payment implies he or she is satisfied with your services and unaware of any defect. Consider this example:

■ Payment of any invoice by the CLIENT to the DESIGN PROFESSIONAL shall be taken to mean that the CLIENT is satisfied with the DESIGN PROFESSIONAL's services and is not aware of any deficiencies in those services.

Withholding Fees for Disputes

If your client insists on language that permits withholding fees for any disputed invoiced amounts, you might use language similar to the following:

■ If the CLIENT objects to any portion of an invoice, the CLIENT shall so notify the DESIGN PROFESSIONAL in writing within _____ (____) calendar days of receipt of the invoice. The CLIENT shall identify the specific cause of the disagreement and shall pay when due that portion of the invoice not in dispute. Interest as stated above shall be paid by the CLIENT on all disputed invoiced amounts resolved in the DESIGN PROFESSIONAL's favor and unpaid for more than _____ (____) calendar days after date of submission.

Please note: The above material is for informational purposes only. Before taking action that could have legal or other important consequences, PSMJ suggests that you speak with a qualified legal professional who can guide you through your own unique circumstances.

PSMJ Best Practices, September 2000.

Finally, choose a team. Estimate members' average experience level by taking the total number of years of experience of all team members and dividing by the number of team members. If the resulting number is less than five years, you may want to add more experienced people to the team or closely supervise the work.

Proposals The proposal presents a firm's proposed approach to a project. As such, it often serves as the basis for the formal written contract. (See Appendix C for a sample killer cover letter for your next proposal.) It follows that your proposal should be subject to the same kind of quality control check as any other part of the practice. Figure 4-9 is a checklist of items to consider when writing the proposal. Use this checklist as a guideline to draw up your own, to be reproduced and followed each time you write a proposal.

Contracts Your first line of defense against exposure to liability is your contract. Spell out exactly what your client can expect of you and what you can expect of your client. State responsibilities and the level of professional services you will provide. In

Proposal Checklist

❏ Make sure the proposal responds to the client's request. First, answer their questions; don't tell them what is of interest to you. If you feel the need to expand on the request, do so after you have met the requirements of the request for proposal.

❏ Determine what issue is most important to the client and how you can respond to it. This may not always be spelled out by the client. You may have to do some research, ask the client representative, or read between the lines.

❏ Beware of irrelevant statements and broad generalizations. Avoid "We use the team approach" and "We are a design-oriented firm." Such generalizations state nothing and usually mean nothing to the client.

❏ Do not overstate your qualifications. The content of a proposal can raise unrealistic expectations in the client as well as expose you to possible litigation later.

❏ Include a cover letter. Not everyone on a selection committee reads the proposal, and this may help sell your firm to them. (See Appendix C for information on creating a killer cover letter.)

❏ Reread the request for proposal to be sure you have included every item.

❏ Allow plenty of time for delivery of the proposal. Do not rely on last-minute delivery services, as there is always the possibility, despite guarantees, of it arriving late.

Figure 4-9
Source: Guide to Quality Control for Design Professionals, by David Kent Ballast.

addition, be sure your contract protects your rights to collect fees due.

Because laws and regulations vary from state to state, you should consult an attorney on all legal matters. Figure 4-10 is a checklist of general considerations applicable to most contract situations, and Figure 4-11 contains information about contract clauses that help avoid problems from the outset of the project.

QUALITY CONTROL FOR THE ACTUAL WORK

Because every design practice differs in the details of the work process, it would be difficult, if not impossible, to include here every phase of work and a checklist for each one. Publications are available with checklists and other advice. You can also develop your own quality control checklists. Be sure to include every step in the design process:

Programming
    Zoning
    Building codes
    Universal accessibility
Design
    Actual design
    Selection of materials and products
    Technical design of individual components and
        details
Construction documents
    Working drawings
    Project manual
    Specifications
    Coordination checking
Bidding
Substitutions
Contract administration
    Site observation
    Shop drawings and change orders
Startup, operations, and maintenance
    Project closeout
    Client follow-up
Postoccupancy evaluation
    Office performance
    Professional services evaluation
    Consultants/contractors evaluation

Also consider including records and information management in the above list.

Contract Checklist

❑ Base your contract on standardized contract forms developed by the American Institute of Architects or other professional organizations. While you should develop your own contract to best clarify your needs, these contracts represent the most current standards of practice and needs of the practicing professional, and are important reference points.

❑ Never start work without a signed contract, even if it is being negotiated and near completion. Unforeseen circumstances can cause the project to be canceled, leaving you with no basis for collecting fees on work already done.

❑ When modifying any standard form, consult an attorney. This is the least expensive kind of insurance you can buy. If your client insists on using another contract form, consult an attorney. Compare it to your contract, paying particular attention to its provisions. Don't hesitate to insist on changes necessary to protect your interests.

❑ Make sure your contract is coordinated with the general conditions of the contract and other applicable contract documents.

❑ Clearly spell out the scope of services. Do not hesitate to attach a detailed list of services you will perform.

❑ Include a detailed description of the owner's responsibilities for delivery of whatever the owner is to provide for the project. Clearly identify the due dates and exactly what data are to be provided. Do not perform services based on a purchase order, service order, or other preprinted form.

❑ Verify that the contract does not contain any language that connotes perfection. Be on the lookout for the following words and phrases that refer to your performance and obligations:
- Guarantee and warranty
- Supervise
- Inspect
- Insure and assure
- Comply with applicable regulations and ordinances
- Complete drawings and specifications
- Will provide as-built drawings (instead, provide record drawings)
- Control
- Direct
- Oversee
- Guide
- Approve
- Right to stop work

❑ Check for words that imply an indirect promise of performance, such as *adequate, safe, satisfactory,* and *suitable.*

❑ Check for words that connote extremes, such as *all, best, complete, every, highest, none.*

Continued on the next page

Figure 4-10
Source: *Guide to Quality Control for Design Professionals,* by David Kent

❑ Check for ambiguous words and phrases.

❑ Carefully review any phrases that involve "hold harmless" or "indemnify and defend" positions. Check with your attorney on these. Ideally, you should negotiate these out of the contract because if you indemnify someone, you accept all of the liability. Make sure all referenced items, exhibits, and other documents are attached to the contracts and that you understand what they contain.

❑ To the extent allowed by the laws of your state, include indemnification clauses to limit your liability to third parties or transfer it to the owner (except for personal injuries). Because this is a complex area of law for construction-related contracts, work with your attorney to devise the best approach for your needs and to be in accordance with local laws.

❑ Avoid contingency clauses that base payment of your fee on conditions over which you have no control, such as successful completion of the contract and approval by a zoning board.

❑ Avoid statements about completeness. Include a clause that limits your liability on a project to the amount of your fee and professional liability insurance, or just your fee, if you don't carry insurance. If the client insists on deleting normal phases of service (such as contract administration), make sure your contract clearly limits your liability for damages and claims arising from changes of improper use of your work or from other actions over which you have no responsibility.

❑ Include provisions for holding you harmless for use of your drawings or other work if your services are terminated prematurely. Include a suspension or termination of services clause after a certain period of nonpayment of fee and implement the clause immediately if the client does not pay according to the contract schedule.

❑ Have consultants contract directly with the client. Not only do you avoid problems with late payment of fees by the client to the contractor but you also avoid several more contractual relationships that can add to your liability exposure. Retain ownership of drawings and specifications, prohibiting their use by the client on future projects without your permission and compensation. Include a holding clause holding you harmless from all liability arising from such future use. Because state laws on indemnification vary, check with your attorney. Include a provision requiring the client to approve, in writing, completion of each phase before work begins on subsequent phases. Changes made by the client after approval form the basis for extra compensation and possible time extension. Verify the existence of certification forms beyond those normally used (such as certificates for payment) that your client may want you to sign during the course of the project. These may come from the client's lending institution, surety companies, and other parties to the project. They usually require the design professional to make statements about construction conditions over which he or she has no control or knowledge and can expand your liability. Again, consult your attorney. If the client insists on you performing this kind of surety, include a clause in the contract limiting liability.

❑ Include a clause providing for payment of extra services if the construction time is extended beyond the original estimate by more than a given percentage.

Figure 4-10 (continued)

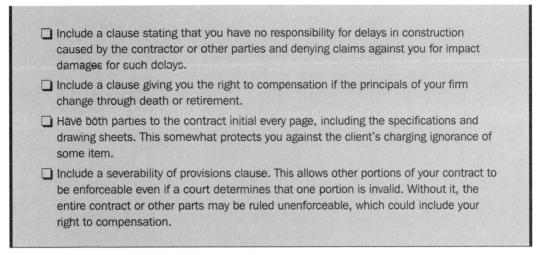

❏ Include a clause stating that you have no responsibility for delays in construction caused by the contractor or other parties and denying claims against you for impact damages for such delays.

❏ Include a clause giving you the right to compensation if the principals of your firm change through death or retirement.

❏ Have both parties to the contract initial every page, including the specifications and drawing sheets. This somewhat protects you against the client's charging ignorance of some item.

❏ Include a severability of provisions clause. This allows other portions of your contract to be enforceable even if a court determines that one portion is invalid. Without it, the entire contract or other parts may be ruled unenforceable, which could include your right to compensation.

Figure 4-10 (continued)

Quality Control Methods In the 1980s, the quality control concepts of peer review and quality control circles were developed. Quality control circles are useful, but peer review is more effective. A brief discussion of each follows.

Quality Control Circles The idea of the quality control circle, which originated in Japan in the 1960s, has been successfully applied in many industries. A quality control circle is a group of employees that regularly meet to identify, analyze, and solve problems related to their work. The premise is that employees are valuable resources and may know, better than management, their immediate quality control problems and how to solve them. Benefits from this process include increased motivation, improved communication, teamwork, more involvement by employees, and higher productivity. The circles should meet once a week for an hour and be flexible enough to accommodate everyone's schedules. Membership should be voluntary.

Additional guidelines to quality control circles are shown in Figure 4-12.

Peer Review Peer review improves the quality of the practice by having its policies and procedures examined by a group of professional colleagues. Peer review does not assess the design quality in the office but rather the firm's ways of delivering services.

One exemplary source of peer review is the American Consulting Engineers Council (ACEC). ACEC's program involves a team of highly qualified professionals who review a firm's written policies of management, development and

Contract Clauses That Pull Their Weight

If our contracts have teeth, we will collect the revenues that we have earned—and that we deserve. In our design process, we create invaluable intellectual property. In our business practices, let's operate on the same value-adding level—to deliver the best service and achieve the most profitable results.

Study the terms below and rewrite them to your own firm's specific circumstances. Each one will take you a step closer to creating a more successful design business.

1. *Limit of Liability:* "It's understood that the total liability of XYZ Associates for any claims arising out of the services performed under this agreement shall be limited to a maximum of the net fee received by XYZ Associates, not including reimbursable subconsultant fees and expenses."
   COMMENT—This is a more reasonable limit of liability than the total fee.

2. *Limitation on Design Alternatives:* "XYZ Associates will… [use one of the following]: (1)…limit the number of design alternatives provided under this contract to three; (2)…limit to___ hours the time expended in design; or (3)…stop developing project design by _____, 20__, upon which time the design will be considered complete."
   COMMENT—Make sure you're not designing all the way through the project, or if you are, get paid for the effort.

3. *Ownership and Copyright of Documents:* "All drawings and documents produced under terms of this agreement are the property of XYZ Associates and cannot be used for any reason other than to bid and construct the above-named project. The client shall be granted a revocable license to use the drawings and documents for the purpose of constructing, maintaining, and operating the [project], and shall not use such documents for any other purpose without the Architect's consent. The client shall indemnify and defend the Architect from any claim, loss, or damage arising out of the client's failure to abide by the terms hereof."
   COMMENT—Documents used for other than their original purpose may result in liability to the original design professional.

4. *Automatic Escalator:* "After _____, 20__, all fees and hourly rates quoted within this contract may increase by ____ percent annually thereafter."
   COMMENT—Most firms include a clause in their contracts to the effect that, after some specific date, all fees will be subject to renegotiations. This is not the same as stipulating a specific percentage increase. Renegotiations could result in decreased fees to the design firm.

5. *Higher Fees Paid for Changes:* "Any changes requested in the attached scope of services provided under this agreement will be billed at a multiplier of 1.25 times customary billing rates."
   COMMENT—Project changes mean a costly remobilization, a greater potential for errors and omissions, and disruption of other project schedules. Seek compensation at higher rates than normal.

6. *Client Signatures at Various Stages in the Project:* "Beginning with the date of project initiation, all drawings produced under this agreement will be signed by an authorized representative of the client each 60 days during the project or at more frequent intervals when appropriate."
   COMMENT—You must document any design changes mandated by the client in order to minimize future misunderstandings about client wants and needs. Notice that the above stipulation calls for signoff at a given date, not at a phase or a percentage of

completion, although leaving the possibility open. It's too easy to end up in an argument with your client over what defines or constitutes completion of a phase. Hence, PSMJ recommends never tying payment of fees to phase completion.

7. *No Backup for Reimbursable Expenses:* "No backup data or copies of bills will be provided for reimbursable expenses invoiced under this agreement. Should backup data be requested, they will be provided for an administrative fee of $100 per monthly invoice requiring verification, plus $1.00 per bill or cost item supplied."
   COMMENT—Supplying backup for reimbursable expenses takes time. The typical A/E/C firm doesn't have staff resources to squander on nonbillable activities.

8. *No Exact Reimbursable Expenses:* "The client will pay 15 percent of each total monthly invoice for professional services submitted by XYZ Associates as a reimbursable fee to cover all typical reimbursable expenses, such as postage, fax, phone, and mail, but excluding models, renderings, or copies of drawings or specifications in excess of ___ sets."
   COMMENT—This clause simplifies your accounting and saves money, and it eliminates having to keep track of mountains of detailed backup.

9. *Stamp Only After Payment:* "XYZ Associates will not stamp drawings produced for any phase of this project under the terms of this agreement until all invoices billed to that point in the project have been paid in full."
   COMMENT—This is one more method to ensure prompt payment.

10. *Hazardous Waste:* "Any hazardous waste or asbestos requiring removal, encapsulation, or containment during the course of this project will result in compensation to XYZ Associates equaling 3.0 times above normal customary hourly billing rates for any plans, specifications, or construction observation services provided. XYZ Associates will additionally be indemnified from any and all liability associated with removal, encapsulation, or containment of hazardous waste or asbestos."
    COMMENT—Discourage involvement with hazardous waste and asbestos, but get paid well if the client requires such materials.

11. *Job Cancellation Fee:* "In order to take this project, XYZ Associates has foregone potentially significant revenues from other projects. Therefore, if this project is canceled by the client, a cancellation fee will be immediately due and payable according to the following schedule: 0–30 days, $____; 31–60 days, $____; etc."
    COMMENT—In the event a project is canceled, get the client's commitment to pay for opportunities you lost by committing to work on the project. This cancellation fee will decrease the longer the project has run, as you should have earned a greater portion of expected revenues.

12. *Project Restart Fee:* "Because of substantial costs incurred by XYZ Associates to stop and restart a project once it is underway, should this project's progress be halted at any time for 30 or more days by the client, for any reason, a project restart fee of $____, or 10% of the total fee earned to date, whichever is greater, will be due and payable immediately."
    COMMENT—The longer you work on a project, the longer it takes to get back to speed after a stop. The longer the stoppage, the more potential for changes. Seek compensation for events beyond your control.

Disclaimer: PSMJ Resources is not in the business of rendering legal advice and intends these contract terms and conditions to be used only after consultation with a competent attorney knowledgeable in contract law in your area of professional practice in your locale.

Figure 4-11
Source: "Stasiowski On...," *PSMJ Resources,* September 1 and September14, 2000.

Guidelines for Quality Control Circles

1. The concept and process must have top management support, including a commitment to seriously consider suggestions made by the quality circles. Any middle management that exists in larger firms must also support the idea.
2. The quality circles must be ongoing activities.
3. Quality circles are not just gripe sessions; they are problem-solving units.
4. Everyone on the committee should get training in problem-solving techniques.
5. Size should be kept small. For larger firms or firms with several service areas, consider more than one circle.
6. Although quality circles can work with any size firm, they are more appropriate to medium- and larger-sized firms. A 20- to 30-person firm could probably benefit from one small quality control circle. Larger firms may institute more.
7. Quality control circles should be considered a means to help employees develop and generally improve the quality of working as well as the quality of the work output.

Figure 4-12

Source: Guide to Quality Control for Design Professionals, by David Kent Ballast.

maintenance of technical competence, human resources, project management, financial management, and business development. The team then visits the office to determine whether employees understand all policies and procedures. Finally, they deliver an oral report to the firm's principals. For more information, visit the ACEC's Web site at www.acec.org, or call (202) 347-7474.

Roundtable Today, more and more firm leaders are learning about qual-
Discussions ity control techniques for business processes in roundtable forums where noncompeting design firm principals get together once every month or quarter to discuss financial, management, and design issues.

Watch out for overkill, however. In a survey of clients, consultant Martin McElroy found that "many corporate officers took note of a tendency for design professionals to perform (and design) to self-imposed standards that are more costly than necessary to meet the client's requirements."[4] This is the infamous "excess perfection syndrome." (See Fig. 4-13.) While it is important to provide excellent service, you must tailor the services to the expectations of the client, because that is all he or she will pay for. Prevent your staff from providing the same level of service for every job or client. That means some jobs get the Chevy treatment and others the Cadillac.

Excess Perfection Syndrome

Most technical professionals suffer from the excess perfection syndrome. Design professionals often do more than is necessary on a particular task.

For example, a project manager is assigned to study the feasibility of installing snow-making equipment at a ski area. To size the pumps, he must know the difference in elevation between the lake and the top of the mountain. The project manager sends a survey crew to level up and down the mountain. They close within a tenth of a foot and charge the project $3500. However, they could have looked at a U.S. Geological Survey map and charged the project $15.

Note that this discussion is not about perfect versus imperfect work. This is about degrees of excellence. Also, less than 100 percent perfection does not mean poor quality control with resulting liability claims. It might very well mean cutting the designer off at 90 percent and giving the remaining fee to the checkers to catch the mistakes.

The excess perfection syndrome is graphically illustrated below. In the early stages of a task, increased effort causes pronounced increases in excellence. But as the task approaches 90 percent perfection, the point of diminishing returns is rapidly reached. In other words, you lose money in the form of personnel-hours with little real improvement of the project.

The question the project manager should constantly ask is, what level of excellence is really needed at this particular time? In the conceptual stages, maybe only 80 percent is necessary, while for a complex structural system, maybe 98 percent or higher is needed. However, it is never possible to achieve 100 percent perfection.

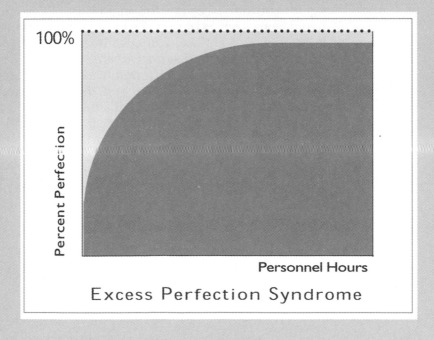

Figure 4-13
Source: "Excess Perfection Syndrome," *The Best of PSMJ.*

Even the Chevy jobs must meet a standard of quality, however. For this reason, be sure to use seasoned personnel as quality control resources. Project managers often do not make good use of the firm's technical resources (in other words, quality control staff), citing cost. When project managers must absorb this cost within their budgets, they minimize the time technical staff spend on the project. This is false economy.

One option for paying for quality control is to take a set percentage of the fee from all projects and pool these funds. The quality control staff then charges time to this pool rather than to individual projects.

In one firm, this solution resulted in project managers using senior staff earlier in the project, when they can contribute more. By removing the cost factor, they found the quality control function more readily accepted as a resource. On the other hand, overhead increased.

Successful firms are distinctively different in the quality control they provide. Emphasize quality control as a process, not as an act after the fact. Figure 4-14 contains ten quality control tips.

INNOVATE EVEN NORMAL ACTIVITIES

Again, you must realize the importance of standing out. Avoid being seen as part of the herd in the way you practice. In today's marketplace, you encounter the same contracts, pricing strategies, and services. None is distinctively different. Position yourself as different in each area of service you perform. Distinction will give you the biggest and fastest return. It will augment the client's perception of your firm providing good service; therefore, it serves as the reason why the client should give you a project. Such distinction allows you to be alone in a niche (see Chapter 2) and to develop a widespread reputation for being in this niche. And, of course, when you are alone in a market niche, you can price your services as high as the market will bear.

Here are ten ways to be different:

1. Give cellular telephones to all technical staff.
2. Guarantee to meet client schedules and budgets or you won't take your fee.
3. Install portable fax machines in project managers' cars.
4. Guarantee to respond to client calls within half an hour.
5. Produce renderings on all projects.

Ten Quality Control Tips

1. Encourage those actually doing the work, not just the principals, to stamp or seal documents. Responsibility and initial quality rise with the signing of plans.

2. Adopt a formal checking system instead of relying on the experience of individuals. Develop or use a more formalized procedure, such as a building code checklist.

3. Build into a project's schedule and budget the time and costs of review by individual(s) not involved with the initial design.

4. Have a final design review after all documents are prepared. Late changes can have a major impact on quality.

5. Get staff to job sites as a continuing training process. This is especially important for designers and drafters working on details.

6. Make sure cost estimates are accurate. Develop in-house expertise, use an outside expert cost estimator when necessary, and continually update and check the cost of items with suppliers and contractors.

7. Schedule postconstruction design reviews by the client's site representative and designer.

8. Do not switch project managers in midproject.

9. Don't allow field decisions to be made under pressure.

10. Have your firm undergo a peer review by your professional association to come up with more ways to improve quality.

Figure 4-14.

6. Build models of all projects.

7. Put a laptop in your client's office.

8. Buy an airplane to guarantee your availability at remote job sites.

9. Know your client's core business as well as your client does.

10. Ask clients how they want you to communicate with them: by email, phone, fax, etc.

Some firms put distinctive characteristics into every aspect of doing business. For example, everyone might participate in signing contracts. Traditionally, architect/engineer firms use boilerplate contracts that tend to be signed in a routine and traditional manner at a private meeting with a client. To be different, you could make the contract-signing a celebration.

Another idea is to handwrite meeting minutes and pass them out the day the meeting takes place. This distinguishes you from other firms, whose minutes are word processed and resemble every other standard piece of paper.

Personal touches make lasting impressions. Have you ever sent a rose to the client's accounts payable clerk when the client pays a bill quickly? You can bet that next time your bill will get paid first.

Being distinctively different makes you easily recognizable and remembered by potential clients, whether you are a firm that does art selection for hotels only, interior hospital architecture, facilities management for chemical plants, or restoration of old movie theaters. Narrowly focus your capability, and prospects will remember you. So will the media. When you are different, it is easier to get published.

As a key part of your service, look at how you hire your staff. Employees who focus on design alone and treat clients as a necessary evil do not belong in your service-oriented firm. Hire extraordinary people who understand the importance of the client and make it a point to concentrate on service as well as design. The next chapter addresses hiring and firing.

SUCCESS CHALLENGES

1. When did you last examine how your service is different from that of your competitors?
2. Do you really know what service your competitors provide?
3. If you are providing a largely generic service, similar to every competitor in your marketplace, how can you change that today to make it be, and to have it appear, better?
4. How can you respond more effectively to clients (through correspondence, on the telephone, personal attention, and in other ways)? Set yourself apart. Say "service" above all.

REFERENCES

1. Harvey Mackay, 1988. *Swim with the Sharks Without Being Eaten Alive.* New York: William Morrow, pp. 43–53.
2. Excerpted from *PSMJ's Advanced Project Management Manual,* ©1999.
3. David Kent Ballast, 1986. *Guide to Quality Control for Design Professionals.* Newton, Mass.: Practice Management Associates Ltd.
4. Martin McElroy, October 1987. "Management: The Architect as FM—Fiction and Fact." *Architectural Record.* Also Martin McElroy, June 1984. "Marketing: How Big Corporations Choose Design Firms." *Architectural Record.*

Chapter 5

Personnel

HIRING

Hiring staff is always a basic ingredient of a good professional practice, but nowhere is this more true than when assembling the staff of a small design firm. The strategic planning aspects of human resources are addressed in Chapter 1. This chapter describes how to recruit exceptional people, how to keep them motivated to perform, how to recognize when a person has reached a peak with you, and why you shouldn't tolerate nonperformance. Successful firms are also not afraid to bring in new people above loyal long-time employees.

One trap that entrepreneurs fall into is to hire people less smart than themselves, people who are not as aggressive, and people who merely follow instructions. They then fail to extend these employees to their full ability or neglect to expose them to clients or to inside business information for fear they may leave and start their own business. Instead, you need to hire people who are smarter than you, whose talents in their area far surpass yours. For example, hire a great specification writer, or hire the best civil engineer or project manager in your city.

Another pitfall of the entrepreneur-led organization is that of intense external focus (on clients) at the expense of internal focus (on operations). The following riddle presents an intriguing way to think of this challenge:

> *Energy focus on*
> *External client problems*
> *Creates excitement*
> *Which causes growth*
> *Which creates stress*
> *Which brings a need for efficiency*
> *Which creates an internal focus*
> *Which loses clients*
> *Which leads to monetary losses*

Why is this called a riddle? Because it begs an answer. How can firms led and energized by an entrepreneur grow without experiencing the peaks and valleys inherent in this business model? A visionary who can bring the firm new opportunities and lead it into new areas is client-focused, paying attention to external needs in the quest to satisfy client demand—but neglecting internal operations.

Successful entrepreneurs have learned the importance of a right-hand man or woman who can counterbalance their external focus with an internal one; think about I.M. Pei and Eason Leonard; Gyo Obata and the late George Kassabaum. These were complementary partnerships that led to the establishment of world-renowned firms.

Hundreds of firms have gone through the peaks and valleys described in the riddle. What's the answer? Spend money on high-quality people who will focus on consistent, internal efficiency. Without this solid base, there's no foundation for building on entrepreneurial dreams.

CONTROLLING YOUR EGO

One of the biggest challenges when hiring smart people is controlling your ego. Understand that, as entrepreneur/main partner/key person in the small design firm, your primary role is as leader. Orchestrate the firm as a coach does a football team made up of a group of stars. The coach cannot try to run every play of the game; the team would soon be losing every game of the year. His job is to create a team to take on the other teams and win the game.

In professional architecture and engineering, your job as head of a small firm is to hire stars. Make sure that you are in control of the shots but that your stars are carrying out the plays—day in, day out—to manage the clients and their projects.

Another way in which you must control your ego is in giving others in the firm recognition. The principal of a firm in Cambridge, Massachusetts, was considered a guru by many of his peers, except for one bad habit. He employed staff who would work as much as 80 hours a week on a project and produce a great product after tremendous amounts of effort. As the project was completed, the firm's publicity campaign would highlight the principal, who in fact had little input into the project, with no recognition going to the actual designers and other staff. The firm soon found itself a seedbed for new firms. Employees would leave and start their own firm or join other competitive firms. It ended up as a fine training ground but a poor example of a successful small design firm.

HOW TO ATTRACT TOP PEOPLE

An August 1999 PSMJ Resources *A/E Pulse* survey of design firm principals supports the pervasive feeling that it's close to impossible to hire good people. Eighty-five percent of respondents revealed that they were trying to hire additional staff. Less than half of those (48 percent) were able to find individuals to fill open positions. The main result of this employment crunch is that firms are offering more incentives to job candidates. For detailed results of recruiting methods used and special treatment extended to potential new hires, see Figure 5-1.

Recruiting at colleges can be an effective way to add members to your team. Here are a few tips for identifying and bringing on board young talent:

- Become an adjunct professor at a local university. This gets you in the door, able to assess talent before it even hits the job market.
- Nurture relationships with professors. Wine and dine a handful of select faculty members to whom you can turn in December and ask, "Out of everyone graduating in May, who's the best?"
- When you interview college students, ask about their entrepreneurial activities in college. This will cast some light on their potential with your organization.
- Hire four or five interns every summer, whether you need them or not. Offer scholarships or pay their tuition if, in return, they'll promise to join your firm on graduation. One firm used such a tactic to effectively shut out the competition from other potential employers. They identified an outstanding student nine months before graduation and offered him a signing bonus of $500 per month while he was still in school in exchange for signing an employment agreement. This had greater impact than waiting until the student got close to graduation because the $500 per month was much more useful while he was still in school. One architect who knew this student commented, "He was serving imported brews at his parties while his buddies could only afford domestic!"[1]

One key to overcoming hiring obstacles is to nurture your image as a dynamic, highly successful firm. Rather than running a tiny three-line ad in the local paper, invest the money necessary to buy an annual spot in a large city or regional newspaper. Create a job ad that is a promotional piece for your firm. This is a fantastic marketing opportunity and image builder.

Recruiting Is a Struggle

Methods Used For Recruiting New Staff	Percent Using
Local paper help-wanted ads	85
Out-of-town paper help-wanted ads	67
Firm's Web site	56
College job fairs	41
Industry help-wanted Web sites	41
College alumni(ae) offices	37
Bonuses to employees for referrals	37
National trade publication help-wanted ads	33
Recruiting firms	30
General help-wanted Web sites	7
National jobs publications	7

Special Treatment Offered Potential Hires	Percent Using
Relocation costs	59
Signing bonus	37
Waiver of vacation and sick leave waiting period	26
Additional time off above firm policy	15
Waiver of waiting period for bonus plan participation	11

Percentage of starting salary paid as a signing bonus: 7
Percentage of interviewed candidates to whom jobs are offered: 44
Percentage of job offers accepted: 74
Currently able to fill available job openings: Yes 48 percent   No 52 percent
Currently seeking to hire additional staff: Yes 85 percent   No 15 percent
Percentage of firms participating in this survey: 87

Figure 5-1
Source: PSMJ *A/E Pulse*, August 1999.

Find the Good People and Steal Them! As one infamous developer (you guessed it—Donald Trump) advises, if you find a good person in a competitor's organization, find a place for her in your organization and steal her, rather than wait for the opportunity for openings in your organization and hope she'll apply. Look for good people in other firms, including their branch offices, and steal them.

How do you steal? One way is to place an advertisement in the newspaper and hope the person sees it, then directly contact him.

If you feel direct recruitment is unethical, remember that you cannot force anyone to go against his wishes. Staff members won't leave their present companies to join yours unless it is clearly in their best interest or you have misrepresented the opportunity offered.

On the other hand, other firms may be attempting to directly recruit your employees. To guard against losing top performers, concentrate on making your organization the best possible place to work by emphasizing open communication and clarity of direction and by constantly letting everyone know where they stand. That way, if an employee meets a competitor at a local AIA meeting and is approached about a position, or gets a call from a recruiter or a former classmate working at another design firm looking for talent, she will remain in your fold.

Identify the stars in other companies and attract them to your team. If you are small, you cannot afford to wait.

One method used by some small firms is a signing bonus. The advantage of the bonus to the firm is that the salary can stay at about the existing level; the bonus is, in essence, a one-time expense.

Develop a process for meeting competitors' top performers. Here are some suggestions:

- Do joint ventures to work directly with your competitor's top people.
- Within peer associations, always be on the lookout for stars from other firms who may be dissatisfied.
- Look into other firms' compensation plans to see how they compare with yours.
- Discover ways to identify people in the competitor's firm who would fit into your organization.
- Incorporate tiny firms into your operation—that is, by acquisition.

DEVELOP TOP PERFORMERS FROM WITHIN

"There isn't anyone in the office who can bring a project in on schedule and on budget, keep clients happy, and hustle new work when things are slow. I want you to find a person who can do those things. Oh, yes, he should be registered, willing to work for a modest salary until he proves himself, and shouldn't be much more than 35 years old, so he'll fit in with the rest of the staff. What I want is a real go-getter, somebody who'll be able to take over my job some day—and, if you can find him, I'm prepared to offer him an associate partnership!"

Search firms hear this description of Mr. Perfect so often they have dubbed him The Man on the White Horse (TMOTWH). TMOTWH has no faults. He manages well. He's technically competent. He is handsome, a born leader, and people like to work for him. He can charm an angry client in 30 seconds flat. He can identify a prospect, write a proposal, lead a presentation, and get a job that all your competitors have been lusting after. There's only one problem: TMOTWH doesn't exist.

Where do search firms find candidates for such positions? Usually, the person who is hired away from a firm has been passed over for promotion by her present boss. The only way to climb the career ladder is to change jobs, with a title and an instant higher level of responsibility at a new office. So the employee changes jobs. The old firm now must find a replacement and calls a search firm.

Twofers, and How to Avoid Them

What occurs next is known as a twofer situation. This happens when two employees working in different firms are each talked into quitting their present job and going to work at the other place. Twofers count only when each person receives an increase in salary, position, and authority. This occurs more frequently than search firms like to admit and, clearly, each firm is better off if such a job swap does not take place. In this situation, the time required for the newcomers to be accepted by present clients and the effort involved in acclimating them to the firm's practices are a waste. In addition, to the higher salary add the search firm's fee (which may go as high as one-third of annual salary), the expense of relocation, the time it takes to interview, and the extra perks. All of this may total 60 to 70 percent of the person's annual salary.

To avoid twofers and searching outside for TMOTWH, assess which current employees have top-performer potential and groom them for a senior position within your firm. For a list of 21 traits exhibited by outstanding employees, see Figure 5-2.

You can help your employees become top performers. Consider these approaches:

1. *Assessment*—Analyze the good and bad things about a person. Make a list of technical skills the person needs to learn or improve, plus a list of social or personality traits that may need changing. Now write down ways such changes can be implemented.

2. *Appraisal*—Advise the employee of areas in performance and personality that could be improved. Outline these areas in detail, but in a nonthreatening and noncritical way. Together with the employee, agree on steps to be taken to erase technical deficiencies and improve social and personality traits.

3. *Motivation*—Clearly explain why the employee should improve in these areas—that he or she is being considered for advancement or promotion by salary or

21 Traits of Powerhouse Project Managers

This list of traits speaks specifically to the attributes seen in outstanding project managers, but it applies equally well to other employee populations. The following 21 characteristics are those of star performers.

1. **Overcommunicate with the client.**
   The clients of powerhouse PMs are never surprised and never feel neglected. A PM at an Atlanta engineering firm establishes a time to call his clients every week. What would you give to get a call every Tuesday at 2:00 P.M. from your doctor?

2. **Lavish praise on the team and show a daily interest in team members.**
   How willing are your PMs to praise success and take blame for failure? Great PMs make this a habit. They also nurture a close relationship with team members.

3. **Possess a religious sense of duty to return calls and emails.**
   A PM who works for a top Midwest design firm guarantees a response within one hour. And he delivers.

4. **Believe each client is a friend, and the project is a stop along the way in that long-term relationship.**
   These PMs send cards for clients' anniversaries and their kids' graduations.

5. **Keep fastidious records.**
   They know exactly how to put their hands on notes or records when they need to get them.

6. **Strive constantly for self-improvement.**
   A project manager who's never satisfied—who seems almost to have a complex that drives her to excel—is a winner. Average PMs complain the firm never gives them enough training; great PMs go after knowledge through courses, books, magazines, and more.

7. **Play hard with their team.**
   A powerhouse PM takes time from his personal life to meet his team for dinner, breakfast, or a softball game.

8. **Focus visually on a schedule.**
   Project managers who never fail to get the job done have a mental image of the project schedule in their head. Almost every powerhouse PM prefers the more visual 8½ × 11 bar chart or network diagram of the project schedule to a milestone chart.

9. **Take a genuine interest in people.**
   Striking up a conversation with a stranger on an airplane, volunteering at a soup kitchen, and belonging to a large network of friends are typical of the powerhouse PM.

10. **Stay physically fit.**
    The best PMs find time to exercise, sleep well, eat well, and take pride in their appearance.

    Continued on the next page.

Figure 5-2
Source: "Stasiowski On...," *PSMJ Resources,* February 23, 2000.

11. Possess curiosity about the details of your clients' business.

This is called going beyond the call of duty. Powerhouse PMs want to know what it takes to get the client to move ahead. They learn the clients' business, their needs, and goals. This is all part of building that long-term friendship.

12. Never are satisfied with their own status.

A great PM isn't content to remain a PM forever. This person wants to be a principal or a firm owner. Powerhouse PMs are workaholics in that they do what it takes to move forward in their career. They're not clock-bound to an 8:00 A.M. to 5:00 P.M. schedule like the average PM.

13. Accept mistakes as part of a learning process.

They admit to a mistake, acknowledge its impact, then correct it. Here's a wonderful idea from a powerhouse PM. Keep crisis files on past mistakes and solutions to them.

14. Work hard to make clients look good.

A PM's job is to lead the client through the maze of changes we define as a project. The project manager who can do this by giving the client credit for successes, involving the client in decisions, and keeping up strong communication with the client will win both herself and the firm a friend for life.

15. Possess a passion outside the office.

What is your passion and those of your firm's project managers? Having a source of pleasure outside the office gives people a mission other than work and makes them more interesting people.

16. Synthesize new work.

Great project managers create work out of nothing. An average PM brings work in off an ad in the paper. A powerhouse PM is always looking for new work and opportunities for the firm in everything he does, everywhere he goes.

17. Bring opportunities to their clients.

Clients don't forget a project manager who has facilitated a partnering arrangement with another firm or put together financing opportunities.

18. Embrace new technology for the firm.

This is in the best interest of the project manager, who can now offer faster, more convenient service and better control projects.

19. Have a penchant for overcoming adversity.

An average PM wouldn't want to take on a job with a loss already prescribed economically on day one, but a powerhouse PM would! Top project managers love to take on a bigger project, a tougher assignment, and find ways to make it all work.

20. Grow easily bored with routine.

PMs with their eye on advancement stop performing routine tasks over and over again by creating a subteam to whom they delegate the work. They control and monitor this team but get less involved in repetitive tasks themselves.

21. Seem to deal with minimal paperwork.

Powerhouse PMs write shorter emails, shorter proposals, and push less paper in general. They manage to accomplish everything necessary, but seem to do it with one-tenth the volume of paperwork of an average PM. The difference is that the powerhouse PM doesn't need to cover herself with paper!

Figure 5-2 (continued)

Now That You've Got the List, What Are You Going to Do with It?

First, help employees focus on how they promise what they deliver. Star performers underpromise and overdeliver. Is your staff making realistic, understated, or overstated promises? If they promise more than they're capable of achieving, they're setting up themselves, and your firm, for failure.

Second, encourage your team members to be as direct and honest as possible in all interactions. Remind them that if they're honest with clients, those clients will want to enter into long-term relationships with your firm. If your employee is direct about her ability to perform and not perform, she'll inspire confidence in others.

Third, ask your employees about fairness. Are their actions fair to themselves, their client, and your firm? No one in the world can argue with fairness. It's what everyone wants, and your employees can give it!

Figure 5-2 (continued)

title, such as becoming an associate, which carries with it higher salary, profit participation, or other perks, such as use of a company car. Even if there are few tangible perks, most staff will be motivated to improve with the promise of management participation. (See Fig. 1-16, which presents one firm's criteria for becoming an associate.)

4. *Coaching*—Work with the employee daily to make the improvements. Help improve job-related areas by assigning work that will give the employee familiarity in new areas. Nothing sharpens project management skills better than assigning more projects to manage. Also, give constant feedback.

5. *Reward*—When the first promotion or increase takes place, the coaching process doesn't stop; it continues until you feel completely comfortable in every respect with the employee, to the point of turning over more responsibility.

Never underestimate the importance of people skills. A survey of firms that promote from within and successfully retain valuable staff stresses the importance of personality traits. These must be at least equal to technical competence as a prerequisite to admitting people to upper management. In a small firm, especially, you have to offer more to a client than just the promise of doing a good job. A client must feel secure about your firm and like dealing with your contact person if the relationship is to continue.

ANNOUNCE POSITIONS WITHIN

When you feel you must look outside, how you search can have a direct impact on your current employees' morale. Announce plans to look for an outsider to your staff before you begin to search. This accomplishes two important goals. First, it gives an opportunity to any current employee who feels qualified for the position to talk to you about the job before it is offered to an outsider. Nothing is more damaging to staff morale than to have the principal announce that a new person has already been hired to fill a position an employee would have liked but did not know was available.

If a current employee does inquire about a position, be honest if you don't think he is ready for the assignment. Be prepared to suggest steps you can take together to help the employee work toward the level of competence required to attain such a position within your firm. If your candid feeling is that the person is unlikely ever to meet that level, you have an obligation to share that feeling, even if you turn out to be wrong.

The second goal of announcing openings is to generate possible referrals from your staff. Someone may know of an outside candidate, leading to an introduction and subsequent hire. Employee referral is one of the most satisfactory methods of recruiting and among the least expensive.

If you fail to find an employee in-house or by referral, then, and only then, should you consider advertising the position, contacting a search firm, recruiting directly, and so forth. See Figure 5-3 for tips on advertising positions, Figure 5-4 for questions to ask in an interview, and Figure 5-5 for making an employment offer.

When you give your staff the first opportunity to apply for a position and, later, to try to help you fill it, they will accept the newcomer more warmly and will be more willing to accept that person as a team member.

DELEGATE!

Entrepreneurs tend to believe that no one can perform as well as they. The solution is to make the goal clear to the subordinate before you delegate the task, then let her find the right method for reaching that goal.

Here are five types of tasks to delegate:

1. *Something that you cannot do*—For example, if you have to design a wastewater treatment facility as part of a project and you have no experience at this, you must obviously hire an engineer who is a specialist.

Job Advertising Do's and Don'ts

- Do write ads that will attract the reader's attention quickly. Keep in mind that your ads should be posted on your Web site, where they give job seekers insight into your organization.
- Do include your company name, address, telephone number, and Web address as well as your company contact person.
- Do request details on the candidate's current compensation package.
- Do provide information on unusual benefits your company has to offer.
- Do make sure your receptionist knows how to respond to calls or visits.
- Do run regular advertising for the positions you historically have had the hardest time filling.
- Do send a letter to all who respond to your ad within one week.
- Do track responses to your various advertising efforts to determine what medium attracts the greatest numbers and quality.
- Don't include salaries or salary ranges.
- Don't oversell your company or your opportunity.
- Don't give the position a title that misrepresents the real duties and responsibilities—for example, Marketing Management Administration Specialist instead of Receptionist.
- Don't include discriminatory language such as *attractive, young,* and *he.*
- Don't ask for salary expectations in the new position.

Figure 5-3

2. *Technical tasks someone else can do as well as you—* Let that person do the task so you can get on to more important issues. Even though you can calculate structural beam depths, it may be more important for you to handle client communications and to delegate the actual calculations to another engineer.

3. *Technical tasks someone else can do almost as well as you—*Be certain that you guide and coach. For instance, if you have been responsible for specifying all details for structural columns, and you now have a new engineer, let her do the preliminary drawings, then review the final drawings together.

4. *Technical tasks someone else can do adequately—* Make sure you delegate items that won't harm the project. Consider assigning someone to assemble drawings from predrawn standard details that are locked into your CADD system so they cannot be destroyed.

5. *Project management tasks—*This is one of the easiest areas to delegate. Such tasks include assembling

Interview Questions

The goal of employment interviews is to find out what a candidate is really like. Asking questions that can be answered with *yes* or *no* will not accomplish this goal. As an interviewer, you should do about 20 percent of the talking and 80 percent of the listening. These questions will help you uncover what you need to know about a prospect:

1. Tell me about yourself.
2. What are your greatest accomplishments?
3. What do you want to be doing three, five, ten years from now?
4. Why did you go into this field?
5. What tasks do you like to do?
6. If we talked with your coworkers, what would they tell us about you?
7. Why should we hire you over someone else?
8. What is motivating you to make a change (if the candidate is currently employed)?
9. What do you like and dislike about your present position?
10. What is your least favorite activity?
11. If you worked for us and we told you that we wanted you to move to Fargo, North Dakota, what would your reaction be?
12. What is a typical workday for you? How long is it?
13. What motivates you to do an outstanding job?
14. What in the work you currently do encourages a lack of motivation?
15. What do you like to do in your spare time?
16. What do you think is more important—technical abilities or communication and management skills? Why?
17. Do you aspire to be an owner in this or any other organization? Why?
18. What have you done that shows your commitment to clients?
19. Are you willing to give clients your pager number and respond to their needs within one hour (if the position requires it)?
20. Please rank the following in their order of importance to you:
    a. the quality of your work
    b. the timeliness of your delivery
    c. giving clients what they want
21. Name some of your accomplishments.
22. Name some of your worst failures. What are you doing to make sure they don't happen again?
23. Do you plan on continuing your education? If so, what do you plan on pursuing?
24. What is more important to you—getting along with people or getting things done?
25. What do you feel is the most pressing issue facing the design profession today?
26. What kinds of projects do you like best? Why?
27. Are you well versed in CADD software?
28. How do you feel about working evenings and weekends if the job requires it?
29. How do you feel about travel?
30. How do you feel about working with people who are younger or older than you?
31. What are you doing to improve your knowledge of your field?
32. Could you give us the names of your supervisors at your previous job? Are they still there? Do you have their phone numbers?
33. Is there anything else we need to know about you?
34. If we made you an offer, when could you start?

Figure 5-4

Making an Employment Offer

Cover these 15 points when extending an offer of employment:

1. Position title
2. Duties and responsibilities
3. Name and title of person to whom employee will report
4. Office location—the location of the particular office/branch to which the employee will be assigned
5. Base pay—salary expressed in weekly, biweekly, or monthly terms, or the hourly rate
6. Whether overtime will be paid, and, if so, whether it is straight overtime or time-and-a-half overtime, or a combination
7. Benefits
8. Date by which to accept or reject offer
9. Start date
10. Work hours
11. Dates of first performance/salary reviews
12. Perks, such as flextime, which expenses are covered, and personal use limitations
13. Specifics of the relocation package, if any
14. Potential for the person to advance beyond the position being offered
15. Written confirmation immediately following the spoken offer

Figure 5-5

meeting minutes, preparing a preliminary budget, and developing or implementing the schedule. Put yourself into a reviewer role.

Make a point of having a good staff of part-time workers on call. As a small business person, you cannot afford to hire all employees on a full-time basis. Work up the flexibility to delegate to a staff of part-time or independent contract employees. This way, other firms or individuals can work on part of a project whenever you are short-staffed. (Figure 5-6 gives insight into the differences, which are not always obvious, between an independent contractor and an employee.)

Delegating means flexibility. You can accomplish more and spend less by working with a group of such outside contractors than with a full-time staff.

Instructions When Delegating Instruct your employees to ask you the following when you are delegating:

Defining Independent Contractors and Employees

The IRS has a tight definition of those who rate as outside contractors rather than common-law employees. You may be held responsible for payroll taxes for more individuals than you think. Here are some of the tests applied by the IRS to determine employment:

1. A worker who is required to comply with another person's instruction is an employee.
2. Provision of training is normally seen as an advantage that comes with employment.
3. A continuing relationship may indicate employee–employer status.
4. Establishment of set hours of work is a control factor for employment purposes. If you control a person's hours, then a person is not an independent contractor.
5. Full- or substantially full-time work is not necessarily the mark of an independent contractor.
6. Work performed on the employer's premises is an indicator of employment, especially if the work could be performed off the premises.
7. The requirement of regular oral or written reports may indicate control that comes with employment.
8. Payment by the hour, week, or month rather than by a lump sum is associated with employment, especially if it is not just for the convenience of a lump sum payment.
9. Working for only one firm is the mark of an employee.
10. The right to fire an individual or terminate his services can be interpreted as employment. An independent contractor normally cannot be terminated without violation of a contract.
11. Unless the individual offers services to more than one firm and to the general public, a business relationship may be considered as employment.

Your firm should review its relationship with outside contractors to see if an employment status has been reached. The IRS examines such issues closely in order to increase revenues, especially FICA taxes. A firm failing to file taxes and reports may be held liable for both interest and penalties. If in doubt, review IRS Rev. Rule 87-41.

Figure 5-6

- What happens if you are away and I have a question about this task? Whom should I consult?
- What is your absolute deadline for completing this task?
- Will there be review meetings between now and the final deadline?
- Can someone help me work on this task or should I do it all alone?
- What do I do if I am pulled off this task by another supervisor?

This approach will ensure that you retain control over the project and its priority. It also is the difference between delegating and abdicating responsibility.

PROBATION PERIOD

As you hire new staff, be sure to set up a restrictive initial three-month period in which you immediately test new hires' abilities. On the first day, everyone is eager to perform. But do not wait two months before you give out tough assignments; do it right away. Also, make sure the new person is learning how to accomplish tasks as quickly as possible and, after the learning period, is achieving meaningful results on jobs that need to be done.

Always give employees a salary target. For example, start the new employee at a somewhat smaller base salary for the first three months. Then implement tough performance standards, to be met rigidly. At the end of the next three months, offer an immediate raise (say, $3000), followed by another three-month probationary period. At the end of that period, give another raise if the employee met your expectations. This way, the new employee knows what he can expect to be making at the end of nine months.

It should also be made clear during probation that if the employee fails to perform, he can be dismissed.

There is merit in setting up a moderately threatening framework for the new employee. Put the person to the test right away; don't tolerate nonperformance. Nonperformance is expensive to you as a small firm.

FIRE INCOMPETENTS

It is difficult to find good staff and, when you have had someone with you for a long time, it's hard to let that person go. It is much easier to keep a mediocre person than it is to fire someone and have to look for a replacement. But, as a small firm, you cannot afford to pay someone to perform a mediocre job.

Successful small firms must have rigid standards of performance that are routinely adhered to. For example:

- All projects will be done on budget and on schedule.
- Whatever the client wants comes before what the firm wants.
- Team performance supersedes individual performance.
- Good design cannot be achieved exclusive of project profitability.

- Communication effectiveness is the cornerstone of client service.
- Client expectations will be explored and understood fully before starting any project.
- The firm's contractual relationships will achieve all profit and cash-flow goals.

Employees who do not adhere to your expected performance criteria (after warnings) should be dismissed. One way to monitor performance is to conduct an annual review with each staff member, focusing on the interview itself rather than on standardized forms. Forms should merely be records of the review process, not the process itself. To monitor day-to-day performance, set up monthly informal meetings with each employee to review the performance of a particular set of mutually established goals.

The willingness to fire is important to staying small successfully. One firm even dares to enforce an annual 10 percent turnover. If, at the end of the year, the partners find only a 6 percent turnover, they fire 4 percent of their staff to meet the quota. It may seem unkind at the end of the year to terminate one out of every ten people, but the impact on motivation, performance, and service is considerable. Although you may not feel the mandatory turnover rate policy is fair, it is an ingenious way to maintain top staffers and fire bad ones.

EMPLOYMENT CONTRACTS

With the increasing importance of a clear understanding of the employer–employee relationship, many more small firms are now choosing to enter into employment contracts with key employees. The primary beneficiary of such agreements is the employee, who receives a documented and explicitly clear written agreement on her role in the firm. Recent court rulings have made enforcing one type of contract, the noncompete agreement, extremely difficult. If you feel obligated to present employees with this type of contract, seek legal advice before taking for granted that your noncompete will protect you from the actions of former employees. Figure 5-7 is a typical employment contract from a small firm. Expect more firms to adopt such agreements in the future as one means of attempting to retain key people in light of the increasing competition the design industry is facing from computer animation shops like DreamWorks, and Web design companies in need of CADD-savvy, creative employees.

THE CAVENDISH PARTNERSHIP, INC.
145 Main Street
Ludlow, Vermont 05149

EMPLOYMENT AGREEMENT

EMPLOYMENT AGREEMENT by and between **THE CAVENDISH PARTNERSHIP INC.,** (Company) and ****, (Employee).

For good consideration, Company shall employ and the Employee agrees to be employed on the following terms:

1.   **Effective Date:** Employment shall commence on ***, 20**, time being of the essence.

2.   **Duties:** Employee agrees to perform the following duties:

*****

Employee shall also perform such further duties as are incidental or implied from the foregoing, consistent with the background, training and qualifications of Employee or may be reasonably delegated as being in the best interests of the Company. The Employee shall devote full time to his employment and expend best efforts on behalf of the Company. Employee further agrees to abide by all reasonable Company policies and decisions now or hereinafter existing.

3.   **Term:** The Employee's employment shall continue for a period of *** years, beginning on the effective date of this agreement and ending on ****, 20**.

4.   **Compensation:** The Employee shall be paid the following compensation:

a)   Annual salary: $_____, paid on the payroll schedule existing for other employees.

b)   Such bonuses, vacations, sick leave, and expense accounts as stated in the Company manual for other management personnel or as may be decided by the Company if said items are discretionary with the Company.

5.   **Termination:** This agreement may be earlier terminated upon:

a)   Death of Employee or illness or incapacity that prevents Employee from substantially performing for *** continuous months or in excess of *** aggregate working days in any calendar year.

b)   Breach of agreement by Employee.

6.   **Renewal:** Should employee remain in the employ of the Company after the termination date of this Agreement, the terms of this Agreement shall remain in full force effect, except that the continued term of employment shall be at the will of the parties, and can be ended at any time, for any reason, by either party.

7.   **Miscellaneous:**

a)   Employee agrees to execute a non-compete agreement as annexed hereto.

Figure 5-7. Typical employment contract (page 1 of 5).
Source: The Cavendish Partnership, Inc. Used with permission.

***   b)   Employee agrees to execute a confidential information and invention assignment agreement as annexed hereto.

***   c)   Employee agrees that during the term of this agreement and for a period of ** years thereafter, Employee will not:

i)   Induce or attempt to induce any employee to leave the Company's employ;

ii)   Interfere with or disrupt the Company's relationship with any of its employees;

iii)   Solicit or employ any person employed by the Company.

d)   The agreement shall not be assignable by either party, provided that upon any sale of this business by Company, the Company may assign this agreement to its successor or employee may terminate same.

e)   In the event of any dispute under this agreement, it shall be resolved through binding arbitration in accordance with the rules of the American Arbitration Association.

f)   This constitutes the entire agreement between the parties. Any modifications must be writing.

8.   **Equal Opportunity:** During the performance of this Agreement, the Company will not discriminate against any employment because of race, color, creed, religion, sex, national origin or handicap.

The Company will comply with the applicable provisions of Title VI of the Civi' Rights Act of 1964 as amended, Executive Order 11246 as amended by Executive Order 11375 and as supplemented by the department of Labor Regulations (41 CFR Part 60). The Company shall also comply with the rules, regulations, and relevant orders of the Secretary of Labor, DOT Regulation 49 CFR 21 through Appendix C, and DOT Regulation 23 CFR 710.405 (b).

The Company shall comply with all of the requirements of Title 21, V.S.A., Chapter 5, Subchapter 6 and 7, relating to fair employment practices to the extent applicable.

Signed under seal this *** day of *****, 20**.

THE CAVENDISH PARTNERSHIP, INC.

_____   _____

Witness   Principal

_____   _____

Witness   Employee

Figure 5-7. Typical employment contract (page 2 of 5).

EMPLOYEE NON-COMPETE AGREEMENT

FOR GOOD CONSIDERATION, and in consideration of my being employed by THE CAVENDISH PARTNERSHIP, INC., I, the undersigned, hereby agree that upon my termination of employment and notwithstanding the cause of termination, I shall not compete with the business of the Company, or its successors or assigns.

The term "not compete" as used in this agreement means that I shall not directly or indirectly own, be employed by or work on behalf of any firm engaged in a business substantially similar and competitive with the Company.

I further agree that this Agreement shall:

1.   Extend only for the following geographic territory:

       ***   For a radius of fifty (50) miles from the present location of the Company.

2.   Shall be in full force and effect for ** years(s), commencing with the date my employment with the Company will have terminated and notwithstanding the reason for termination or the party terminating.

Signed under seal this ** day of ****, 20**.

_____   _____
Witness   Employee

EMPLOYEE INVENTION AGREEMENT

FOR GOOD CONSIDERATION, and in consideration of the undersigned being employed by THE CAVENDISH PARTNERSHIP, INC., (Company) the undersigned hereby agrees, acknowledges and represents:

1.   The undersigned, during the course of employment, shall promptly disclose in writing to the Company all inventions, discoveries, improvements, developments and innovations whether patentable or not, conceived in whole or in part by the undersigned or through assistance of the undersigned, and whether conceived or developed during working hours or not, which:

       a)   Result from any work performed on behalf of the Company, or pursuant to a suggested research project by the Company, or

       b)   Relate in any manner to the existing or contemplated business of the Company, or

       c)   Result from the use of the Company's time, material, employees or facilities.

2.   The undersigned hereby assigns to the Company, its successors and assigns, all rights, title and interest to said inventions.

3.   The undersigned shall, at the Company's request, execute specific assignments to any such invention and execute, acknowledge, and deliver any additional documents required to obtain letters patent in any jurisdiction and shall, at the Company's request and expense, assist in the defense and prosecution of said letters patent as may be required by Company. This provision shall survive termination of employ with the Company.

Signed under seal this ** day of ****, 20**.

_____   _____
Witness   Employee

Figure 5-7. Typical employment contract (pages 3 and 4 of 5).

CONFIDENTIAL INFORMATION AGREEMENT

IN CONSIDERATION of being employed by THE CAVENDISH PARTNERSHIP INC. (Company), the undersigned hereby agrees and acknowledges:

1.   That during the course of my employ there may be disclosed to me certain trade secrets of the Company; said trade secrets consisting of:

   a)   Technical information: Methods, processes, formulae, compositions, inventions, machines, computer programs and research projects.

   b)   Business information: Customer lists; pricing data; sources of supply; and marketing, production, or merchandising systems or plans.

2.   I shall not during, or at any time after the termination of my employment with the Company, use for myself or others, or disclose or divulge to others any trade secrets, confidential information, financial or other data of the Company in violation of this Agreement.

3.   That upon the termination of my employ from the Company:

   a)   I shall return to the Company all documents relating to the Company, including but not necessarily limited to: drawings, blueprints, reports, manuals, correspondence, customer lists, computer programs, and all other materials and all copies thereof relating in any way to the Company's business, or in any way obtained by me during the course of my employ. I further agree that I shall not retain any copies of the foregoing.

   b)   The Company may notify any future or prospective employer of the existence of this Agreement.

   c)   This Agreement shall be binding upon me and my personal representatives and successors in interest, and shall inure to the benefit of the Company, its successors and assigns.

   d)   The unenforceability of any provision to this Agreement shall not impair or affect any other provision.

   e)   In the event of any breach of this Agreement, the Company shall have full rights to injunctive relief, in addition to any other existing rights, without requirement of posting bond.

Dated:_____

_____   _____
Witness   **Employee**

Figure 5-7. Typical employment contract (page 5 of 5).

SUCCESS CHALLENGES

1. Rank your employees according to top, middle, and bottom thirds by performance, not by position. Reflect why you are keeping those in the bottom third. Are all those in the top third adequately compensated for their efforts?
2. How is your training program organized? Is it clearly different from those of your competitors?
3. Are you managing your benefits package differently?
4. Are you able to attract employees because of your distinctive personnel policies?
5. Do you know of a top employee in another firm you would like to hire? Make the contract.

REFERENCES

1. Dave Burstein. "Recruiting the Best and the Brightest New Grads," *PSMJ Best Practices*, November 1999, p. 13.

Chapter 6

Compensation

Successful firms compensate their staff with more than money. An analysis of payroll burden based on annual total revenues, annual net revenues, and direct labor is shown in Figure 6-1. Figure 6-2, analysis of general overhead expenses, also includes data on payroll burden. This chapter presents ideas for motivating and rewarding employees for performance, and highlights some innovative small firm business policies.

MOTIVATING DESIGN PROFESSIONALS

Many people think that to motivate design professionals, bonuses or other forms of incentive compensation are necessary. An extreme example that calls this assumption into question is the story of Hal Ahlberg, former leader of a Dallas-based firm. His company acquired a series of five- to ten-person firms in the geotechnical field and instantly, upon acquisition, eliminated all incentive bonuses. He began paying his staff at market or slightly above, based on the salaries in the communities where the firms were located. Believing that design professionals are more motivated by recognition and control of interesting project work, he found he lost no staff and, in fact, started to acquire more because he compensated for the loss of bonuses by giving his staff more autonomy on their projects, bigger and better jobs, and greater final say in project outcome.

Ahlberg's philosophy was that a bonus is the employer's way of borrowing money from the employee interest-free, until year-end, when such monies are due anyway. He felt people should be paid a fair salary and motivated with quality projects. Ahlberg's success with the firms was demonstrated by the fact that he acquired the additional firms over a two-year period and sold the entire operation for a net gain of $30 million.

A small-firm principal can learn from this example of a larger firm.

Another useful practice was instituted by the principal of a Michigan firm. The principal invited employees from the firm to breakfast with him once a week. They talked about what they wanted, and he listened. Then he wrote a personal

Analyses of Labor Overhead

	Based on Gross Revenues		Based on Net Revenues		Based on Direct Labor		Based on Total Payroll		Based on Worked Payroll	
	Median	Mean	Median	Mean	Median	Mean	Median	Mean	Median	Mean
Payroll Taxes	3.43%	3.48%	4.46%	4.42%	12.86%	12.99%	8.11%	8.33%	8.78%	8.95%
Vacation, Sick, Holiday	3.80	3.87	4.91	4.86	13.80	13.34	8.92	8.64	9.80	9.54
Group Insurance	1.91	1.95	2.69	2.74	7.93	7.69	5.01	5.12	5.55	5.78
Retirement Contribution	0.92	1.09	1.19	1.40	3.16	3.85	2.17	2.62	2.36	2.84
All Other Fringe Benefits	0.36	0.56	0.48	0.68	1.33	1.72	0.85	1.22	0.93	1.33
Total Payroll Burden (without incentive/ bonus)	10.37	10.08	13.65	12.87	39.34	37.13	24.58	23.94	26.73	25.82
Incentive/Bonuses (retirement plan contribution)	0.37	0.97	0.47	1.23	0.97	2.87	0.94	2.39	0.99	2.61
Total Payroll Burden (including discretionary retirement plan contributions)	13.34	13.34	15.76	15.06	43.82	42.97	31.46	31.55	35.40	35.37
Incentive/Bonuses (paid currently)	3.81	5.25	4.30	5.10	9.82	10.19	5.57	6.08	8.16	8.76
Incentive/Bonuses Total	3.06	3.50	3.67	4.04	10.61	11.23	.6.30	7.23	7.71	8.53
Total Payroll Burden	14.83	15.88	19.09	19.54	55.07	53.72	32.09	32.75	37.55	41.11

Individual items are not additive.

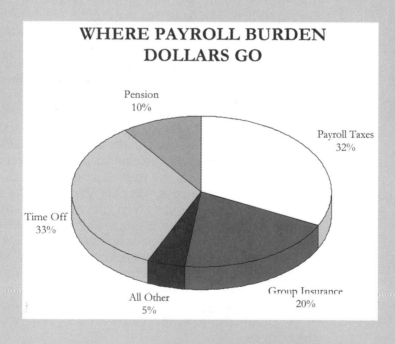

Figure 6-1. Analysis of payroll burden.

Analyses of General Overhead Expenses

	Based on Gross Revenues		Based on Net Revenues		Based on Direct Labor	
	Median	Mean	Median	Mean	Median	Mean
Indirect Labor	8.95%	10.19%	11.46%	12.42%	34.74%	36.4%
Computer Costs	0.00	1.20	1.08	1.55	3.20	4.60
Payroll Burden (without bonus or discretionary retirement)	10.37	10.08	13.65	12.87	39.34	37.13
Space Costs	3.48	3.59	4.50	4.63	13.04	13.71
Telephone	0.77	0.84	0.96	1.08	2.79	3.00
Professional Liability Insurance	1.51	1.87	1.59	1.92	2.58	3.43
General Insurance	0.26	0.40	0.33	0.53	1.01	1.49
Interest Expense	0.44	0.68	0.55	0.86	1.61	2.24
Bad Debt Expense	0.31	0.46	0.39	0.55	1.17	1.59
Training and Education	0.34	0.43	0.44	0.52	1.37	1.58
Legal and Accounting	0.48	0.62	0.61	0.79	1.73	2.33
Registration and Licenses	0.19	0.25	0.24	0.33	0.74	0.90
Taxes and Permits	0.20	0.49	0.23	0.62	2.02	3.08
Production Supplies	0.53	0.63	0.74	0.90	2.27	2.67
Office Supplies	0.75	0.87	1.00	1.13	2.99	3.27
Marketing Costs	3.48	4.06	4.81	5.32	12.84	14.47
All Other General Overhead	3.79	4.37	4.74	5.61	8.82	8.89
Total Overhead	39.52	39.07	50.79	50.35	146.52	142.99

Individual items are not additive.

WHERE OVERHEAD DOLLARS GO

Figure 6-2. Analysis of general overhead expenses.

letter to each employee explaining why certain concerns could or could not be dealt with. Such meetings are a form of reward in themselves and can be morale builders for design firms. More ideas on motivating design professionals appear in Figure 6-3.

Salary as a Motivator (or Demotivator) In successful small firms, the spread between the salary of the owner(s) and those of the employees is relatively narrow compared to that in unsuccessful firms. In successful firms, the second person in command earns about 80 percent of the salary of the top person. This is a well-balanced compensation scheme. If a compensation scheme favors the top owners in spite of good performance by junior employees and the spread is wide (30 to 50 percent between owners' and

---

Motivating Design Professionals

One way to motivate is not to demotivate. The following checklist helps you avoid demotivating ambitious, achievement-conscious professionals:

1. Encourage them to complete what they start—don't assign more project/tasks than can be completed with above-average effort.
2. Don't assume your staff cannot handle an unfamiliar project.
3. Keep your people informed. Tell them about the firm, their department, new or lost projects. Pass on both good and bad news.
4. Be frank about individual performances. Give thorough performance appraisals when they are due, but also have regular informal conversations to let employees know how they are doing and what their future is.
5. Give commitments regarding advancement. Tell employees what it will take for them to advance to the next level. Then back up your commitments; do not rationalize lack of action.
6. Give plenty of stroking. Frequent spoken praise, memos to personnel files, letters, bulletin board postings, and so on, all help keep motivation levels high.
7. Explain why people are promoted. Most companies fail to take advantage of this great opportunity to reinforce patterns of behavior they want to perpetuate.
8. Offer your best people a piece of the action. Most design firm principals will share information about ownership with their best people, but few get around to offering it.
9. Build management expertise from within, if possible. Promote from within, when you can, for management positions.
10. Reward performance with tangible rewards. Tie compensation as much as possible to performance. Do not allow your top people to be dragged down by your nonperformers.

Figure 6-3

the next-ranking employees' salaries), the result is often a high turnover rate, low morale, and other related problems.

BENEFITS

A comprehensive benefit package is taken for granted by today's employees. Winning the hiring wars frequently comes down to how far your firm will go in terms of flexibility and responsiveness to employee needs. A handful of design firms offering unusual benefits includes:

- A California firm that provides a concierge service, which takes care of dry cleaning, car washing, and so on.
- A Massachusetts firm that allows employees to bring dogs to the office
- A Texas firm that provides child care services

Many firms offer flextime and telecommuting as well. One caveat when extending these types of benefits to employees: Don't discriminate! If you want to ride your bike into work and hang it from your ceiling on bicycle hooks, allow your employees to do the same.

Some companies opt to pay no benefits at all. Instead, they pay salaries high enough for employees to purchase their own benefits. This accomplishes two goals: The employee gets a higher rate of pay and the employer saves money otherwise spent on group benefits.

If you choose to include benefits, be sure they are equitable. Firms are legally obligated to demonstrate that their fringe benefits are not discriminatory.

Benefits and costs for all groups in a firm must be proportional. For instance, you can no longer give top management significantly different benefits such as country club dues, expensive cars, multiple vacations, or high life-insurance coverage without running the risk of having the IRS tax a portion of those benefits as compensation. If you do not pay such taxes on these benefits, members of the highly paid group will have to recognize a portion of their benefits (free health insurance, etc.) as income. Here are suggestions for coping with this law:

- Minimize the number of optional benefits (e.g., dental coverage), as each option creates a separate plan group that must be tested.
- Per a 1999 Supreme Court ruling in a case involving Microsoft, a full-time employee eligible for benefits is one who works 20 hours per week for any five months of a year. For tips on how to deal with this wrench in the works of relations with independent contractors, see Figure 6-4.

Success Tips for Working with Independent Contractors

To avoid inadvertently entering into an employee-employer relationship with independent contractors, use these tactics for success:

■ Have independent contractors perform work outside your offices (such as working at home).
■ Have them perform tasks your staff cannot perform, or tasks that aren't part of regular employees' job duties.
■ Have them work on discrete tasks rather than jointly on tasks with regular employees.

Figure 6-4
Source: "This Ruling Affects You," *PSMJ Best Practices*, February 2000, p. 10.

■ Eliminate extra coverage for managers and principals that could be considered discriminatory.
■ Expect to spend $2000 to $2500 in data gathering and paperwork for each plan you offer.

TIMING PAY RAISES

Part of the compensation package includes motivating design professionals with pay raises. Some urge separating discussion about the granting of salary increases from performance evaluations. Others feel this approach could be worse than not having performance evaluations at all.

The problem with separating performance and salary discussions is that to most employees in design firms, the only recognition for good performance is increased salary. Not talking about it is like talking about the scope of a new project for a client without discussing the fee.

You should discuss performance and money during the same meeting, but structure the meeting differently from the standard performance evaluation:

1. Begin performance reviews by concentrating on the future. Ask each employee to bring to the meeting a written list of goals for the next six months. The employee should note what will be done and when.
2. Listen. Make the employee explain even the most absurd idea.
3. Ask probing questions, but don't tell the employee what you think until all of the employee's goals are fully explained to you.
4. Come to a mutual agreement with the employee on goals and objectives, and then ask her to tell you

what she thinks she is worth if all goals are met satis-factorily. Whether this figure is below or above yours, you should discuss it and agree on an amount.

5. After agreeing on the amount, discuss how the differ-ence between current income and future income will be paid. Should part be salary and part bonus, or should all be bonus?

If you have been open about setting up a mutually agreed-on scope of work with each individual, and if the amount and terms of payment are clearly understood, the employee will be able to self-evaluate prior to the next ses-sion and tell you whether or not increased compensation was earned. This process is like writing a contract with a client.

This approach is feasible, but it has two drawbacks:

1. It takes time and requires that each person be allowed to set up individual goals.
2. It takes courage and honesty to discuss salary as part of a performance review if you have never done it, especially in light of the commonly held opinion that you should separate such discussions.

INCENTIVE COMPENSATION

Incentive plans should be set up with one goal in mind: to recognize superior performance. W. L. Vanderweil of R. G. Vanderweil Engineers once explained how he accomplished that within his firm:

A key to our success is the emphasis we put on marketing to existing clients to generate repeat business. Of our six principals, only the principal who is in charge of opera-tions gets a bonus that is heavily weighted towards profit-ability. The others receive the major part of their bonus from marketing existing clients and the amounts of repeat business they bring in. We do find that money is a very good motivator, particularly when you pay bonuses that are very significant in proportion to an employee's salary, as we do. This emphasis on repeat business makes the key people in our firm focus on keeping the client happy. By doing this we get most of our business from existing clients (83 percent in 1988) and also find that their referrals result in a fair amount of new business. To date, this philosophy has served us well.

Avoid the following compensation practices, which are known to result in poor profitability:

▪ All employees get the same raise. When profits drop, some firms limit all raises to a given percentage—but this way, you reward your worst and your best per-formers equally. Eventually, the good performers will either leave for a firm that rewards performance, or their performance will drop to average, as it makes no difference to their salary. Equal raises look fair and appealing, and not having to apportion limited salary dollars will save time, but they will only prolong poor financial performance.

▪ Bonus plans that pay the same percent of salary to all eligible participants. The same factors apply as in the above scenario.

▪ Pay bonuses where the average is 5 percent (or less) of salary. If you make $40,000 a year, will a $2000 (or less) bonus really motivate you? Compensation stud-ies have shown 15 percent of salary to be the mini-mum necessary to trigger a significant positive staff reaction. This is especially true if bonuses are tied to performance. If you are going to hold out bonuses as a reward, make sure they are big enough to get an employee's attention.

During hard times, when there are not enough salary and bonus dollars to satisfy every employee, you must be even more careful to make sure good performers are rewarded favorably. This means your poor and average per-formers may get no raise or bonus at all.

Incentive Bonuses Incentive bonuses, used to reward key people, should be at least 10 to 15 percent of a person's salary.

When budgeting, set aside 10 to 15 percent of your total expected salary expense for incentive bonuses. Although this figure may seem high, you will receive the benefit of superior performance before spending your first bonus dollar. The very fact of establishing the budget underscores your commitment to your key staff.

Begin cautiously. A poorly established and managed plan is worse than no plan at all. Start by carefully defining each job in your firm and make sure that your people understand clearly what is normally expected of them. Establish regular performance appraisals to confirm your understanding and theirs of what is meant by normal expected performance. After standards are set, define your bonus incentive reward process clearly. See Figure 6-5 for a look at how one wildly successful firm in the Southwest "incentivizes" its people.

One Midwest firm rewards its project managers on a per-project basis using a formula that includes variables for profitability, quality of design, service to client, and staff performance. Another firm gives team bonuses to an entire project team when it achieves better performance than

The Connection between Happy People and High Profits

"I can get my group together tonight to tell them I've got a client that needs something Monday morning. I promise you everyone would say 'I'll stay.'"

The leader of a 32-person A/E firm in the Southwest told me this at 6:30 P.M. last Friday. At the same time, he shared with me his firm's average profitability since opening in the late 1960s: 42 percent. The output of this firm is on par with that of a 140-person firm. What's their secret weapon? An output-based compensation program that really works!

This VP told me, "When I sit down in an interview with someone, I tell them, 'We pay lower than anyone. But we also pay compensation based on your production.' That weeds out about 50 percent. I've had people get up right then and say, 'See you later!' Which is great, because we're looking for the people who are looking for this kind of deal."

Here's a firm that pays its architects about $20,000 per year and expects its design professionals to pay for errors and omissions out of their own pockets. Still, the highest-paid PM made $350,000 in 1999 and the lowest-paid made $192,000.

Speed, accuracy, and accessibility during project delivery are firm trademarks—a dedicated team of six construction experts hired away from general contractors is on every job site, servicing the client during construction and reporting back to the firm's production team about job errors and how they were fixed. In the last ten years, one employee has left the firm. This is its recipe for success:

- *"We pay each member of the team a portion of every job that comes in on budget."* Everyone is paid a graduated percentage of the project according to time they worked and their output. The firm also provides every employee with a 401K plan, an employee stock option program, life insurance, short- and long-term disability, and health insurance.
- *"We put a tremendous amount of time and effort into firmwide employee training."* The firm's liability carrier makes a yearly presentation. Each month, outside speakers share information on topics of interest to the staff. "We also contact contractors after they build jobs for us and ask, 'Comparing us to other firms, what was the weakest part of our work?' If their answer is poor masonry specs, we'll bring in a masonry expert and find out how to do it better."
- *"We promote and talk about the fact that the company's very profitable, and I'm making a lot of money. That's nothing to hide—I think it's awesome. What it means is, they're making money."*

Figure 6-5
Source: "Stasiowski On...," *PSMJ Resources,* April 6, 2000.

expected. This helps build team spirit. Your plan must reflect your goals for reward based on your process for delivering service. If you perform services as a team, reward the team, not an individual. If you act as individuals, reward individually.

Do not vary from standards. Do not reward one project manager $500 and another $1000 for superior performance on similar projects despite the second manager's greater experience. Never consider longevity a factor in making incentive rewards. Doing so will demotivate a hardworking younger employee.

Consider using bonus rewards other than monetary reimbursement:

- Added vacation time
- A paid trip for the top achiever and family
- Books or subscriptions
- Extra education, such as seminars and night courses
- Special use of company recreation facilities, such as country club privileges for a month
- A company car

Here are two other ideas that are not incentive-related but positive:

1. *Profit sharing*—This rewards all, including poor performers.
2. *Christmas bonuses*—Personnel often count on this as a salary requirement.

Finally, be sure to communicate your incentive plan to the entire staff.

Stock Bonuses

In a growing business, cash flow is often a trouble spot because of long accounts receivable and work-in-process turnover. Making matters more difficult is the fact that small firm owners must pay their employees, most often before the firm has collected its fees.

An alternative method to paying large cash bonuses is available to incorporated design firms that may not have cash on hand. It consists of issuing to employees bonuses in the form of stock instead of cash. Doing so allows a firm to take an immediate deduction on its books for the expense of the stock bonus without actually paying out cash. Thus, cash flow is preserved and taxes deferred.

One Northwest engineering firm provides its employees with both cash and stock as an annual bonus. For each dollar of bonus, the employee receives 40 percent in cash and 60 percent in stock. This move allows the employee to pay personal income taxes with the cash and, at the same time, lets the company take an immediate deduction for 100 percent of the bonus value while paying out only 40 percent in cash.

The additional benefit derived from such a plan is that it encourages all employees to increase the value of your stock by working harder to make the firm profitable. Paying a stock bonus requires a well-developed ownership and leadership transition plan that allows for stock distribution among key employees on this basis. Closely held businesses with one or two partners may find it difficult to incorporate such a bonus arrangement.

Quarterly Bonuses A variant on the stock bonus theme is a quarterly incentive compensation plan that pays each project team a bonus based on accrual team profitability for the past three months, even if cash is not yet collected.

A design firm in New York City has a slightly different approach. At the end of each calendar year, employees learn of the bonus they've earned, but they don't receive it right away. The firms opts to dole it out over the coming year. An employee receives one-quarter of his bonus each quarter. If the employee leaves, uncollected bonus monies are forfeited. A common term for this type of system is *golden handcuffs.*

Such a frequent-payment plan is best for using money as a reward. The closer the timing of the reward to the activity for which it is given, the greater the motivation.

Deferred Bonuses The end of the fiscal year is often the time to distribute bonuses. One type of bonus is deferred compensation. Under this program, regular weekly pay is lower than market rates, or at least less than the value the firm applies to the individual's efforts. This discrepancy is made up at the end of the fiscal year with a cash bonus payment that is widely distributed throughout the firm.

Here are seven advantages to using a deferred bonus program as part of your total compensation program:

1 Deferred compensation reduces cash flow out during the year until the end of the fiscal year, when the firm may have more cash available. This can help borrowing requirements during the year or, alternatively, make more cash available for short-term investment.

2. Firmwide compensation can be linked to profitability by tying individual compensation to the overall financial achievements of the firm. This is an excellent way to motivate employees to act in accordance with the profit objectives of the firm.

3. In price-competitive marketing situations, you can quote lower hourly rates for your employees. This may need to be offset by a higher multiplier to cover eventual bonus payments, budgeted as part of your overhead, but you have an initial advantage over competitors.

RETAINING YOUR BEST EMPLOYEES

"A people plan is as important a tool in today's marketplace as a marketing or financial plan."
—*HR Focus*, October, 1997

The problem of employee shortages in our industry has become intense. It's not just lack of people that's plaguing business—every employee who leaves costs your firm anywhere from one to two years' wages and benefits. As you juggle the demands of a growing business, you must also take the time to keep employees in your organization.

What Do Employees Want?

Employees want to be challenged to do their best work.

■ They want an environment, resources, training, evaluation, coaching, and mentoring that support them in being their best.

■ They want to be fairly compensated for their efforts and the results they produce.

■ They want honest and straightforward communication from their supervisor and the company.

■ They want you to communicate their opportunities within the firm, and they want you to help them get there.

■ They want to belong to a family, a team, and have fun while learning and producing.

In this environment, employees will give you their best, and chances are better that they'll remain loyal to the company. By creating an environment where quality service is delivered by your employees, your firm is utilizing the least expensive marketing approach to create loyal clients. With satisfied employees and clients, your firm will have all the repeat business you can handle.

What's an Employer to Do?

It's management's job to identify and remove obstacles to employees' success. What could be better than unleashing your staff's talents and helping them excel? Employees need you to be conscious of their struggles and successes.

Questions to Ask During Employee Reviews

You need to review the progress of your employees regularly. Here are a few of the questions to ask:

■ Is there anything in our company's culture that gets in the way of your doing great work?

■ What can you do about it?

■ How can we help?

■ What is needed to remedy the situation?

Follow this with:

■ You are a valued employee. How can we help make our company the place you want to be in the future?

■ Where do you see yourself and the firm five years from now?

Close by sharing your realistic vision of the opportunities for the employee within the firm and your vision of where the firm is headed.

Employees Have Responsibilities

Encourage employees to solve their own problems. Be aware that if a firm's culture is insidious and presents too many stumbling blocks, it may encourage your employee to respond to those headhunter's calls, where the grass looks greener and the pay is slightly higher.

A Word of Caution

Don't ask your employee for the kind of input I've suggested unless you are truly willing to listen. Scoffing at or arguing with an employee's reality will hasten their retreat. You must be able to listen nonjudgmentally. If you can't do this, get an outside party to help.

Management's job is to know which resources will enable employees to do a great job. Training, equipment, work/life balance, compensation, acknowledgment, coaching, career tracking—they're all part of the picture. Your belief in your employees and your excitement about their progress and achievements are what make it all worthwhile.

Sandy Blaha, "Retaining Your Best Employees," *PSMJ Best Practices,* January 2000, p, 9.

4. By delaying compensation for a year, you are able to tie compensation more effectively to actual performance. Deferred compensation payments can be adjusted up or down depending on the individual employee's actual achievements.

5. Because payments are made at the end of the fiscal year, employees are encouraged to stay with the firm until that time rather than lose the bonus.

6. By deferring compensation and combining it with more discretionary bonus payments, you are able to make bonuses significant enough to truly motivate employees the following year. Small bonus payments are poor motivators.

7. Deferred compensation can serve as an enforced savings program for employees. By allowing a company to take an immediate expense reduction, this puts aside a future amount of compensation for an individual.

Bonus payments may also be used for such items as IRA contributions or stock purchases for those seeking equity positions in the organization.

CAREER TRACKING

Successful design firms create career tracks for employees. This tactic recognizes that your firm is made up of both professional management positions and technical positions and that both must be rewarded. Successful firms reward their professionals according to their respective career tracks.

In firms that use career tracking, salary levels are assigned by ranges, and all employees are paid within those levels. No one knows exactly how much each individual makes, but the salary level structure is a published document that shows the ranges corresponding to job positions within the firm. This is feasible even in the smallest firm.

CREATING AN ATMOSPHERE OF ACHIEVEMENT

As a design firm principal, you should try to create an environment of achievement in your firm. The purpose is to get your staff motivated. Do not, however, start a massive motivational campaign. Instead, start with yourself. Look at the little things you can do daily:

- Listen more than you talk. Practice by learning to ask more questions.
- Tell employees or project teams often that they are doing a good job, if they are. Appreciation and recognition are the most valued but least available commodities in most design firms.
- Thank staff and their spouses for overtime work. A nice touch is a handwritten thank-you note sent home

to a spouse. Such a practice will set you apart from the average.

- Be seen. Take your coffee break and walk around the back room. This is not a waste of time but a sound motivator.
- Start each project with a team meeting to discuss goals for the project, goals of the client, and specific goals of each team member. If the team assumes ownership of the project requirements, the time you spend in this meeting will be amply returned by the participants.
- Stay flexible. When one of your staff works until 2:00 A.M. on a project, accept it when she comes in late the next morning. Learn who are your morning versus your night people and realize that a night person may work all night but have trouble coming to the office on time in the morning.
- Never tolerate poor performance, or you will encourage your best performers to do less and end up with a group of nonperformers. When people do not perform, tell them immediately. The second time, let them know it is the second time, and the third time, consider termination.
- Ask yourself if all staff members really know what is expected of them. If the answer is *yes*, you probably don't have anything to worry about. If it's *no*, begin planning performance criteria and revise job descriptions to reflect expected performance.

Successful small firm entrepreneurs recognize performance as a key issue. There are five elements to measure in performance:

1. Hard work
2. Work effectiveness
3. Loyalty to the company
4. Work ethic
5. Emotion

One of the most difficult entrepreneurial challenges is to replace a loyal, hardworking staff member who has reached his or her maximum capability in a growing firm. Successful firms are able to hire people and position them over employees of long standing as the company grows. Many firms build around loyalty in the absence of other performance standards only to find their profit growth severely limited by a group of people who have maximum capability. The Peter principle Dr. Laurence J. Peter's theory that "in a hierarchy, individuals tend to rise to their levels of incompetence,"[1] hurts these firms dramatically. How a firm motivates its employees is a measure of is success in the marketplace.

The simplest form of motivation is recognition. Praise your staff for the smallest examples of good performance. Do it in writing so they can show it off at home. On the other hand, reprimand privately and orally promptly after poor performance.

SUCCESS CHALLENGES

1. Does your second in command receive 80 percent of your salary, or is the spread too wide to encourage close team relationships?

2. Does your bonus system motivate people to perform, or are you wasting your money on holiday and other expected bonuses? How could you restructure the same bonus money in a way that would more effectively motivate staff to perform?

3. Are you giving bonuses to 100 percent of the people in your firm, or are you giving bonuses to the top performers only, as you should?

4. If you could do as much work in the marketplace with fewer people, how can you compensate people less to help you do so? Can you use independent contractors to accomplish some of the tasks full-time salaried people are doing now?

5. Can you employ two part-time people rather than one full-timer, thereby saving on the overhead of fringe benefits and the lack of productivity that occurs during a full eight-hour day put in by one person?

6. As you look to the future, do you have in place compensation plans that allow for career tracking—for both the technical and management professionals to advance in their respective directions—with defined, appropriate salary levels?

7. Do you have a training program that will allow you to retain key people who are now highly compensated but unchallenged?

REFERENCE

1. Laurence J. Peter, 1985. *Why Things Go Wrong or The Peter Principle Revisited.* New York: William Morrow.

Chapter 7

Managing the Bottom Line

As Wayne Schmidt, president of Schmidt Associates Architects, Indianapolis, says, "Running a sound business that is efficient, results-oriented, cost-effective, and accountable to timeliness is as important. . .as providing top-quality professional skills."

William Carpenter, former CEO of a successful engineering firm in South Carolina, once said, "Profit is the only measure of successful design." Carpenter's philosophy was that no matter how you define success, the bottom line is the ultimate yardstick for measuring it. Thus, a focus on bottom-line financial performance, which includes setting and managing budgets, prices, contract terms, and financial results, is an integral part of becoming and staying successful.

A significant profit goal is a must in every firm's planning process. As stated in Chapter 1, average small-firm profits are in the 14 percent range. However, outstanding firms have goals of 40 percent and, because they aim for higher-than-average goals, they naturally produce higher-than-average results. This chapter tells you how to achieve the profit goal you set in your strategic plan (Chapter 1) through simplified financial planning, measuring your progress with five simple elements, and improving project profits.

Sound financial management is the basis for a successful practice. One of the dangers small firms face is in allowing a client to approach them with a fixed budget, asking how much design it can get for the price. When faced with this approach, a firm is forced to put together a top-down budget and work plan. Built into this method are several pitfalls:

- *Leaving out profit*—The client's quote includes your profit. Immediately set aside your required profit, then determine your scope of work.
- *Underestimating direct costs*—Under this approach, there may be no reimbursable items. You may need to pay for everything out of your fee. Make sure you allow enough for all your costs.

- *Assuming incorrect consultant fees*—Do not assume you know how much a consultant will charge. Get firm quotes on scope and fee.
- *Trying to squeeze into the fee a scope you would want if you were the client*—The fee quoted should determine the project scope. Do not overestimate your abilities to produce and perform. (See "Excess Perfection Syndrome," Fig. 4-13.)
- *Leaving no room to negotiate*—Instead, the client may well expect to negotiate, either to an increased scope or a lower fee.

A far wiser approach is to focus on the bottom line. Regardless of goals for design quality, staff performance, or professional recognition, what counts is a bottom-line strategy that involves effective financial performance measured against predetermined goals. Small and large firms alike must realize the importance of the bottom line. W. L. Vanderweil of R. G. Vanderweil Engineers (Boston) once stated:

> We must run our operation as a sound financial business. One of the things that personally disappoints me in the architecture/engineering business is the attitude that many firms have that makes profit secondary to the quality of design. In fact, they should be equal, as they go hand in hand. To get our share of work, our fees must be competitive, but we try hard not to lowball the client. We stress to our staff that they must run their projects like a business, which is sometimes difficult because many people in our field do not always approach things in a businesslike fashion. By making good profits, we find we are able to pay our people what they deserve, give them the motivation to serve our clients well, invest the money we need for our business to grow, and keep our top people in what is a tightly held business.

Under a top-down budgeting method, firms are in danger of unconsciously giving away too much. There is too much room for the client to win and for the firm to lose. It is imperative that the firm assess its overall strategy relative to the scope of work being provided on the set fee determined by a client.

Design firms typically have great difficulty reducing their scope of services from the standard suggested by professional societies or by our traditional way of doing business. The successful firms have found a way to cut scope (when the client has a budget) without cutting quality, thereby allowing for an equal level of profit margin on a small project as on a big one. Be certain you focus on the issues of margin and retain the same percentage of profit on a project even if the client's fee seems low in relation to fees received for similar projects in a market.

Finally, simplify. Financial planning need not be complicated. In the smaller firm, it is a straightforward process to monitor:

- Utilization of staff resources
- Billing and collections of receivables
- Negotiation of the details of a contract

SIMPLIFIED FINANCIAL PLANNING

Most design professionals recognize the need to plan the operations of individual projects—to develop time schedules, programs of work to be accomplished, staffing plans, and budgets. But most firms fail to devote enough attention to planning and monitoring the financial results of the firm as a whole. In many firms, the focus of firmwide financial management is merely on cash management and maintaining good borrowing relationships, often the byproducts of mediocre financial results. You must develop and monitor a financial and operating plan that is simple and straightforward and that frees architects and engineers to focus on architecture and engineering first and finances second. Financial planning begins with formulating the statement of profit goals and other key financial measures. Using these goals as a guide, the next step is to calculate an annual budget, to be turned into a pro forma annual budget. The final step is to formulate a reporting system to measure progress toward your financial goals—basically, the goal for your bottom-line profit (set during the strategic planning process, Chapter 1).

BUDGETING

Design firms have two ways of setting their annual budget: the *contracts method* and the *size of staff method*, also known as *realization budgeting*. Here you will see that the second is the better method of the two.

Contracts Method A common budgeting method is to anticipate the contracts a firm will get in the coming year as the basis of the financial plan. This is difficult to calculate because it assumes that current contracts will carry a firm for three to six months, but the remainder of the year's work is unknown. When you don't know what contracts your firm will procure six to eight months from now, you can only guess at their profitability, scope, and schedule. Therefore, estimating the number of contracts that will materialize in a year can be based only on what you have in your pipeline. Such a pipeline bears many uncertainties—a market can change and a sure-thing project may or may not materialize, depending on the whims of the client. The immediate contracts probably account for only one-quarter to one-third of a year. Thus, to estimate for the entire year, you would multiply the project costs of the first three months by four:

3 months (all projects, all costs) × 4 = annual plan

This is an inaccurate, unpredictable method of estimating an annual budget. Very small firms, in particular, commonly use this method because they are unaware of alternatives.

Size of Staff Method A more stable planning factor is realization budgeting, which is based on staff size. The number of employees and their ability generally do not change dramatically in one year. Consequently, financial planning using achievable billing capacity per employee is a much sounder basis for planning accuracy.

Realization budgeting is a conservative method strongly recommended for the small firm (and for any firm) because it does not include extra profit that might be made on a current project but not another, future one. It also does not count on overtime efforts, making overtime an entirely extra income producer.

The following steps for realization budgeting correspond with the column numbers on the form shown in Figure 7-1:

1. List the people in your firm.
2. Figure each employee's target utilization (or chargeability) rate. What percentage of total time will each person spend on billable projects? Total time includes technical time, vacation, sick days, fringe benefits time, administrative time, and so on. The PSMJ Resources *2000 A/E Financial Performance Survey* (PSMJ Resources, Inc., p. 60) reported a median chargeability of 62.5 percent. In the example (Fig. 7-1), the firm consists of ten people and the average median utilization ratio is 74 percent. The utilization ratios in Figure 7-1 are considered goals and are purposefully set slightly higher than the industry average for each position they represent. (If your firm has a lower average utilization ratio than 62.5 percent,

Realization Budgeting

Staff	Pay Rate ($/year)	Target Utilization (2080 hrs)	Available Hours per Year	Target Billing Rate ($)	Potential Fees ($)	Availability	Totals ($)
Timmons	165,000	60%	1,248	186.30	232,500	100%	232,500
Warner	115,000	75%	1,560	126.68	197,625	100%	197,625
Yeh	115,000	75%	1,560	126.68	197,625	100%	197,625
DiFoggio	83,000	80%	1,664	95.38	158,720	100%	158,720
O'Keefe	75,000	80%	1,664	89.42	148,800	100%	148,800
Perkins	60,000	85%	1,768	74.52	131,750	100%	131,750
Lakey	60,000	85%	1,768	74.52	131,750	100%	131,750
Rodriguez	55,000	85%	1,768	71.54	126,480	100%	126,480
Vladir	50,000	85%	1,768	67.07	118,575	100%	118,575
Alberts	35,000	30%	624	50.67	31,620	100%	31,620

Total	**$1,475,445**
Loss to Effective Multiplier (.048 × Total)	**$ 71,393**
Total Available Revenue (Total – Loss)	**$1,404,053**

Figure 7-1

find out why. Take into account your type of business and your profit margin. For instance, interiors firms tend to have lower utilization ratio but higher hourly billing rates. They thus have a higher-than-average profit margin.)

3. Determine available hours per year. A standard work-year is 2080 hours (40 hours × 52 weeks). Multiply this by each person's target utilization ratio to achieve the billable chargeable hours for each person.

Standard workyear × utilization ratio for each person = billable chargeable hours per person

For example, if your typical workyear is 2080 hours and your person works at a 75 percent utilization ratio (person #2 in Fig. 7-1), that employee will generate 1560 hours of time over the next year that are billable to your clients.

4. Determine a targeted hourly billing rate. This can be complicated if you are using a multiplier or a variety of billing rates per individual. If you cannot easily figure the billing rate for each of your employees, standardize the rates—for example, simply charge $100/hour for everyone. In the example, person #2, with 1560 hours and a 75 percent utilization ratio, has a billing rate of $126.68 per hour. This person, if in your employ for the entire year, will generate $197,625 in fees.

5. Write the total fees generated for the year based on availability in the next column.

6. Assess availability. If a person is available for 100 percent of the year, he will generate 100 percent of the total billable rate. Give these individuals 100 percent billable ratings. If, however, you are planning to add three persons six months into the year, they each will have a billable rating of 50 percent. Multiply the total revenue generated amount ($197,625, in the example for person #2) by the availability rate (100 percent).

7. Add each employee's individual revenue amount to determine the firm's total available revenue generated. In the example, this is $1,475,445. This is the total amount of money your staff can generate based on your target utilization ratios (explained further in the upcoming section entitled "Key Financial Measures"), which can be easily measured using a time card.

8. Remember two added factors:

   ■ *Writeoffs*—You may not get paid for a certain percentage of time (hours charged on the time cards). This ratio should be calculated and subtracted from the total generated revenue amount at this point. Look back over last year's time cards and determine the percentage of hours you had to write off. In the example, the percentage is 2 percent.

   ■ *Bad debts*—Look over last year's books and determine the percentage of debts you had to write off. For the example, 2.8 percent of debts are bad. Add the writeoff percentage to the bad-debts allowance. In the example:

   2 percent writeoffs + 2.8 percent bad debts
   = 4.8 percent

Subtract the writeoffs from the total amount of revenue generated (TRG). In the example, that would be:

TRG   4.8 percent = total available revenue

9. Calculate total available revenue. In the example, 4.8 percent is $71,393:

$$\$1,475,445 - \$71,393 = \$1,404,053$$

The Pro Forma Annual Statement Now you are ready to develop a pro forma annual statement using the revenue figures and subtracting all allocable expenses from the total revenue generated (see Fig. 7-2):

1. Salaries from column #2 in Figure 7-1
2. Benefits such as bonuses, overhead, raises, and other expenses associated with salaries
3. Rent
4. Heat
5. Light and utilities
6. Reimbursables (add income you'll get if you mark up your reimbursables by, say, 15 percent)
7. Consultants, part-timers, outside personnel, and other services

Having done all this, you now have an annual financial plan (budget) based on an estimate of firm staff size. With only staff size as a variable, adjusting your plan becomes much simpler than trying to anticipate the probability of future contracts.

Pro Forma Annual Statement

Total annual revenue:	$1,404,053	
Total budget expenses:	$1,229,103	

1. Salaries	$813,000
2. Benefits and salary-related expenses	$ 90,000
3. Rent	$ 50,000
4. Heat	$ 8,000
5. Light and utilities	$ 18,000
6. Reimbursables	$ 32,000
7. Consultants, part-timers, outside personnel, and other services	$218,103

Expected profit = $174,950 (12.5% of total annual revenue)

Note: This budget is greatly simplified for explanatory purposes only.

Figure 7-2

Realization budgeting is a simple and rapid planning method. If your firm consists of ten employees, as in the example, developing your financial plan should take no more than 30 minutes. Figure 7-3 is a more realistic, more complex budget for a larger firm.

Professional Design Firm Realization Budget

Account Number	Title	Original Annual Budget	Budget per Month
3000.00	Income		
3100.00	Professional Fees	$ 1,137,348	$ 94,779
3200.00	Expense Realization	$ 40,000	$ 3,333
3300.00	Other Income		
3300.01	Bad Debts Recovered	$ -	$ -
3300.05	Interest Income	$ 3,000	$ 250
	Total Income	$ 1,180,348	$ 98,362
4000.00 to 7000.00	Expense (100%)		
4100.01	Professional Salaries and Wages (58%)	$ 568,522	$ 47,377
4200.01	Management Salaries and Wages (7%)	$ 66,804	$ 5,567
5100.00	Management Expense (25%)		
5100.01	Rent and Utilities	$ 75,000	$ 6,250
5100.05	Equipment Rental & Repair	$ 10,500	$ 875
5100.10	E. & O. Insurance	$ 40,000	$ 3,333
5100.90	Photography	$ 485	$ 40
5100.92	Meals and Lodging	$ 2,500	$ 208
5100.94	Postage and Freight	$ 3,500	$ 292
5100.95	Miscellaneous Expenses	$ 2,500	$ 208
5100.96	Office Management Travel	$ 4,200	$ 350
6100.00	Marketing Salaries and Wages (3%)	$ 27,375	$ 2,281
7100.00	Marketing Expense (7%)		
7100.01	Cost of Projects not Obtained	$ 29,026	$ 2,419
7100.05	Graphics	$ 25,000	$ 2,083
7100.06	Publications	$ 1,200	$ 100
7100.10	Conventions	$ 3,000	$ 250
7100.15	Travel Expenses	$ 7,000	$ 583
7100.20	Public Relations	$ 2,000	$ 167
7100.25	Miscellaneous	$ 500	$ 42
	Total Expense	$ 869,112	$ 72,426
Profit (Loss)		**$ 311,236**	**$ 25,936**

Typical Fiscal Staff Utilization Budget

1 Year = 2080 Hours

Name	Target Budget Chargeable	Chargeable Hours	Non-Chargeable Hours	Breakdown				
				Sick	Vacation	Holiday	Mktg	G.O.
Jones	55%	1,144	936	60	160	80	520	116
Smith	70%	1,456	624	60	160	80	200	124
Walker	85%	1,768	312	40	120	80	50	22
Curtis	5%	104	1,976	40	120	80	136	1,600
.	.	.	.	.	.	.	.	.
.	.	.	.	.	.	.	.	.
.	.	.	.	.	.	.	.	.
Burton	75%	1,560	520	30	80	80	30	300
Taylor	65%	1,352	728	30	80	80	138	400
Leonard	85%	1,768	312	30	80	80	0	122
Russell	90%	1,872	208	30	80	80	0	18
Total	72%	77,640	23,249	3,500	6,000	4,000	6,720	3,029

Typical Fiscal Year Utilization Revenue Projection

1 Year = 2080 Hours

Employee	Name	Billing Rate	Budget % Chargeable	Chargeable Hours	Fiscal Availability	Revenue Production
1	Jones	$ 110.00	55%	1,144	100%	$ 125,840
2	Smith	$ 110.00	70%	1,456	100%	$ 160,160
3	Walker	$ 65.00	85%	1,768	50%	$ 57,460
4	Curtis	$ 57.50	5%	104	100%	$ 5,980
.	.	.	.	.	.	.
.	.	.	.	.	.	.
.	.	.	.	.	.	.
15	Burton	$ 54.50	75%	1,560	100%	$ 85,020
16	Taylor	$ 46.00	65%	1,352	10%	$ 6,219
17	Leonard	$ 40.00	85%	1,768	10%	$ 7,072
18	Russell	$ 37.00	90%	1,872	25%	$ 17,316
	Firm Totals		72%	77,640		$ 1,338,057

Total Chargeable: $ 1,338,057
Total Billable (88%): $ 1,177,490
Total Collectable (85%): $ 1,137,348

| (1) Rate | X | (2) Hours | X | (3) Availablity | = | (4) Revenue |

Figure 7-3. Example of a complex budget.

Spreadsheet programs such as Microsoft Excel make financial planning flexible. You can change the utilization ratios, the standard year, and other factors to determine variations of your financial plan.

Clients' selection criteria for choosing design firms includes price competition or bidding. With an accurate budget, you will know exactly what your costs are and where to set your bid. Without a reliable budget, it is difficult to plan for bonuses and other important expenses throughout the year.

Banking Relationships One good reason to develop an accurate budget is to maintain banking relationships. Without an effective financial plan, bankers will not understand your business. Most will request to see your annual budget or financial plan. Design professionals are different from most businesses bankers deal with. They have no inventories; rather, they have work-in-process. They have projects that take, at minimum, many months to complete, not including construction time. They must meet a payroll every two weeks, whether or not the client pays its bill. A financial plan built around your staff count provides a solid tool for demonstrating control over your finances.

KEY FINANCIAL MEASURES

Armed with an annual financial plan (the budget) for the firm, you can begin setting financial goals and take steps to implement those goals. To set goals, first look at your firm's present financial picture and assess the key financial measures of your firm. Then compare your firm's actual performance with the targeted performance on a monthly basis using a brief (one-page) report.

To obtain an up-to-date financial picture, the smaller architectural or engineering firm should use five key financial measures to evaluate its operations and profitability:

1. Utilization ratio
2. Ratio of accounts receivables turnover
3. Work-in-process turnover
4. Accrual profit and loss
5. Project profitability

These measures were identified by Moritz Bergmeyer, founder of Boston's Bergmeyer Associates. Calculate each ratio once a month and compile a one-page report containing the results of each ratio. Figure 7-4 shows a sample monthly report/profit and loss statement. If your firm is divided into profit centers or project teams, you can request a similar report from each division leader.

Utilization Ratio The utilization ratio is the proportion of staff time that is chargeable to specific projects compared to the total time employed by the firm. In most cases, the firmwide utilization ratio should not exceed 65 percent. As mentioned earlier, PSMJ Resources' *2000 A/E Financial Performance Survey* showed that the median utilization ratio was 62.5 percent. When a firm's utilization ratio goes below this figure, profitability becomes difficult and the firm struggles financially.

The utilization ratio for the entire firm is a mix of ratios for each individual position. For example, project managers should aim for a utilization ratio of 65 percent, while technical staff should hit 90 percent. These ratios will differ for each firm. A principal may also be a project manager or marketing director. With that in mind, compare these ratios with those of your firm's utilization goals to see if they are realistic. Here are ways to increase utilization ratios:

1. *Get more work.* You'll have more available hours on which the employee may charge time against a project.

2. *Cut back on overhead time and overhead staff.* This means reducing the amount of time spent on marketing, general office activities, and office education and training in relation to the productive hours charged against the project.

3. *Eliminate overhead staff entirely*—that is, all accounting and administrative staff and other nonchargeable personnel.

4. *Shorten schedules.* Condense the amount of hours worked on a particular project. Have more people working more hours on the project to increase schedule performance. Doing so stimulates people to work at a greater capacity per hour.

5. *Get principals involved in the projects.* When the principal becomes entangled in overhead tasks, the utilization ratio can be very low.

6. *Get your overhead staff to charge their time to a project.* For example, when an assistant works on a set of meeting minutes, time should be charged to the project instead of to the general office overhead.

7. *Bring in some of the outside subcontract work.* For instance, if your firm is an engineering firm that subcontracts survey work to others on an independent-

contract basis, you may find the utilization rate of your staff can increase if you hire your own survey crews and keep them busy, with your engineers as supervisors of the survey crews.

8. *Reduce the total number of hours being charged by all staff.* Cut back from a five-day week to a four-day week, requiring staff to charge a bigger percentage of their time directly to projects. This is not an advis-

Monthly Summary Income Statement

	Current Month Budget	Current Month Actual	Year to Date	Frank P.C. 1	Jan P.C. 2	Alissa P.C. 3	Darius P.C. 7	Hannah P.C. 8
Income								
Gross Fee Income		$159,613	$ 1,381,822	$ 38,380	$ 22,159	$ 53,998	$ 15,191	$ 27,253
Net Fee Income	$152,876	$139,056	$ 1,177,795	$ 35,652	$ 17,248	$ 44,720	$ 13,273	$ 26,218
Work in Process		$ 6,489	$ 28,989	$ (1,008)	$ 2,632	$ 3,497	$ 983	$ -
Expenses								
Reimbursables		$ 24,056	$ 189,144	$ 10,733	$ 2,140	$ 9,193	$ 1,049	$ 941
Dir. Labor - Overtime	$ 51,272	$ -	$ -	$ -	$ -	$ -	$ -	$ -
Direct Labor		$ 42,778	$ 367,900	$ 8,761	$ 7,709	$ 13,714	$ 2,841	$ 7,043
Other P/C Labor		$ 18,488	$ 106,004	$ 1,075	$ 2,290	$ 2,212	$ 1,059	$ 1,319
Corporate Overhead		$ 57,587	$ 476,339	$ -	$ -	$ -	$ -	$ -
P/C Overhead		$ -	$ -	$ 1,174	$ 2,426	$ 2,153	$ 856	$ 863
P/C O/H Transfer		$ -	$ -	$ 865	$ (1,366)	$ 811	$ (1,139)	$ (250)
CADD Transfer		$ -	$ -	$ 1,843	$ 1,554	$ 2,690	$ 578	$ 1,529
Int@10%/Over 60 Recvs		$ -	$ -	$ 157	$ 1,000	$ 787	$ 364	$ 272
Corp. O/H Transfer		$ -	$ -	$ 11,476	$ 9,678	$ 16,753	$ 3,603	$ 9,523
Tot O/H (Excl Reimb)		$118,853	$ 950,243	$ 25,351	$ 23,291	$ 39,120	$ 8,162	$ 20,299
Profit								
Gross Profit		$ 16,704	$ 242,435	$ 15,772	$ 8,960	$ 25,915	$ 10,525	$ 17,337
Profit	$ 15,784	$ 16,704	$ 242,435	$ 2,296	$ (3,272)	$ 5,685	$ 5,980	$ 6,013
P/C YTD Profit			$ 232,435	$ 21,858	$ 44,513	$ 106,360	$ 47,063	$ 22,641
P/C% - Tot YTD Prof			100.0%	9.0%	18.4%	43.9%	19.4%	9.3%
Analysis								
Net Profit on Net	10.3%	12.0%	20.6%	6.4%	-19.0%	12.7%	45.1%	22.9%
Net Profit on Gross	0.0%	10.5%	17.5%	6.0%	-14.8%	10.5%	39.4%	22.1%
Current Multiplier	2.98	3.25	3.20	4.07	2.24	3.26	4.67	3.72
Breakeven Multiplier	2.67	2.86	2.54	3.81	2.66	2.85	2.57	2.87
Breakeven + 15%	3.07	3.29	2.92	4.38	3.06	3.28	2.96	3.30
Overhead Rate	160.0%	178.0%	158.0%	189.0%	202.0%	185.0%	187.0%	188.0%
Avg. Billing Rate	$ 42	$ 50		$ 57	$ 33	$ 47	$ 75	$ 54
Bill/Charge @ $42/hr	129.8%	118.0%		135.4%	79.3%	111.6%	177.5%	127.4%
Direct Labor %	33.5%	30.8%	31.2%	24.6%	44.7%	30.7%	21.4%	26.9%

	Current Month		Year to Date	Frank P.C. 1	Jan P.C. 2	Alissa P.C. 3	Darius P.C. 7	Hannah P.C. 8
	Budget	Actual						
Staffing								
Backlog (Manweeks)								
Backlog Tech. Staff								
Tech. Staff		22		3	6	6	3	4
Total Staff		28						
Weeks in Month		4						

Efficiency	Goals	Actual	Hours					
Total Hours			4686					
Chg Hrs/Tech Staff/Wk		31.88%						
Chg Hrs/Tech Hrs	90.0%	91.9%	3053					
Chg Hrs/Total Hrs	70.0%	61.2%	2805	627	518	954	178	490
Staff O-H Hrs/Total Hrs	6.0%	5.4%	248					
Admin Hrs/Total Hrs	18.0%	16.6%	761					
HVS Hrs/Total Hrs	10.0%	11.3%	520					
Promo Hrs/Total Hrs	3.0%	2.9%	131					
CADD Hrs/Total Hrs	2.0%	2.7%	122					

Balance Sheet	Current Month	Previous Month	Goals					
Cash	$ 104,558	$ 70,236	$ 41,717					
Accounts Receivable	$ 649,180	$ 658,719	$ 347,640	$ 69,444	$ 166,760	$ 214,266	$ 77,452	$ 97,307
Total Assets	$ 829,591	$ 820,051	$ 861,053					
Accounts Payable	$ 69,713	$ 73,092	$ -					
Total Liabilities	$ 346,865	$ 353,028	$ -					
Net Worth	$ 483,726	$ 467,023	$ -					

Accounts Receivable								
Accts Rec 0-60	$ 319,658	$ 350,261		$ 50,475	$ 46,261	$ 119,461	$ 33,618	$ 64,555
	49.2%	53.2%		72.7%	27.7%	55.8%	43.4%	66.3%
Accts Rec Over 60	$ 329,523	$ 308,458		$ 18,969	$ 120,499	$ 94,805	$ 43,834	$ 32,753
	50.8%	46.8%		27.3%	72.3%	44.2%	57.0%	33.7%
Average Collection Period	111	110		68	153	101	110	113

Figure 7-4

able way to cut back on overhead or increase utilization. It can decrease morale and cause the better people in your firm to leave.

9. *Raise awareness.* By creating a spot on time cards for staff to calculate and fill in their utilization ratio, they will become more aware of how they are spending their time. (See Fig. 7-5.)

Controlling Utilization Ratios with Time Cards

Use time cards to measure utilization ratios weekly or biweekly. It might be helpful to design your time cards with a percentage-chargeable entry in the lower right-hand corner. Explain to employees the formula for determining this ratio:

chargeable hours ÷ total hours = utilization ratio

Inform your employees of the target utilization ratio. Ask them to be sure that a certain percentage of hours on the time cards is not only chargeable but also billable. Communicate the utilization ratios to each staff member and negotiate them each year so each person knows his target ratio. This way, you can control the salary expense of your firm, your biggest expense item.

Figure 7-5

Ratio of Accounts Receivable Turnover The accounts receivable turnover formula measures the number of days from the time an invoice is sent to a client to the time it is paid. The average for design firms has, for years, hovered around 65 days from the time the invoice is received to the time it is paid. (See Fig. 7-6.) To determine this figure, first calculate the average daily revenues (annual gross revenues divided by 365 days) then divide the average accounts receivable balance by the average daily revenues.

To reduce accounts receivable turnover, try collecting a portion of your fees in advance. This lowers your accounts receivable turnover, thus, in effect, reducing the number of days between the time you send out, and get paid for, an invoice. Some firms request a 10 percent retainer up front, to be applied to the last invoice. Still others, for small enough projects, request a substantial portion, if not the total fee, up front.

Another way to reduce accounts receivable is to adopt rigid collection procedures. Stop work when a client is in arrears. While this practice may seem harsh, it is the one way for the small firm to guarantee prompt payment. Obviously, judgment must be used on a project-by-project basis before stopping work, to assure that factors such as lost checks are not reasons for nonpayment.

Work-in-Process Turnover Unlike accounts receivables turnover, this is the measure of the number of days between when the work is done and when an invoice is sent to a client. Aim for a work-in-process turnover of 10 days. This means that every 10 days, invoices should be generated. To reduce the turnover to less than 10 days, your firm must be paid money in advance on all con-

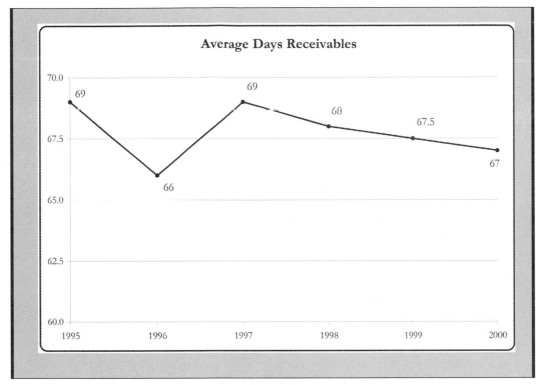

Figure 7-6

tracts. One firm has even achieved a negative work-in-process balance; by collecting fees in advance, it actually owes it clients money. According to PSMJ Resources' *2000 A/E Financial Performance Survey*, the median work-in-process turnover is 27.5 days. This is an increase of 2 days from 1999 figures, indicating that firms are taking more time to process and issue bills to clients. Even more problematic is that, in general, smaller firms have larger unbilled fees. For tips on reducing work-in-process turnover, see Figure 7-7.

Accrual Profit and Loss To determine accrual profit and loss, look at the amount of revenue generated versus the expenses generated. This differs from looking at the amount of revenue received versus expense paid, or the cash-basis profit. The basic difference with accrual and cash accounting is timing. On an accrual basis, you measure money earned in a specific period; on a cash basis, you measure fees collected.

Measuring profit and loss on a cash basis can be highly inaccurate, as a design firm may plan to pay a bill one month but postpone payment until two months later, thereby affecting the cash-basis profit simply by the timing of its payment

Two Ways to Improve a Long Work-in-Process Turnover

1. The days related to work-in-process reflect the internal process of collecting costs and billing clients. The faster and more efficiently you get bills to the clients, the more you improve the work-in-process situation. The firms in the lower quartile bill frequently (i.e., every 2 weeks) or as soon as a lump sum task is complete (no matter what day in the month it occurs). Time and expense reporting systems are automated and on-line. Time charges and expense accounts are collected every day and errors are corrected rapidly. The focus is to get the bill out as soon as possible.

2. Improving the collection period begins *before* the bill is sent to the client. Sample bills are reviewed with new clients to ensure they are understood and acceptable as part of starting a first project. Bill formats are simplified (e.g., minor expenses are lumped together into unit prices, backup expense data are eliminated from bills, project progress reports are not attached to bills but sent directly to client project managers). A phone call is made to the client's payables department seven days after sending each bill to ensure it was received and is being processed. Discussions between the firm's project manager and the client always include the subject of invoice payments.

On average, 64.6 percent (almost two-thirds) of your firm's assets are tied up in the combination of work-in-process (which you haven't billed yet) and accounts receivable (which you have billed, but haven't been paid). Your ability to generate cash is more critical than making a profit, so keep your eye on your cash flow measurements!

Figure 7-7
Source: "We Made a Profit, but Where's the Cash?" *PSMJ Best Practices*, May 2000, p. 11.

of invoices. A firm can also accelerate or postpone the receipt of funds from clients, pushing clients to pay or backing off. Accordingly, the accrual basis is more accurate in measuring the firm's actual performance. Figure 7-8 shows the relationship of accrual financial statements to cash financial statements.

The accrual profit and loss statement shows the performance of the company regardless of the timing of payments and expenses. It is an early indicator of potential cash-flow problems. Figure 7-4, the monthly financial measures report, is calculated on an accrual basis.

Project Profitability This key measure must be taken at regular intervals for each project. Analyze project profit and loss, looking carefully at the specific man-hours charged to the project for each task at each phase of the job.

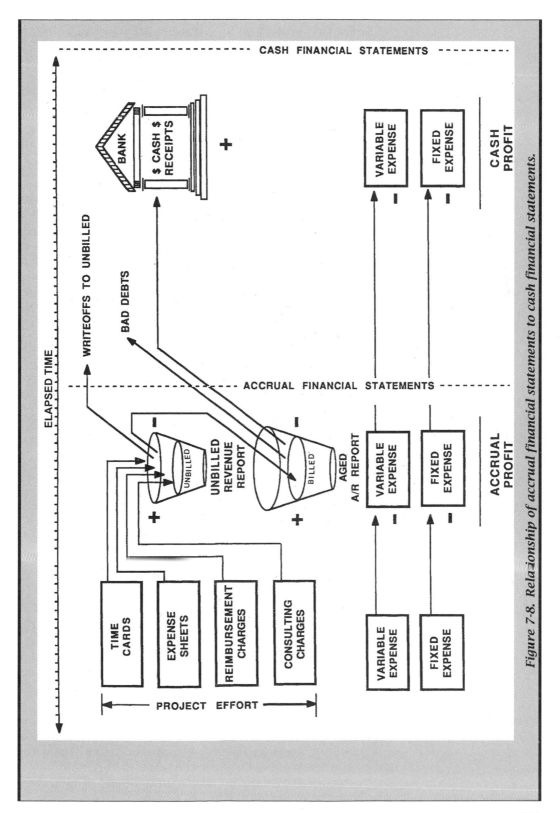

Figure 7-8. *Relationship of accrual financial statements to cash financial statements.*

191

Simplified profit and loss statements include:

- The number of hours used versus the number of hours targeted
- The number of fee dollars used versus the number of fee dollars targeted (See Fig. 7-4.)

The profit/loss statement should be no longer than one page. Reports that exceed that length are seldom read and easily forgotten. You can readily hang a single-page report on the wall to view your financial progress at any time. If you use a computer format, remember that one of the biggest criticisms of computer-generated reports is that they provide too much data; page after page of information can often overwhelm the recipient, and, frequently, no clue is offered as to which figures are most important. Keep the report simple.

Get a Complete Picture By measuring the above five elements, you will attain a complete financial picture that allows you to control your firm in the fastest, most effective manner. Bergmeyer found that a simplified one-page-per-month financial report consisting of these five key ratios, in addition to reading the best and worst of the project reports, was enough to help him manage the firm's operations. (See Fig. 7-4 for the sample monthly finance report.)

By looking at the key indicators, you can then ask critical questions about follow-up financial reporting. The next section further explains how to improve profitability.

PROFIT IS EVERYTHING

The yardstick of success in any operation is its profitability. Most of the design firms examined for this book have a healthy respect for bottom-line profits. Clear, high-profit goals are the key to financial success.

Successful firms do not sacrifice profits to improve design. They build a profit ratio into the design budget. This section explains how to set profit goals and suggests ways to monitor and improve profits.

Goal setting for profit is twofold; it addresses both the firm's annual profit goal and individual project profit goals.

Preparing the Firm Profit Plan Preparation of the profit plan begins at the annual planning meeting. As suggested in Chapter 1, you should hold a strategic planning meeting at least once a year, usually near the end of the fiscal year. Discuss economic forecasts and the general business climate. Establish guidelines for the principals to use in preparing the annual business plan. For example, you might set a profit goal of 20 percent pretax overall, with specific percentages for individual market segments.

The main point to remember is to set profit goals high, so your firm must stretch itself to reach them. As stated in Chapter 1, if you set your goal at 35 percent profit and achieve only 29 percent, you are still producing more than twice the profit of the marginal firm that sets its profit at 14 percent (the average).

Other factors affecting your company profit are:

- *Capital expenditures (rent versus buy decisions)*—It is generally less expensive for the small firm to rent rather than buy equipment or other capital items. Small firms are typically stretched for capital, and buying a piece of real estate or even computer equipment and software requires an expenditure of funds that many don't have. Furthermore, buying ties a firm to a particular direction, whereas renting or leasing allows a firm total flexibility and, thus, adaptability to the marketplace.

- *Investment in other ventures*—When a firm invests in another firm, it ties up resources that it could put into the development of its own resources, thus affecting profit. Therefore, the decision to invest in another venture—whether related or unrelated (i.e., real estate)—is a very important one.

- *Estate settlements with deceased owners*—Many small firms are strapped with heavy payments to the estates of the founders of a particular firm. The impact on profit can be significant; hence, the way in which the buy/sell agreement (see Appendix A) is established is critical to the liability that the second set of owners will have to the initial founders of a particular company.

- *Lease/purchase equipment*—Purchasing equipment ties up funds that might be better utilized to "grow" the firm; for example, the moneys might be spent on marketing or the pursuit of new projects. By leasing, you can avoid tying up funds and build in flexibility.

- *Market diversity*—When a firm is diverse, it must expend funds in several directions simultaneously. Accordingly, a firm focused on a niche or particular service has an advantage over the diverse firm.

- *Economic climate*—This greatly influences a firm's profitability. Some firms succeed in spite of themselves just by being in the right place at the right time. Others fail even though well managed.

- *Merger versus acquisitions*—A merger or acquisition can often enhance a firm's ability to market itself to a new group of clients, thereby improving profitability.

▪ *Staff Turnover*—Both positive and negative factors relate to staff turnover. A certain percentage of staff should turn over each year, allowing the elimination of people who are not performing to standard. Beware, though—too much staff turnover is negative. This may suggest that the firm cannot retain staff or that its employment policies are not in line with those of the competition. The median turnover rate in the design industry, according to PSMJ Resources' *2000 A/E Financial Performance Survey* (p. 207), is 18 percent.

▪ *Branch office philosophy*—For firms with branch offices, branch office management will greatly affect profitability. Firms that operate branch offices as profit centers (explained later in the text) generally make more profit than those that operate on a cost-center basis. This decision, however, must be made in light of the firm's culture; if a firm wishes to have a single company image in all its branches, then perhaps the cost-center method is best. If the firm, on the other hand, wishes to maintain multiple offices in competition with each other, then perhaps profit-center arrangement is more appropriate.

Once prepared, incorporate the profit goals into the strategic plan (see Chapter 1). Review profit goals at least monthly to measure your firm's financial standing. Compare budget to actual performance (found on the one-page key financial measures report, Fig. 7-4) and investigate variances.

Project Profit Project profit, in general, is a reflection of your firm's overall profit plan. Goals are typically set by the principals. Decisions on whether to accept a greater or lesser profit goal are generally outside the jurisdiction of the project manager, who is rarely a principal. The profit goal for a project is set in the negotiation stage and carries over into the budget.

At the negotiating stage, many decisions are made that affect how a project will be carried out. For example, if only $10,000 is allocated to a project, then the budget must reflect the fact that only $10,000 worth of team time is allocated. Many firms do not relate the budget to the actual fee negotiated in the project contract, thereby creating a problem before a project even starts. The project manager must match the scope of services, the budget, and the actual fee generated for each portion of the project. Otherwise, it is almost impossible to achieve the project's targeted profit goal.

Profitable projects result from five factors:

1. *The right market*—Some projects a firm should shun. The style of operation it takes to conduct the project profitably may be in direct conflict with the firm's style. For example, not all firms are able to produce government work profitably, even if the job is won.

2. *The right client*—Even within your company's natural market, some clients can lead to losses. Clients with too large a project, too small a project, or unreasonable expectations are problems for firms seeking profits.

3. *The right price*—Through negotiation, a price must be secured from clients that permits the firm to achieve its profit goal and cover all costs. Specialty firms with limited markets typically must secure high margins.

4. *Control*—Control your projects so resources committed are in line with the price you secure. Control means planning and budgeting so that each scope task is assigned specific time guidelines, thus allowing for easy measurement of actual versus planned results.

5. *Collection*—No project is profitable until fees are collected. Up to that time, profits are theoretical rather than actual.

Overall, it takes a good project manager to implement each of these.

Identify Unprofitable Projects Reject projects that represent unacceptable risk. Here are six reasons to turn down a project:

1. *The project is too small*—Every firm has its fee floor for profitability. A fee floor is generally determined by calculating the firm's liability exposure versus the amount of fee to be collected. Below this floor, the firm, by its nature, cannot produce profits, as it will automatically invest too many resources. Turn these projects over to even smaller firms that will not compete with you on larger projects from that client.

2. *The project is too large*—Any project that represents more than 25 percent of a firm's annual gross is too risky. Ask yourself whether, if that project is a failure, the whole firm risks failing. Instead, consider participating in a joint venture.

3. *The project is from the wrong client*—Don't accept work from a client who is wrong for you, whether the reasons involve financial instability, litigiousness, unreasonable expectations, or personality conflict.

4. *The client won't pay*—A strong reason not to accept a project is that the client is not likely to pay the bills. Assess the client by knowing the industry they're in and finding out from others their reputation for on time bill payment. Also, ask the client what its source of money is. This will immediately reveal potential problems. If you still want to do the project, even when the client's financing seems dubious, get paid in advance.

5. *The project involves professional liability risk*—Certain types of projects are high risk. Asbestos-connected, hazardous-waste, rehab, and condominium projects may all carry high liability potential. Evaluate your risk before accepting such work by estimating your firm's capacity to defend a destructive lawsuit under each category of project being considered.

6. *The project calls for expertise you do not have*—Do not accept such work. You may be unable to meet your client's expectations and will probably subject yourself to unexpected costs, such as those for research and consultants.

Improve Project Profitability On average, 60 to 70 percent of a design firm's total payroll goes into project labor. As a result, how well each project is managed is the major determinant of a firm's profitability. Successful firms need to control, at least semimonthly, the personnel-hours needed to complete the work. They also need to assess continually the chances of overruns in time to prevent them. This section shows how to measure profit by analyzing certain trends of the ratios presented in the section "Key Financial Measures."

Note first that utilization is not the key to profitability. Each personnel-hour you charge to a client is not necessarily profitable just because of the multiplier used to establish billing rates. That hour, if it is in excess of the time that the project should have taken, encroaches on the bottom line—the contribution to overhead and profit of that project. So, in effect, that hour and its costs constitute a loss.

If that single personnel-hour overrun is, mistakenly, included in direct charges to projects, it distorts utilization. You will then agonize about how profitability can be so low when everyone is so busy working on projects.

Next, look at the net effective multiplier and, rather than assume your profit problems are the fault of the competitiveness of the market or the reluctance of clients to pay enough for your services, look at the three most prominent red flags of project financial failure:

1. High work-in-process (i.e., not invoicing clients fast enough)
2. Low receivable turnover
3. Low effective multipliers

Work-in-process is a common hiding place for overruns. It postpones the point at which the project manager discovers the project is incurring more personnel-hours than planned. It claims that an overrun, usually at billable rates, is an asset and not a loss because charged amounts are not yet written off, as invoicing has not occurred.

Low receivable turnover is the result of too much work-in-process and lax follow-up on collections. It is a symptom that the client is holding up payment on invoices that bill personnel- hours spent on project work performed so long ago that the client cannot remember the details. The invoice becomes suspect and you lose time proving it valid.

An *effective multiplier* is a multiple of direct labor salary paid to an individual, which creates a fee per hour chargeable to a client. In general, the multiples charged for architects and engineers are in the range of 2.9 times the direct personnel expense. This is the amount paid per hour to the CADD operator or designer, plus the cost of the fringe benefits paid to that person. This amount, combined with overhead and profit factors, equals the total multiplier or billing rate chargeable to the client.

A low effective multiplier reveals these problems:

- The personnel-hour budget was established after the fee was agreed to.
- The personnel-hours needed were established as a percentage of the fee and ignored the time needed to get the work done.
- The work was planned before the fee was agreed to, but the project manager failed to compute the average base personnel-hour cost of the project team or failed to use the firm's net effective multiplier goal when negotiating the fee. (In general, a project manager figures an average rate for the people on a given team and applies that average rate to the total number of hours to be performed on a job, thereby eliminating the need to produce a finite estimate of the cost involved. This creates an acceptable effective average multiplier.) If the project manager fails to compute

the correct average personnel-hour multiplier, this can reflect problems in project profitability.

- The project manager considered the personnel-hour budget padded, so she artificially cut the budget as a basis for fee negotiation. This was wrong—the budget was, if anything, set tight to get the job and improve the backlog.
- The principals felt the project important enough to obtain regardless of the personnel-hour budget.
- The project manager, with the fee already set, failed to assess the degree to which the working budget could be reduced to attain the net effective multiplier target.
- The project manager failed to provide, either to consultants or the client, a clear understanding of the scope needed to meet the client's expectations for the project.

All the above problems result in projects heading for a substandard net effective multiplier before the work is even begun. Overruns are unavoidable from the outset.

To avoid these problems, check the net effective multiplier on each project at least once a month. This helps focus principals' attention promptly on problem projects so they can be corrected. Such a review can reveal a host of other problems:

- Poor productivity
- Untrained project team members who are not clear about the scope of work they are to perform or the work plan intended when the personnel-hour budget was established
- Use of more highly paid people than needed or planned for
- Failure to agree on the personnel-hour budget with those assigned to the work
- Tendency to goldplate—that is, doing more than the standard of quality the client actually expects and agreed to in the contract (See "Excess Perfection Syndrome," Fig. 4-13.)
- Internal rework to meet quality standards
- Work performed gratuitously beyond the scope agreed to with the client
- Rework caused when the client or firm changes its mind about the design or design criteria. The added work is then performed free or for a meager fee that lowers the net effective multiplier
- An unrealistic semimonthly estimate of personnel-hours to complete the work

- Failure to rebudget work packages or tasks included in the project as soon as the budget must be modified for any reason (in such cases, clearly document the reason for such budget changes
- Too much staff on project teams or excess overtime when agreed schedules are in jeopardy

High utilization and low overhead rates, though good indicators, will not guarantee high profitability. High overruns, on the other hand, assure poor profitability and distort the accuracy of the other two measures of effectiveness because utilization looks good while bottom-line performance is eroded.

Profit Analysis by Market As mentioned earlier in this chapter (under "Key Financial Measures"), firms that operate in several markets should consider breaking down their profitability analysis by market. For example, an architectural firm may design schools, industrial facilities, and office buildings. It makes sense to measure a firm's profitability in each area.

Do this by measuring the year's profit on each project. Subtotaling the profit for each market and comparing these subtotals to the firm's total profit can demonstrate each market's importance to the company. Relating each market's profit to the gross revenue from that market will, in addition, reveal its relative profit margin. (See Fig. 7-9.)

Measure your firm's profitability from several perspectives. With this kind of management information, firms can decide on their investment in marketing and areas with growth potential.

These markets can be turned into separate profit centers and managed as such by developing a monthly key financial measures report for each center. From the example in Figure 7-9, it is clear that housing and office buildings have different measures of profitability. You can also break down market profits into more finite measures for each project:

- Utilization rate
- Cost factors
- Market share firm

This gives you an idea of how the firm is doing in each market, not just how the overall firm is doing. For instance, if you have three markets, two performing at 25 percent margin on gross and one achieving only 5 percent margin on gross, you must define exactly why you stay in the lesser market when other markets are achieving better performance for you. Many small firms remain in lesser markets for long periods, dragging down their overall profitability, at

Relative Importance of a Market to the Firm

	Office Buildings		Housing		Health Care		Total	
	Target	*Actual*	*Target*	*Actual*	*Target*	*Actual*	*Target*	*Actual*
Revenue	$1.2M	$.9M	$.8M	$2.IM	$.5M	$.6M	$2.5M	$3.6M
Profit margin	$ .4M	$.09M	$.2M	$1.05M	$.1M	$.2M	$ .7M	$1.16M
Profit margin by %	33%	10%	25%	50%	20%	33%	29%	33%

Note that office buildings were targeted for the largest percentage of profitability (margin) at 33 percent, with housing targeted for only 25 percent, but that housing actually achieved a 50 percent margin. More importantly, housing generated more than two-thirds of the firm's total dollar amount of profits at $1.05M. Thus, while office buildings were originally planned to be more important to the firm, the yearly results revealed housing to be a more significant market.

Figure 7-9

the expense of entering other key markets in which bigger dollars might be earned.

One 27-person firm is organized into profit centers by building type. These profit centers are like small businesses and are fairly autonomous. They are responsible for managing themselves, negotiating contracts, hiring and firing their personnel, and making a profit. The umbrella firm is there to provide the overall goals, information to run the profit centers, marketing support, and other administrative functions.

This is an effective approach as long as the principals make certain that the overall firmwide goals are being accomplished. Profit center managers must not be allowed to get into situations where their individual goals or competition with other profit centers interferes with the firm's best interest. For example, preference should be given to sharing available work among profit centers when that is best for the firm as a whole, even if certain tasks might be accomplished outside at lower cost.

Resolution of this problem requires a balance between competition and collaboration. Part of this is accomplished through the compensation policy. The firm illustrated in Figure 7-9 believes in sharing profits (when there are profits) with all employees. At present, half the profit is kept by the firm and the other half is distributed. The bonus distribution not only takes into account profit center performance but also recognition for achieving firmwide goals.

The firm described in Figure 7-9 is moving toward an incentive management system where more and more of a person's salary is tied to performance and her value to the firm. Management is looking for the incentives that motivate people, that can be measured, and that are correct for the firm. Such incentives might include rewards for being profitable in a profit center at the time profit is billed, recognition for design work when published, advancement based on client satisfaction, and prizes for innovative ideas.

SHARING FINANCIAL INFORMATION

Sharing financial information with staff improves morale and, indirectly, project control and cost control. This practice was encouraged in Chapter 1 and is reviewed here to stress its importance. Here are four suggestions for sharing financial information with employees:

1. *Publish a simple annual report* for employees that highlights the key financial results of the firm. This financial report need not show all of the detailed accounting and the general ledger, but should include general results of the operations.

2. *Make sure financial reporting is done regularly* using the method explained earlier in this chapter under "Key Financial Measures." Share these measures in a one-page report at least monthly with key persons in the firm. This ensures that all information is current and that all are abreast of the status of overhead, salaries, and project results. With this information, company managers can better adjust activities to actual financial circumstances. (See Fig. 7-4 for a sample monthly financial report.)

3. *Note that financial reporting does not normally include payroll reporting.* Payroll should be confidential.

4. *Share with employees* such necessary information as project profitability, firmwide profitability, and overhead expense.

SUCCESS CHALLENGES

1. Look at your present financial reporting system. How long are the reports? How readable?

2. Review your current budgeting method. Are you calculating your firm's revenue based on expected income or on staff size? If you are using a revenue approach, draw up a plan using a staff size approach and compare the two.

3. Write up a one-sheet view of your firm's financial status. What are the key financial measures you use? Do you use such measures correctly?

4. Review your firm's accounting system. Could you benefit from a new financial management software package?

5. When was the last time you shared financial information with your staff? Set a date today to dispense financial information.

6. Does your firm view profit as the most important bottom line? How could you divide your firm into profit centers?

Chapter 8

Information Technology

CADD is an everyday part of small A/E firm daily business in the 2000s. So are other technologies, like email, Web sites, information networks, and complex database programs. Despite the ubiquity of technology, it remains a large trouble spot for many firm leaders. The amount of money required to keep up with technological advances coupled with the confusion over which products should be purchased and how they can be used most effectively makes the issue of information technology (IT) a frustrating one.

Most firm principals accept the importance of technology to everyday business operations. However, their commitment to getting the most out of that technology is lower. PSMJ Resources' *Office Automation and Information Technology Survey*, ©2001, shows that 82 percent of responding firms established budgets for hardware and software upgrades, while only 43 percent had an automation training plan.

For the owner of a small firm, the prospect of spending even more money on technology—by sending employees to training programs—may not sound appealing. Kristine Fallon, founding member of CAD for Principals, however, believes that few firm owners are getting what they paid for out of their systems—they just don't understand them well enough. Kristine makes the following recommendations for delving effectively into the world of IT.[1]

Set up your basic system—and forget about it.
Your IT system has certain basic components—plumbing—on which your business depends. These include file servers, backup systems, email service, communications servers, firewalls, and Internet connections. No matter how fancy, however, they will have no effect on your bottom line. Yes, you'll need these components in the right sizes and configurations. But spending extra money on them is like buying designer storage cabinets for your supply room.

Try to make these components disappear. Neither management nor IT staff should give them much time or energy. Focus on reliability and lowest *total* cost of ownership (purchase cost plus maintenance plus related staff expenses). Consider redundant hardware components in your server (that automatically take over if their twin part fails). These

INFORMATION TECHNOLOGY IS YOUR LEVER TO A MORE DYNAMIC BUSINESS

Is e-collaboration really in the cards for the A/E/C industry? Three converging trends tell us that it is:

1. According to projections, overall Internet business-to-business transactions will reach nearly $2 trillion by 2002. And, in a survey of contractors, 70 percent of respondents thought at least 25 percent of their business would be conducted via the Web by that same year.

2. Firms everywhere are talking about the pace at which clients expect them to perform. The one way to find more time is to use IT to gather input, document decisions, and communicate information faster.

3. The use of intelligent 3D modeling from design through construction has proven to enhance constructibility and to reduce the number and cost of field change orders.

How can your firm prepare for the electronic fast track? Try these four steps:

1. Enlighten your IT gurus.

Ten or more years ago, someone in your firm had an uphill battle to convince your manual drafters that 2D CADD was a powerful technology. Today, you may be finding that your CADD experts and managers are the most reluctant members of your firm to adopt new and unfamiliar software products; they have become comfortable with their skills and work processes.

As a principal, you must provide the leadership and motivation to encourage these individuals to take the next step, particularly in the area of intelligent 3D modeling. Good technology planning and training will ensure that their transition is successful.

2. Extend your technology to all project players.

Studies as early as the mid-1980s showed that IT brings benefits an order of magnitude greater when applied to overall business processes rather than to individual tasks. Rigorous work process modeling efforts by the CAD for Principals Council Best Practices Committee, headed by Ken Stowe, have shown that when an architect and a builder share intelligent CADD models via a project Web site, the duration and cost of design and construction planning can drop by 7 percent and 12 percent, respectively. But the committee also found that by including subconsultants, subcontractors, and owners in the communication,

time savings reached 18 percent and cost reductions, 23 percent.

When choosing and implementing your Web-based project communications system, make sure your technology solution extends to and adds value for all team members. If the new process takes additional effort with no apparent benefits to the user, getting buy-in and participation will be an uphill battle that will sap the anticipated gains.

3. Choose your project Web site for its payoff.

Somewhere between 100 and 200 vendors are vying for attention as project Web site providers. Consolidation of once competing firms is already taking place. Make sure the vendor you choose is financially secure and has a good-sized customer base. Also, be sure you can get and use your data if the vendor ceases to do business. Once you have a short list of vendors that meet these criteria, keep your site simple. Do not accept any vendor's list of features as what you need. Instead, focus on those features that will yield results for your team. To spark collaboration and pick up your project pace, look for:

■ Strong drawing and document management with on-line viewing and markup

■ Interactive communication tools, such as Web-based drawing reviews, conferencing, and discussion forums

■ Accountability tools that issue alerts when someone does not respond promptly, particularly to requests for information, shop drawing submissions, change order requests, and other time-sensitive communications

4. With intelligent modeling software, be smart.

On the intelligent modeling side, the field is much smaller. Until now, the biggest stumbling block to adopting this powerful next-generation CADD has been the extremely steep learning curve. But vendors are wising up, and new, easier-to-use technologies are emerging.

In choosing software, demand a powerful product that is also intuitive and easy to use. *Intelligent modeling software simulates a real building, not a drawing.* It is designed for experienced professionals who know how buildings go together—not for entry-level designers or drafters. Senior staff members who never mastered 2D CADD and who have no time for weeks of training will benefit most from this technology, so get them involved in selecting and using it.

Kristine Fallon, "Crank Up Your Operating Speed Electronically," *PSMJ Best Practices*, November 2000, p. 9.

PROTECTING YOUR INFORMATION SYSTEMS

- Are you legal? Do you have all your software and hardware licenses? Can a disgruntled employee turn you in if you don't?

- How do you handle backups of data? How often and which data? Who does the backups, and where do they get stored?

- What happens in case of an emergency, such as the IT people do not make it into work?

- How do you handle a crisis, such as if your network goes down or your Internet connections go down? Who does what in these cases?

- How are you secured from outside intruders on the Internet? Do you have a firewall?

- Do you have an audit of your entire network, and is it diagrammed?

Linda Joy Weinstein, "Is Your Approach to Technology Sabotaging Your Firm?" *PSMJ Best Practices*, March 2000

cost virtually nothing compared to the cost and downtime required to manually rebuild a failed hard drive.

Make sure you evaluate all available options. Outsourcing can be an excellent strategy for these components, although selecting a good source and structuring a sound agreement are both critical and difficult. Look for total solutions and avoid long term contracts especially for communications components. New products are coming online quickly, and prices are dropping.

Keep upgrading your equipment *and* your people.
Continuous IT improvement in both productivity and quality is essential to business survival, and this includes training. You can acquire cutting-edge desktop technology—critical to competitive service delivery—with an upgrade plan. But that same technology also needs to provide leverage for your design professionals, to allow them to deliver more services more quickly and with greater precision in the same number of hours.

For all this to happen, you'll need a unified software/training plan that:

- Defines your firm's goals in buying new or upgrading existing software. If there is no business benefit, why spend the money?
- Drives the hardware upgrades necessary to support the new software.
- Identifies which staff will use the new or upgraded software.
- Defines the training required for the target user group to successfully use the target features.

Don't let the marketing furor surrounding hot new technologies distract your firm from focusing IT investment on continuous improvement in your core competencies—design, project delivery, and client relationship maintenance. In these areas, targeted IT spending will yield bottom-line results.

Create an IT strategy.
In the current economy, you cannot afford to do without a strategic technology plan. Your firm should always devote a portion of its overall technology budget to looking toward the future. Whether the funding is to send your principals to an IT seminar, to have a consultant review your current technology status and recommend next steps, or to give your staff time and budget to run pilot IT projects, the investment will support your firm's competitiveness and future profitability.

Get familiar with technology *today*.

In the past three years, the Internet has transformed the economics of project communications for geographically dispersed teams, and a new generation of CADD software has come to market. Each of these developments has implications for staffing, workflow, fee setting, and competitive positioning. Small design and construction firms are using the Internet to provide up-to-the-minute project status information to their clients, any time of the day or night, without adding staff. Large organizations have employed Web-based workflow controls to maintain project quality and service while they open new offices and add hundreds of new staff members. Powerful, easy-to-use next-generation CADD software is permitting senior staff and firm principals to regain control of their operations. Have you missed these opportunities? Has your competition? Be one of the first to take advantage of new developments—you'll reap large rewards from being positioned to service clients more effectively and run your firm in a more profitable manner.

DEVELOPING YOUR STRATEGIC INFORMATION TECHNOLOGY PLAN[2]

You should assess your technology plan within a business-directed focus by examining the following:

- How your prioritized objectives fit into a business plan
- Your technology assets
- An inventory of software
- Your network capabilities
- The schedule for managing the process
- Your firm's loss prevention plan

What Is Your Plan for the Next Two Years? Thinking beyond the initial development of the plan, you must consider which technology policies you now have in place, whether those policies are in lockstep with your other firm policies, and what the role of management is in carrying the plan into the future. Also look at:

- Budgeting (between $2,000 and $7,000 per employee per year for new technology)
- Assigning specific staff members and committing hours toward implementation of the plan
- Providing periodic review, maintenance, and upgrading of all systems
- Providing periodic training of the technology staff

Deciding Who Will Manage the Process A small-firm leader is wise to move control over information resources away from the technical guru and into the hands of diverse business constituencies and end users, such as the CADD department and others, including outside consultants and team partners. What really matters applies both to the external view, or your position in the marketplace, and the internal view—your people, processes, and structure that deliver on the strong market position that managing information technology gives you.

Leadership's IT Challenge The IT challenge for firm leaders is not to make the strategic technology plan and the business plan dovetail but rather to assess the technology plan along these key points:

- Market-driving capabilities
- The plan's role and impact
- Current IT investments

Evaluation Principles IT projects should build capabilities rather than improve ongoing operations. Your firm's technology should:

- Open new channels.
- Produce happier customers.
- Manage services and documents.
- Support business development.
- Enable new means of production.
- Support expanded services/territory.

Position for Competitive Advantage
- Leadership must be clear about every IT project/initiative that crosses its path.
- Leadership must understand what is being bought/implemented or developed. Clarity is key!
- Leadership must ask, "Is this the cost of doing business?" or " Is this an investment in our competitive advantage?"

Additional Considerations
- *Align with your clients*—Your IT vision responds to your client's needs. Is another firm providing services to your clients? Would your clients prefer you to provide these services?
- *Align with your firm's values*—Does IT mirror the culture of your workplace? Is access to IT equitable? Is IT management isolated or integrated within the various departments?
- *Align with your people*—Do you provide the tools and power your team needs? Do you provide training, support, input, and possible buy-in?

> ■ *Align with your business goals*—Is your IT funding adequate to meet business goals? Are all your business groups, both internal and external, represented?

UNDERSTAND YOUR SYSTEMS[3]

To make a sound decision about the technologies in which you and your firm should invest, it is helpful to place the myriad systems and software in context. Here's a basic rundown:

1. *Base Technologies*—These are technologies that a firm must master to effectively compete in its chosen market service area. Your staff must have strong skills in these areas to be competent with the other technologies you'll need to utilize in the future. These skills are:

   ■ Necessary to do business but are not sufficient to achieve a competitive advantage.
   ■ Widely known and readily available (e.g., word processing, CADD)
   ■ Easily acquired by your competitors
   ■ Of little marketing value
   ■ No different from commodity products

   Generally speaking, base technologies are almost all that small firms invest in, and the vast majority of design and construction firms (regardless of size) overinvest in them. As a general guide, about 40 percent of your technology budget should go toward maintaining this base technology, both in systems and in staff skills.

2. *Key Technologies*—These are technologies that provide competitive advantages. They:

   ■ Permit a firm to improve work efficiencies.
   ■ Allow a firm to get into markets that other firms cannot.
   ■ Are not widely used.
   ■ Require a high level of sophistication to use well.

   While base technologies tend to be viewed as normative and usually get classified as overhead, key technologies are the ones that clients may include as prequalifications in their RFPs and RFQs (and are probably willing to pay additionally for).

If planned, implemented, and managed properly, these technologies can provide a firm with tangible competitive capabilities that can improve performance and profitability. However, if planned, implemented, and managed improperly, these technologies can inflict great damage to the firm.

As a rule of thumb, about 45 percent of your technology budget should go toward developing and utilizing key technology, both in systems and in staff skills.

3. *Pacing Technologies*—These could become tomorrow's key technologies. They have several unique characteristics. They:

■ May be cutting-edge or experimental.
■ Are often high-risk investments.
■ Are often part of a research and development (R&D) effort.
■ May be too expensive for many (particularly smaller) firms.

As a general guide, about 15 percent of your technology budget should be invested in pacing technologies. This will help you form a core R&D effort focused on identifying and exploiting progressive technologies that the firm will need to maintain (or increase) its strength in two or three years down the road.

STANDARD ISSUES

Basic Hardware Other than voice mail and a fax machine, the most ubiquitous examples of base technology in any A/E/C operation include:

■ *PCs (personal computers)*—Although they offer less flexibility, desktop computers generally have longer shelf lives than laptops, especially if you intend to use CADD applications. Ideally, a project manager will have a desktop computer *and* a laptop (or, increasingly, a PDA—a personal digital assistant) for when he is out of the office. Work then can be copied to the desktop, with its easier connections to peripherals.
■ *Scanners and digital cameras*—The PM should have the means to turn hard copy into digital (electronic) information that can be downloaded, updated, and easily distributed around the globe, if need be. Both

scanners and, for site condition updates, digital cameras are indispensable.

- *Modems*—The modem is the device used for the actual transmission of your digital information. Speed is an essential consideration here and, although it will seem slow with time, the fastest available modem should generally be considered. Large offices require connections that are more advanced than standard telephone lines, such as ASDL, ISDN, or a (partial or full) T1.

- *Fileservers*—Offices with two or more people generally require networks to allow everyone access to shared devices such as printers, plotters and modems. Adding a fileserver to this network will provide a central location in which to store files, enabling you to organize all project files in one location while allowing users access to those files. A fileserver will also enable you to back up files more effectively.

Basic Software   Software is always being revised. Most software manufacturers release a new version of their most popular programs every year, with several minor intermittent updates between each release.

To ensure that archived electronic files are always accessible, users should be mindful of any and all application software changes. Here are a few of the most pertinent packages:

- *Spreadsheet Packages*—Consisting of large sheets of cells into which you enter numbers, text, and dates as well as sums and calculations that reference other cells, spreadsheet software packages are electronic versions of the traditional green grid paper used by bookkeepers. Generally, they also offer more advanced capabilities, including automatic charting and graphing of spreadsheet data, search and retrieval tools formula verifications, and methods for intelligent data entry.

  Obvious uses for spreadsheets include detailed budgets, task lists, specification schedules, and many types of quantitative data collection, such as square footages of end-user spaces. Spreadsheets also provide graphic formatting capabilities that can produce attractive schedules and columnar reports. Most spreadsheets allow you to export or publish data into word-processing documents, slide presentations, and other software file types.

- *Databases*—Databases are files composed of records containing fields of information about a topic, whether project contacts, a door schedule, or a shop drawing submittal. Among good database software's most powerful features is the ability to present the same information in multiple formats, ranging from detailed reports and summary lists to mailing labels and, increasingly, Web pages. This enhances productivity because users need enter data only once but can circulate it in many forms.

Another advantage is the database's quality control function. You can specify that database fields accept only certain types of information, such as numbers, dates, or values from a predefined list of acceptable entries. The database then can be programmed to alert you to inconsistent data entries, overdue dates, and outstanding issues.

Database software ranges from simple flat-file packages to complex relational (multifile) databases, and from user-friendly intuitive (but often feature-limited software) to high-level tools that only experts can program. Regardless of the particular software or scope of data, a well-conceived database can be a project manager's best friend, providing useful ways of storing data and making it available as required while minimizing redundant and inaccurate data entry.

Such tools also may be shared by more than one user, so that the project team has access to current project information while performing tasks. In this way, the database also becomes an important project team communications tool.

■ *Project managers/schedulers*—Unlike spreadsheets and databases, which are often generic software packages designed to be tailored to a range of uses, project management and scheduling software is intended specifically for the planning and running of projects. It is widely used in construction-related industries, which depend on effective scheduling.

These packages can range from simple schedulers that produce basic milestone bar charts and wall schedules to highly complex packages that link project milestones and tasks to start and completion dates, and track fixed and variable costs and staff assignments. The latter enable you to compare actual to planned schedules. Through both tabular reports and graphs, the program highlights when the project is encountering cost overruns, scheduling crunches, and staffing crises.

While the more complex scheduler/project manager packages can be overkill for short, simple projects, they can be indispensable tools for tracking and managing projects of significant scope and time frame. By providing multiple ways to look at the elements of a project and by providing alerts to any variance from the original project schedule, they enable project managers to be proactive.

Many of these software packages also allow project managers to combine multiple related projects under a single project file so that the impact of a change in one project can be shown on another. In fact, it would be possible, especially for smaller offices, to track all office projects in a single project management file, thereby facilitating officewide project coordination.

■ *Financial management packages*—For a discussion of financial management software packages, see Figure 8-1.

COMPUTER-AIDED DRAFTING AND DESIGN (CADD)

The single most important application that you will select and use in your practice, CADD, lies at the heart of today's design firm. Not just a documentation tool, CADD is also an effective design tool. A design can be easily and quickly altered to provide numerous variations on the original concept.

When selecting a CADD application, you should thoroughly evaluate the different products on the market. Here's a list of criteria that should be considered when evaluating CADD applications:

■ Interface/setup
■ Layering
■ Drawing tools
■ Modifier tools
■ Hatches/fills
■ Dimensioning
■ Text
■ 3D modeling
■ Referencing/linking drawing
■ Symbols/libraries
■ Plotting
■ Translations/compatibility with other CADD applications
■ Support
■ Cost

Guidelines for Selecting a Project Management/Financial Software Package

Most financial software packages are quite capable of nuts-and-bolts accounting. If properly chosen, however, a good project management/financial software (PMFS) package will assist a firm with other important tasks, like project management, resource management, budgeting, and cash flow projections.

The task of selecting a system that is right for your firm is by no means a simple one, but these eight steps can serve as a guide to how the selection process is best accomplished.

1. Involve the Right People

Too often, decisions about PMFS packages are assigned to the accounting or systems manager, with little or no involvement from others in the firm. In order to derive the maximum benefit from any financial package, all areas of a firm should be represented in a selection team.

In addition to representation from accounting and information systems (IS), project managers and the managing principals should play key roles in the process. This selection team approach will ease implementation and increase the likelihood of firmwide satisfaction with the new system.

2. Define the Problem

As with any journey, it is best to have a destination in mind before embarking on the trip. It is important, in the initial phase of selection, to specifically define the goals and objectives you wish to accomplish by implementing a new financial software package. These should include needs not currently being met, areas in need of improvement, and anticipated future requirements.

Once your selection team has determined what should be accomplished, the list should be prioritized and a requirements document created. This document will lead much of the evaluation criteria and should be examined continually throughout the process for necessary modifications.

Questions to be answered include:

■ How flexible is our firm in its current processes?
■ What do I need to manage my projects and staff?
■ What do I need to accurately forecast and control my cash flow?
■ What should be automated in order for the firm to grow?
■ What information is required to make strategic decisions?

3. Select System Architecture

Although the system choice is primarily an IS-driven decision, some thought must be given to existing hardware, network, and operations software, along with sophistication of the end users. At this point, the team should decide whether to examine only packages compatible with the existing platform or to expand the search, mindful of additional hardware/software expenditures necessary for proper implementation.

Continued on the next page

Figure 8-1

Source: M. Bonnie Squibbs, "Guidelines for Selecting a Project Management/Financial Software Package"
PSMJ Best Practices, November 1999, pp. 14–15.

4. Choose a Consultant

It is wise to take advantage of the skills and experience of one of the individuals or firms that specialize in project/financial management for A/E firms. Select a consultant who is familiar with many, if not all, financial software packages available and their respective strengths and weaknesses.

While some firms, depending on their level of comfort at this stage of the process, will wait to choose a consultant until after a software vendor has been selected, it is wise to use the consultant's expertise to assist in the selection process. In either case, you will want to know the following about your consultant:

- Has the consultant successfully implemented financial software packages at companies similar to yours?
- Is the consultant a software reseller or independent operator?
- Can the consultant provide references?
- Does the consultant listen and communicate effectively?
- Do the selection team members feel they can work with the consultant?

5. Evaluate System Performance

While evaluation is one of the most complex and important steps of the selection process, proper execution of steps 1 through 5 will significantly ease completion of the task. At this point, the selection team should have gathered basic marketing materials on available packages and narrowed its focus to a short list of potential software vendors.

Representatives from these vendors should be scheduled for presentations so their products can be further scrutinized. In addition to how well the software can achieve the goals and objectives you have defined, the following areas should be examined:

- Ease of input and use
- Data validation
- Error handling
- Ability to modify input
- Multiuser support
- Security (front- and back-end)
- Reporting capability/flexibility
  - —Project management reports
  - —Earned income and work in process
  - —Ratios, indicators, productivity, and so on
- Ability to import/export to other programs
- Documentation/manuals
- Availability/cost of customization
- Ease of learning system operation
- Other features often desired:
  - —Consultant tracking
  - —Resource/project scheduling
  - —Electronic time sheets/expense reports

Special attention should be given to the flexibility of reporting and invoicing within the system, as these functions can become costly customizations if those included in the base package are inadequate.

Also, take note of how well the vendor tailors its presentation to your firm's needs, as this can be a good indicator of its familiarity with similar companies.

Figure 8-1 (continued)

6. Evaluate the Software Vendor

Continued satisfaction with any software package is dependent on adequate continued support following implementation. This support is critical for financial software packages, as delays due to technical glitches can be costly or even devastating to a firm. In order to lessen the risk of such delays, your selection team will want to evaluate the vendor as closely as the software itself.

Some questions to keep in mind when evaluating software vendors include:

- Does the vendor have a strong background in the A/E industry?
- What types of technical support options are available (and how much do they cost)?
- How are software upgrades handled (included with tech support package or purchased separately)?
- If you require customizations (or expect to in the future), will they be included in upgrades?

7. Estimate Return on Investment

Remember that the PMFS package you are selecting is an investment and not an expense. As with any other investment, consideration should be given to the expected return. The return generated by a well-chosen package will come from a variety of areas, including:

- Ability to manage projects, track budgets, and project profitability
- Invoicing that is both timely and accurate
- Reduction in project managers' indirect time through better reporting
- Ability to estimate staffing needs
- Increasing future cash flows

8. Implementation

This is quite possibly the most daunting task associated with a new financial software package. Decisions will need to be made well in advance of final implementation regarding items such as:

- What historical data need to be available in the new system and how will the data be converted?
- Will the conversion be manual, electronic, or a combination of both?
- Will the new system go live initially, or will it be run parallel to the existing one for a test period?
- What training of personnel will be carried out? How and when will it be done?

It is at this stage when assistance from an outside consultant experienced in new system implementation can be extremely helpful (and cost effective). Regardless of firm size, this is also a stage at which the involvement of personnel from a variety of areas within the organization should be sought.

Remember that selecting a new project management/financial software package can be a lengthy and difficult process, so don't rush it. However, if the process is executed with care and proper planning, you may well find yourself wondering how you were able to operate so long without it.

Continued on the next page

Figure 8-1 (continued)

Point System for Software Evaluation

When evaluating software packages, use a point system to rank the most important criteria. Rank each item on a scale from 1 to 5 (with 5 being highest):

___ Financial strength of firm
___ Technological development
___ Ease of use
___ Overall best fit

Specific Areas

___ Accounting reports/usage
___ Project management reports
___ Project management budgeting
___ Invoicing flexibility
___ Interface with other packages
___ PMs' ability to access reports
___ Report writer/customizing reports
___ Difficulty in converting
___ Telephone support
___ References

Costs

___ Additional hardware cost
___ Base program
___ Additional modules
Conversion/Implementation
___ Electronic
___ Manual
___ Training
___ Support

Total Points_____

Figure 8-1 (continued)

This review should cover not only the application itself but also the company behind the application and the support it will provide you. When implementing a new CADD application, it is worth paying for support. Your time is too valuable to waste trying to work out problems. Having a service agreement enables you to resolve issues so you can continue providing the services expected of you.

VIRTUAL REALITY

Virtual Reality (VR) has become a viable means for design and construction professionals to improve the quality of their designs, reduce coordination errors, compress construction times, and help clients promote a project.

By definition, VR is a realistic computer-generated representation of a physical environment, existing or proposed. Individuals can place themselves in this environment, move through it, and interact with it in real time. The degree of realism provided by the virtual environment is dependent on the existence and level of the following key factors:

- Real-time interaction
- Immersion or presence
- Model complexity
- Photorealism

Additional elements or features that directly contribute to the level of these factors present in a virtual environment include:

- Viewer navigation
- Object motion
- Object manipulation
- Object deformation
- Newtonian physics (gravity, friction, mass, etc.)
- Localized sound
- Tactile feedback (sensor gloves/suits)
- Head display, stereo viewing
- Viewer head/eye/body tracking

As the amount and sophistication of these features increase, the virtual environment becomes more realistic. However, as the degree of realism increases, the system's cost and complexity increase. Still, with growth in computer price/performance and advances in software and peripherals, VR technology is a viable solution for many simulation problems.

Two of VR's significant benefits are:

1. The sense of immersion
2. Real-time interaction with the model

VR allows the user to immerse himself into a computer-generated environment and to interact with model elements as desired. This can be an effective way of reviewing proposed design alternatives, assessing the impact of alternate construction staging methodologies, even simulating physical environments where measurement of human factors and reactions are important. Typical applications include:

- *Planning and design*—VR has obvious applications in the conceptual phase of a project, where planners, designers, and developers try to assess a project's conceptual or organizational aspects. As planning moves into schematic design, try to get a better understanding of the project's physical nature, in terms of spatial relationships; then, as virtual models are built, design errors, omissions, and conflicts can be identified and resolved.

- *Preconstruction review*—VR has many potential uses when it comes to familiarizing subcontractors with the proposed project. It is possible to bring together HVAC (heating, ventilation, and air conditioning), structural, and mechanical staff and literally let them get into the building in cyberspace. They then can observe how their systems will integrate with a structure, thereby enhancing their understanding of the project.

- *Staging/traffic planning*—VR can aid in the development of temporary traffic plans during construction. These can be an effective means of communicating the impact of construction to a business community, property abutters, and reviewing agencies, and can include accurate three-dimensional (3D) models of existing buildings, roadways, landmarks, proposed work zones, and temporary structures. Construction equipment, vehicles, and pedestrians are added and animated to create a greater degree of realism.

- *Signage simulations*—VR is an effective way to combine accurate 3D models of proposed structures, static and variable message signs, and sign support structures to simulate a proposed roadway environment. Actual sign content, roadway striping, lighting, and vehicles can be added to provide a realistic environment, allowing a virtual driver to evaluate the proposed signage for unobstructed views, readability, and comprehension in real time.

- *Progress tracking*—VR can be used to analyze, comprehend, and communicate progress of physical work. Construction elements may be color coded to represent themes such as construction status, equipment installation status, and equipment testing status. Schedule simulations can compare baseline scope and schedule with revised scope and schedule to help analyze these revisions and communicate them to multiple contractors.

- *Communication*—On large-scale public projects, VR can show key project concepts to a neighborhood association or a planning board—people who ordinarily might be unable to read two-dimensional drawings. The same techniques can be used when a building owner wants to experience how a new building is going to work.

Questions can be posed and answered, such as, How will people or equipment move around the building? What is the best way for equipment or furniture to be brought into the building? How are fire or security systems going to work? VR can help contain costs and reduce risks by simulating specific scenarios in advance.

- *Sales*—VR has great potential in the actual sale of hotel or time-share/condominium-type projects. When potential buyers can't physically get to the project, VR can get the project to them.

USING YOUR COMPUTER AS A PRESENTATION TOOL

When making presentations to clients or bidding on new jobs, firm leaders are faced with the challenge of presenting complex, technical information in a clear, concise, and interesting manner to nontechnical, cross-functional audiences.

Fortunately, with presentation-smart programs such as PowerPoint, Persuasion, Freelance, and Harvard Graphics, you can boost presentations with an almost endless array of visual and audio elements ranging from the simple to the dazzlingly slick.

Visuals have been proven to increase understanding of a concept, show relationships, highlight importance, simplify or clarify, capture interest, and increase retention. Detailed statistics are easier to grasp when displayed on a bar chart or pie chart. Flow charts can clearly show processes or procedures, and organizational charts can depict functions and relationships. Bulleted lists of key words can captivate, emphasize, strengthen, and motivate.

While your computer can be used to generate traditional visual aids such as slides, acetates, and handouts, state-of-the-art presenters employ the computer itself, in various modes, to display their visuals. Cards can convert computer video into video that a television can handle, allowing the screen to be hooked up to a projection television system. Alternatively, a special projector can send sharp computer graphics onto a screen. A lower-tech means of projection employs an LCD (liquid crystal display) panel laid on top of an overhead projector.

No matter the form, visuals should be used to enhance and positively affect the desired outcome of a presentation. They need to reflect a presenter's main ideas without being merely a written repetition of a spoken message.

COLLABORATIVE COMPUTING

Collaborative computing is a way of using computer technology to ensure a more efficient workflow. It enables two or more parties to transfer information and interact online while effectively breaking down hierarchical and geographical boundaries.

A collaborative environment is project-oriented, fostering organization and teamwork regardless of physical location. It allows project managers more control, faster access to information, and open communication to the team, client, vendors and the public.

Collaborative computing opens doors to firms of all sizes to competition and participation in a global work arena, albeit for a price. Although their costs vary from free to prohibitive, collaborative technologies offer tremendous opportunity and significant cost offsets. Shipping, travel, and telephone expenses can decrease significantly while productivity and efficiency are greatly improved.

Whether you're aware of it or not, chances are good that your firm already functions, to some degree, in a collaborative environment, which continues to change the way architects, engineers, and construction contractors work. For example, email, the most common collaborative technology, is now incorporated into the work processes of most firms. Acceptance of other collaborative technologies still remains to be seen.

- *Internet Access*—Increasingly, you cannot survive without access to the Internet. This enables you to establish one or multiple email accounts, research the World Wide Web and other online sources, and share information with your external project team and clients.

  The Internet has been proven to enhance communication among internal and external team members, clients, and contractors. Internet access accounts are available for both single and multiple users. The simplest type of Internet account is through dial-up access. Your Internet provider will give you instructions on how to configure your computer to automatically dial into its servers.

- *Email*—Electronic mail (a.k.a. email) is literally that— an electronic way to send instantaneous messages and letters next door or across the continent. Email has quickly become the preferred form of project communication, allowing for quick response to issues while leaving a "paper trail."

This reduces the need to write that additional memo or telephone report to document important decisions or issues. It is important to remember to save copies of your email within the digital project directory and print a hard copy to be stored in the project paper files.

■ *Desktop Faxing*—Desktop faxing can eliminate steps in distributing information. If you fax a document directly from your computer, you eliminate the need to print it first and then use a fax machine to distribute it. If you can receive faxes via desktop, the documents can arrive in digital format. They can be viewed on screen and then stored in a digital project folder. Digital faxes can also be retrieved remotely if you are not in the office when they are sent to you.

■ *GroupWare*—GroupWare is the next step up the collaborative continuum. GroupWare is software that allows two or more people to work together as a group. The application can be designed to support departments, project teams, or entire firms. The best-known GroupWare program is Lotus Notes. Others include Microsoft Exchange, Novell GroupWise, and (to some extent) Netscape Communicator.

GroupWare encompasses email and adds other features such as document and revision management, group calendars, scheduling features, and the ability to plug in other capabilities specific to your needs. However, its real power is in its document management capabilities. The system manages the documents, keeping track of changes, additions, and usage. This kind of sharing and document management can significantly boost a project team's productivity.

While GroupWare's strength is improved productivity, its drawbacks are organization and cost. These programs, along with the many plug-ins providing additional capabilities, can be expensive. Implementing the application requires extensive up-front organization and information gathering. However, depending on the problems you're trying to solve, GroupWare may be a wise investment.

■ *Whiteboards*—Whiteboards are at the center of many old-fashioned, face-to-face meetings, where conferees use multicolored markers for outlining. Whiteboard Internet conferencing programs let remote participants work in much the same way. Participants at different locations simultaneously write and draw on an on-screen notepad viewed by everyone.

Basic whiteboard programs provide freehand drawing tools around an electronic canvas. Participants' annotations appear on all conferees' screens, nearly in real time. Most whiteboards can paste files copied from other programs, such as word processors and spreadsheets, providing a useful review function.

You can usually print and save the whiteboard file. Most programs keep pasted data separate from annotations, so you can mark up a pasted memorandum and then clear your scribbles without losing the memo. Advanced whiteboard features include:

1. Screen capture capabilities
2. A remote pointer that you can use to highlight without actually marking
3. Screen synchronization, which lets everyone look at the same location
4. Image compression, which speeds data transfer between participants

Whiteboards are often used in conjunction with an audio- or videoconferencing connection. An audio-only connection can be a separate telephone call or be transmitted with the data using simultaneous voice and data (SVD) modems.

■ *Videoconferencing*—Videoconferencing is an interactive video communication session among several parties who are geographically separated. At its most basic level, videoconferencing can be limited to talking heads, a simple exchange of images and voices, the video portion of which is presented on a TV-like monitor.

Advanced videoconferencing allows images of documents and objects to be exchanged, and PCs at each end can share files or let participants work concurrently on a single computer application. By combining the power of computers, documents, faxes, video, and voice, videoconferencing provides a degree of interaction previously available only in a face-to-face meeting.

FROM INTERNET TO EXTRANET

The first wave in Internet technology came with corporate Web sites, which have rapidly become as commonplace as business cards, and as essential as a listing in the Yellow Pages. The Web site provides a new means of external communication, allowing businesses to compete in a global marketplace with economic ease and complete convenience.

Next came the intranet. Intranets dramatically improved interoffice communication by providing instantaneous access to corporate data. With a single mouse click, up-to-the-minute information, ranging from client lists to human resource data, reaches every member of an organization.

Both corporate Web sites and intranets have bottom-line advantages for small firms and Fortune 500 companies alike, reducing man-hours, improving performance, and creating forums for online feedback and collaboration that were formerly impractical. But what happens when you apply the best of both these technologies to interactions with project team members around the country, partners, customers, suppliers, and vendors in far-flung corners of the world?

Enter the extranet—or, as it's commonly referred to, the project-specific Web site. This, the third wave in internet technology, extends the communication benefits of an intranet to people outside the organization. Think of it as an intranet that is open to selective access by outside parties; unlike a corporate Web site, it does not provide universal access to potentially confidential and proprietary information. Neither is it purely externally oriented.

Project-specific Web sites involve a balance of internal and external information. Because they use standard Web technology, even the most technologically challenged members of a project team can participate and collaborate. Standard Web browsers provide a point-and-click interface and complete independence from global access to proprietary hardware and software, and they require only nominal entry fees. For more information about extranets, see Figure 8-2.

INTERNET/INTRANET STRATEGIES

While the prospect of monitoring Web sites that team members have visited or curtailing access to specific Web sites might be distasteful, failure to properly manage employee use of the Internet can leave your firm open to liability on several fronts.

Consider this worst-case scenario: An employee downloads pornography using company equipment, thereby exposing the company to a harassment suit by another employee who notices it.

The issue of copyrighted material is another potential liability. Access to the Internet offers an all-too-easy opportunity to republish copyrighted material without the con-

What Can an Extranet Do for You?

With the Internet's potential to bring together A/E/C players into virtual meeting rooms and thus to speed and improve project delivery, and with the burgeoning number of extranet (project-specific) Web sites clamoring for clients, it would seem that now is the time for A/E firms to go fully online, to ramp up into knowledge-based production.

But with so many extranet services available, what should you look for? What can an extranet really do for you? According to A/E/C industry IT consultant Kristine Fallon of Chicago's Kristine Fallon Associates, an extranet can serve your firm in three principal ways:

1. Speed Document Access and Distribution

An extranet acts as a central clearinghouse for all project-related documents, simultaneously serving all team members, whether they are in Philadelphia or the Philippines. Just by clicking, you can view and redline memos, meeting notes, drawings, sketches, schedules, specifications, field reports, and more. So, rather than waiting for snail mail or FedEx, you can have instantaneous posting of and access to exactly each document you need at the moment you need it.

Thus, no one on the team need wait for commercial printing and delivery of new drawings whenever a change is ordered. Instead, notes Bob Tedeschi of the New York Times News Service, "the most up-to-date blueprints can be posted on the site, with email notifications going out to anyone who needs to know. Work schedules can also be emailed or posted to a particular page on the site, so that different teams can track how the job is proceeding."

In other words, an extranet links you to everyone else on the project. By helping team members to focus on the most critical tasks rather than on paperwork, it can boost efficiency, improve project workflow, and reduce time to market.

2. Streamline Organization and Workflow

An extranet creates for each document an audit trail that shows everyone who posted, revised, viewed, downloaded, or redlined it, with the dates of all those transactions. It thus illuminates roles and provides a clear record of events. With this record, says Dr. Joel Orr in an April article on www.hpac.com, "history is preserved. All communications are archived in a form that cannot be edited. Just think of the lawsuits that could be avoided by the mere existence of an indisputable record of all project communications."

The system also strengthens accountability. If a request for information elicits no response by an agreed-on time interval, it is flagged, and the recipient or the PM receives an email.

3. Promote real-time collaboration

According to current research from the CAD for Principals Council, a key requirement for future A/E/C electronic processing is that "We no longer draw; we create a digital model. We must collaborate on the model, not on drawings. This collaboration must include team members from outside organizations."

For architects and engineers, this means the long-range goal for extranets is for design team players in all locations to meet and work together on models, solve problems, and agree on changes—all without having to leave their offices. By fluidly interacting with other project principals in the conceptual design mode, they will be able to apply creative thinking throughout and see their best concepts become reality.

Although the realization of this dream is down the line, it will mean that, with an extranet, you will ultimately base your team's modus operandi on a 3D model whence all changes begin. The user will be able to extract dimensions and quantities from the model or update the model by changing a dimension. In other words, a good extranet source will enable a top-down approach to project management. It will allow you to think like an architect, not a draftsperson.

While you wait for this reality, an extranet site can still help you collaborate. Your team members can conduct a dialog by posting questions and answers on the site. They can set up online design reviews, hold threaded discussions, and email each other from within the site. They can interactively redline and comment on drawings without necessarily being a CADD user. And by doing so on line, they save measurable costs and inconve-

Figure 8-2
Source: "What Can an Extranet Do for You?" *PSMJ Best Practices,* August 2000, p. 8.

sent of the original author. The Internet's development is so fluid today that new situations arise daily, and firm management must find ways to reduce its exposure to risk.

One way to begin is the adoption of a policy restricting use of the Internet to activities consistent with the project. By analyzing the URL accesses from your Web server, you can see who does not follow policy and take appropriate action.

If such a policy is enacted, you may want to consider providing free Internet usage during a designated period. For example, you may choose to allow your staff members to use the Internet for their own purposes after business hours or during lunch, as long as their activities are not a liability. This personal usage encourages your staff to become familiar with Internet technology.

IMPLEMENTATION ISSUES

Collaborative computing has many benefits, including:

- On-demand project information—from anywhere, 24 hours a day, 365 days a year
- Reduced turnaround time
- Maximized productivity
- Expedited project decision making
- Reduced overhead costs

What are some of the drawbacks or issues keeping firms from implementing these technologies?

- Security of information on the network
- The rapid pace of technological change

- Challenges to the adoption of the technology
- Bandwidth (speed)
- Compatibility
- Cost

Existing and emerging technologies clearly provide excellent opportunities to improve a project team's ability to get the job done efficiently and creatively, and at a reasonable cost. As the cost of these technologies continues to decline, more firms will find them strong options for improving their competitive posture in the market.

SUCCESS CHALLENGES

1. Does your firm have a strategic technology plan?
2. Are you allocating time and resources for your employees to be trained in the technologies available in your firm?
3. Do you know about the many software and hardware options available for enhanced communication and productivity?

REFERENCES

1. Kristine Fallon, "How IT Can Keep Your Firm on the Cutting Edge," *PSMJ Best Practices*, October 2000, p. 8.
2. Linda Joy Weinstein, "Is Your Approach to Technology Sabotaging Your Firm?," *PSMJ Best Practices*, March 2000, p. 4.
3. From *PSMJ's Advanced Project Management Manual*, ©1999.

Chapter 9

Growth

Too many firms, in mapping out their long-range plan, get trapped into the cliché of growth, both financially and with respect to personnel. Many leaders believe that their firm will not survive if it doesn't grow. In a January 2000 *PSMJ A/E Pulse* survey, firms responding to the question "What is the percentage of growth you hope to achieve in 2000?" indicated hopes for a 14.9 percent increase in revenues and an 11.3 percent growth in staff. For the complete survey results, see Figure 9-1.

The issue of firm size is important. This chapter addresses the questions of when you should grow and how quickly. It also points out the merits of a small organization that you risk losing with growth.

BENEFITS OF SMALL FIRMS

Take the following benefits of small firms into account when deciding whether or not to grow.

Flexibility The larger a firm, the more it is weighed down with high overhead and rigid operating procedures. These procedures reduce the firm's ability to respond quickly to changing markets and technology.

The classic example is a large firm that forms a committee to study a decision for months, whereas the same decision could have been made in a small firm in a matter of days.

Motivated Employees Employees of small firms can see the relationship between the firm's success and their own contributions. Every day, they are directly involved; they work on projects, meet clients, and see the results of their efforts in the built environment. As a firm grows, however, employees may lose sight of their work's contribution to the overall project. If this happens, employees lose personal interest in the success of the firm.

Creativity Small firms are innovative in meeting market demands because of the close contact among marketing, design, and

The Lowdown on Growth

Types of Growth Firms Are Considering in Order to Meet Their Goals

Area of Planned Growth	Definite Growth Factor	Considering as Growth Factor	Not Considering for Growth
Work from additional clients	82%	14%	5%
More work from existing clients	73	27	0
Expanded geographic service area	55	27	18
Strategic alliances with other firms	50	36	14
Work from existing backlog	50	27	23
Added project types, existing services	41	32	27
Strategic alliances with clients	32	50	18
Added client types, existing services	32	36	27
Acquire another firm	23	23	50
New geographic office	14	23	64
Add additional scope of service	9	36	55
Add another discipline	9	23	68

Percentage of growth per target areas in 2000:   Revenues 14.9%   Staff 11.3%

Number of firms participating in this survey: 73

Figure 9-1
Source: *PSMJ A/E Pulse,* January 2000.

management personnel. As the firm grows, this contact is lost, and with it goes much of the company's competitive, creative edge. When was the last time your firm had a design review in which the entire team was present to critique a project?

Ease of Decision Making Growth dictates that top managers become more and more removed from day-to-day operations. Information must be formalized through reports and procedures, and channels of communication become cluttered with paper. As top managers become less familiar with many of the firm's activities, they are less able to interpret information that is received. Thus, decisions may not be made quickly or correctly. As a result, the perception of those in the market-place may be that the quality of your work is slipping.

Effective Young, aggressive design professionals who start up new
Management firms are able to manage one or two projects effectively. However, as a firm grows, the demand for sophisticated management capability increases exponentially. Design professionals are not equipped, in most cases, to meet the demands of high-level management placed on them by the growth of their own practices.

DEFINING YOUR GROWTH

Before planning growth, be sure you understand what kind of growth is best for your vision and your firm. Do you want to increase staff size, dollar volume, or quality of work?

Some firms find that growth in size has not been good for them, and have reduced their ranks while trying to retain or increase dollar volume. Many firms grow only by a percentage margin each year to cover cost-of-living increases for employees. Others strive to improve staff knowledge and motivation in order to successfully pursue higher-end projects.

WHEN TO GROW

In considering growth, be sure your firm has the resources to handle expansion, particularly these three important elements:

1. The firm should have enough retained earnings to support growth in accounts receivable without having to borrow more than one-third of the total accounts receivable. If a firm is forced to borrow more than this amount, the interest charges will detract from its profitability and stunt the growth.
2. The firm should have enough available talent to enable growth. Firms often commit to growth only to find that they don't have enough design professionals to sustain expansion.
3. The firm should have a well-developed organizational plan. Growth without a well-defined plan will result in chaos, which will undermine profitability and eventually diminish the firm's size.

THE RULE OF 150

While there is no optimal size for design firms, there may be an optimal *maximum* group size at which large human groups perform best. Firms can be bigger than this but would be wise to subdivide in increments of this maximum. Evidence from history and many disciplines supports the idea that this maximum is about 150 people.

Microsoft's Bill Gates keeps business units to a 200-person maximum, a limit that he believes allows most people to know each other by name and allows tracking of their contributions within the accountability structure.

Morgan Crucible, an £850 million U.K.–based engineering and materials company with 120 plants in 40 countries, splits itself into 150 subsidiaries, each employing up to about 150 people.

Brigham Young divided his 5,000 followers on their trek from Illinois to what became Utah into group sizes of 150 in order to provide independence and maximum efficiency in coordination of activities.

Military commands over the millennia stabilized in World War II with company size at around 170 men (the United Kingdom at the low end with 130, the United States at the high end with 223).

Booz, Allen & Hamilton's COO Brian Dickie recently observed, "I sometimes think we've reached the limit at the present 240 partners. There's definitely a qualitative change at around 40 between the founders and the next generation. Then there's another change at 120 to 150, when a lot of the partners will not have worked with other partners in the firm."

The Amish and the Hutterites have each evolved a communal, agrarian fundamentalist Christian life over 400 years in Europe and in the American Midwest and northern Great Plains. The mean size of their communes is slightly more than 100. This is because they always split the communities when they reach about 150. They have found that at larger sizes, it is difficult to control their members by peer pressure alone.

Gore Associates, of Gore-Tex fabrics fame, is perennially listed as one of the best-managed American companies, with an employee turnover rate one-third its industry average. Its founder, the late Wilbert "Bill" Gore, stated that "We found again and again that things get clumsy at 150." Whenever a plant exceeds 150 employees, Gore starts a new one. In Delaware, for example, the company has 3 plants within sight of each other and 15 within a 12-mile radius. One employee summed up Gore Associates' long-term planning: "We put 150 parking spaces in the lot, and when people start parking on the grass, we know it's time to build a new plant."

The peer pressure that lies behind the wisdom of the 150 number [anthropologists call it the Rule of 150—see Robin Dunbar's provocative 1996 *Grooming, Gossip, and the Evolution of Language* (Harvard University Press) to explore the biological foundation of these ideas] is one of people knowing other people well enough that what they think of each other matters. The operative rule of thumb, arrived at over centuries and without the benefit of organizational theorists, appears to be that functional units larger than 150–200 people cannot be effectively managed nor can their members build critical bonds of support, loyalty, and a sense of mutual reliability. A current best seller, *The Tipping Point: How Little Things Can Make a Big Difference* (Little, Brown, 2000) by *New Yorker* writer Malcolm Gladwell, elaborates on these points.

Gore succeeds without the usual layers of middle and upper management because informal personal relationships are more effective. As a Gore employee illustrates, "Peer pressure is much more powerful than a concept of a boss. Many times more powerful. People want to live up to what is expected of them....It is not just do you know somebody. It's do you really know them well enough that you know their skills and abilities and passions." Gladwell points out that "It's knowing someone well enough to know what they know, and

WAYS TO GROW

Here a few ideas on growth that go beyond the typical track of diversifying:

- *Grow geographically within a particular service or specialty*—It's much easier to spread geographically than to diversify your services.
- *Grow through your clients*—Allow clients to take you to different locales by taking on bigger projects farther

knowing them well enough so that you can trust them to know things in their specialty. It's the re-creation, on an organization-wide level, of the kind of intimacy and trust that exists in a family." He asserts that this makes a company incredibly efficient, that cooperation is easier, decisions get made faster, teams assembled more quickly, that the expertise, impressions, and experience of people in different parts of the company are available and accessible on a moment's notice. Information and new ideas can go from one person or one part of a larger group to the entire group all at once.

There is also evidence in design firms that crossing the 150 line is a small change that makes a big difference, as the accompanying chart from PSMJ Resources' research clearly illustrates. Don't fall into the cliché of growth for growth's sake

Carl Petrich,"Keeping Things Down to Size," *PSMJ Best Practices*, September 2000, p. 8.

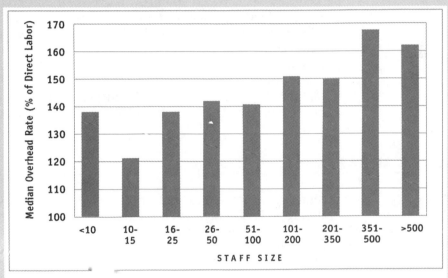

PSMJ data reveal that as nonbillable management hours accumulate with increasing staff size, overhead rates inevitably creep upward. Remember, as you evaluate your firm's growth options, this increase is not linear. Note the inflection points at ~12, ~50, ~150 and their potential implications to your firm's financial health.

from the home office. Growth via clients allows you to establish a presence in other locales, which can yield subsequent work in that area. This presence can take the form of either a project office that continues its existence after final completion or a branch office designed to permanently serve a new geographic area.

■ *Acquire a business*—Finding a firm with a similar culture to yours, with a specialty you'd like to add to your roster and in an area of the country you would like to do business, is a way to grow both your staff and your revenues.

■ *Enter into a strategic alliance or partnering agreement—* Joining forces with a likeminded, noncompeting firm can extend your geographic reach, increase the size of projects you win, alleviate staffing shortages, and raise your revenues.

GROWTH RATE

Plan expected growth rate carefully. Generally, growth in excess of 10 percent gross revenue per year will put significant strain on a firm. Growth is best controlled at 5 to 10 percent per year. When you grow more than 25 percent per year, you place significant pressure on the overall resources of the firm; capital is required to support receivables growth, new talent is needed, and interoffice relationships and management structure will change. Such significant growth could injure the firm rather than help it. Some firms, in fact, have grown to their detriment; they find themselves either out of business or significantly reduced in size.

STAGES OF GROWTH

Design firms that increase their staff size pass through several stages. Each stage is characterized by the activities of the firm's owner, principals, and managers. Determine where your firm is among the following stages.

Stage 1 Most firms are started by one or two people who have secured a project. All the firm's energy is centered on the promotion of a single design service. The organization is an informal one in which all employees tend to be jacks-of-all-trades rather than specialists. The owners/founders are involved in design and carry out most of the activities within the firm, resulting in an intensive work effort to produce good service for the client.

Decisions are made quickly and are based on an intimate knowledge of the firm and its people. Complexity is limited because projects are few, and clients are served well because time is adequate to meet their needs.

Stage 2 Because of the energy and enthusiasm displayed by the owners/founders, the firm begins to grow. Word of mouth sparks interest among other clients. A more structured organization and control procedures become necessary to keep track of operations. Specialized business expertise, such as financial and marketing management, becomes necessary.

When the firm reaches 20 to 30 people, the owners/founders can no longer remain involved in the day-to-day supervision of each employee. When the staff grows to 40 members, business managers are brought in and tasks become specialized, with lines of communication formalized by monthly management procedures and reporting. Overhead starts to increase.

Stage 3 To maintain growth, authority must be shared with lower-level management. Project management systems are developed to encourage lower-level employees to become involved in the authority/responsibility chain and to take on client responsibilities.

At this stage, many design-firm CEOs are unhappy as managers because they are removed from day-to-day design and client work. Rather, they find themselves in professional management positions for which they are untrained. Increased specialization leads to further penetration of markets and the beginning of a defined image for the firm.

Stage 4 Strong departments are developed along with a project management system. Many managers lose sight of company goals, instead focusing on personal and departmental ambitions. Because the firm's corporate management is still young and has not fully matured, the interpersonal relationships among managers are not dealt with expeditiously, resulting in lower morale. Consultants are hired to improve operations, personnel, and marketing management.

This stage is often the most traumatic because the CEO must decide whether professional outside management is needed to help the firm expand.

Stage 5 Formalized long-range planning and budget procedures become the cornerstone of a design firm at this stage. The firm's future depends on a coordinated plan/direction, which requires input from a management team to achieve well-thought-out goals. Many top managers desire to recreate an environment similar to that in Stage 1. Typical activities include the aforementioned long-range planning as well as market and financial planning.

As a design firm moves through the five growth stages, it can undergo a tremendous amount of stress, financial and otherwise. The firm's product—design—may suffer in the process. Many firms have gone bankrupt because they've grown too fast, while others have gone out of business because of the benefits lost with growth.

RISKS INHERENT IN GROWTH

Financial Difficulties Firms that grow too rapidly encounter trouble. Growing too fast can wipe out a firm financially because of the cost of financing work in process and accounts receivable growth. It can hurt compensation policies because lack of cash can cause delays in implementing raises or giving bonuses. Growing too fast can also bring about quality control problems that may prove fatal to the firm.

Lack of Efficiency Another side effect of growth is lost efficiency. Adding employees typically translates into more procedures, more levels of management, and encroaching bureaucracy. Streamlined communication among team members, knowledge of what everyone in the firm is working on, and fast turnaround on project tasks becomes substantially more difficult with more people in the office.

Increased Liability If your firm adds revenues much more quickly than staff, you run the risk of increased liability from inattention to details. Obviously, a quality control program goes a long way toward diminishing the potential for trouble, but when employees are under the gun to deliver, fatigue coupled with long hours and stress can lead to trouble.

Demoralized Staff On a related note, increased project load can cause your staff to become demoralized. Too much work, too little downtime, and too much job-related stress can turn your office into a pressure cooker.

SUCCESS CHALLENGES

1. Consider your firm size. How big (or small) would you like your firm to be? Set up a planning meeting to discuss how to reach and maintain that goal.
2. Can your staff be motivated to perform more work, work more hours, or use time more efficiently to increase firm profits? Consider sharing profits with employees to motivate them toward higher productivity and revenue growth without a growth in firm size.

3. Make a list of the reasons why you started (or joined) your small firm. If the firm grows, how many of these attributes will be lost?

4. Could you expand your services to a larger geographical area? Consult marketing professionals and references that will help you put together a geographic expansion plan. Set a date today to discuss these plans with key people.

Chapter 10

The Psychology of Winning

When analyzing professional sports, the traits of winning coaches and players are easily identifiable. In basketball, consider Pat Reilly's fiery stance on the court, his drive toward winning at every opportunity, and his intolerance for lack of performance. The psychology of winning is evident. Design firm principals must also have such a desire to win. They must have an internal focus bent on challenging each and every competitor in the marketplace and on succeeding at all costs. This psychology is identified in all successful small firms and their principals; it is missing in those doomed to failure or mediocrity.

Successful firm principals often disdain generalizations on how to approach the design practice. Instead, they focus on a winning attitude and position their firms such that they wipe out all competitors.

A PSMJ Resources survey of 25 firm principals, all of them successful small business entrepreneurs in first-generation firms, showed that a common trait of the principals was their struggle between self and company. In a successful firm, that struggle translates into the principal's conflict between his roles as guru and as chief. This seemingly small concern is, in fact, a key ingredient of the successful organizations examined while researching this book.

In the star-focused firms, the principal passes up the traditional management organization in favor of becoming a star, with every part of the firm supporting the march to stardom. Principals of fledgling firms often have not yet decided whether to build a managed organization or be the star. This is the worst possible scenario. When the chief vacillates between building an organization with multiple partners on one hand and becoming a guru on the other, the result is constant changes in policy and operations. Choose one or the other.

Both types of firms can be successful. Also, variations exist. For example, the principal does not have to be the guru; she might position two or three project managers in such roles and, instead, control the design firm's day-to-day operations. On the other hand, star-focused firms have one high-profile leader, with day-to-day management handled by others.

If you are a small-firm entrepreneur, examine your role within your firm. Have you decided that:

■ You don't want any partners?
■ Yours will be the name on the door?
■ The organization will always be under your control?
■ You must be involved in every design?
■ Your financial system must be under your own control?
■ Your presence in every client presentation is essential?

If you answered *yes* to these questions, then you are clearly the control-directed guru in your small firm. If, however, you've decided that:

■ You want your firm to have many partners,
■ You will develop operational procedures,
■ You want detailed multipage contracts, and
■ You want well-trained project managers,

then your focus is on management of your internal operation. Guru firms are externally focused on their clients. Operations-centered firms are internally focused on their management procedures. This is revealing when it comes to measuring success. A small guru-centered firm has a better chance of success than a small internally focused firm. The drawback of guru firms, of course, is that they usually have no transition plan. Internally focused firms can be relatively successful and have great transition plans.

OWNERSHIP TRANSITION

In a partnership of three people aged 40, 45, and 50, there's a 57 percent chance that one of them will die before age 65. The circumstances that trigger ownership transition—death, disability, retirement, voluntary separation, or need to fire a partner—make it an easy subject to avoid. But even if your firm beats the odds stated above, there's no doubt that one of these circumstances will come to bear on your organization. Planning for transition is as important as satisfying customers, finding new clients, and running your firm.

The essence of ownership transition is leadership. Too often, a first-generation owner transfers control to second-generation followers. What does this mean? These are the loyal employees who've looked to you for leadership for 10 or 20 years. By their very nature, they usually aren't strong decision makers with the same bold spirit that propelled you and your firm to success. Look, instead, at your tireless, charismatic young branch office manager who is already running a mini-firm of her own.

Before taking any action, outline and document your firm's culture, your expectations of leaders, and the criteria they must meet in order to become a principal. Chapter 1's list of leadership attributes from Setter Leach and Lindstrom is a good example, as is Chapter 5's "21 Traits of Power-house PMs."

After you've identified the person to whom you'd like to transfer ownership, formalize the process in a buy/sell agreement, which should be updated and evaluated every three to five years. (See Appendix A for PSMJ Resources' sample buy/sell agreement.) This agreement spells out how ownership will be transferred under circumstances such as death, retirement, or termination.

Too often, firms are poised to offer buy/sells prepared by lawyers or accountants to meet the departing owners' needs but that jeopardize the future health of the firm. The participation of these professionals in the ownership transition process is necessary, but it's also important to hire an adviser who can marry the strategic plan of your firm to the legal document. The fundamental purpose of the buy/sell agreement is to lay the groundwork for the continued success of a firm led by new owners. For a list of PSMJ's recommended buy/sell agreement terms, refer to Figure 10-1.

A key element of the buy/sell is the valuation of your firm. Try using the most basic method possible: either [1.25 × accrual book value] or [accrual book value + weighted average of the last 5 years' profits]. Once you've found a formula you like, stick with it, and calculate it once every year.

When you extend an offer of ownership, do it in confidence on a one-on-one basis to avoid group negotiation. Give the potential owner ample time to review and comment on the offer and to line up financing for the transaction. This is a major ownership transition issue that must be given as much thought as the selection of new owners and the overall exit strategy of departing ones. Many firms pay high salaries and bonuses to junior principals to help them buy stock. One golden rule: Ask potential owners to invest some of their own funds. What people get for nothing they treat as nothing.

COMPETING WITH YOUR PEERS

Successful small-firm entrepreneurs share similar traits. One of the most important is knowing how to compete with peers. Here are seven competition success tips:

PSMJ| Resources, Inc.

PSMJ Resources, Inc. 10 Midland Avenue Newton, MA 02458 **Call** 800.537.PSMJ **E-mail** info@psmj.com

SUGGESTED BUY/SELL AGREEMENT TERMS

During the last twenty-five years of investigating design firm buy/sell agreements, PSMJ has accumulated a wealth of knowledge on ownership transition. The following terms are many of those that we recommend for a design firm transition. Although we collaborated with the law firm of Baer Marks & Upham LLP on this publication, PSMJ strongly recommends that you consult with your own legal counsel before implementing any of these suggestions. However, as you read the list, examine your own buy/sell agreement to determine whether or not these items are included.

If you have any questions about ownership transitions or would like input from PSMJ, please call 617.965.0055.

1. **Commitment from Owners** – Most buy/sell agreements observed by PSMJ did not contain performance standards for owners, and a buy/sell agreement may not be the appropriate document for setting forth performance standards for owners. Yet, many owners find themselves in the inevitable position of having to decide how to judge the performance of a partner. For this reason, we recommend that the buy/sell agreement be accompanied by an employment agreement or other document that provides for minimum performance standards.

Such standards should include requirements that an owner will devote 100 precent of his/her effort to the corporation. They should also include the number of hours that an owner will put into the organization, as well as the primary job responsibilities of the particular owner. (Counting hours worked is not typical for senior executives/owners. The requirement to devote 100 percent should take care of this concern.) Although establishing these standards may limit a firm's flexibility, that limitation needs to be weighed against the benefit of such standards in the unfortunate event that an owner is asked to depart the firm for cause.

2. **Valuation Formula** – Any buy/sell agreement must include the formula by which the shares of the firm will be valued under various circumstances. It is expected that the same formula may well apply to all internal transition scenarios. It is recommended that the buy/sell agreement include a formula for valuation rather than a specific number or a general requirement that owners agree upon an amount on an annual basis.

3. **Death** – Any buy/sell agreement should include the valuation process for any shares held by an owner upon the death of that owner. Death provisions may include extra considerations for insurance held by the company on the life of the shareholder. There should be express statement of the terms by which the shareholder's estate receives any value. The buy/sell should provide for the option to purchase shares in the event of death, disability or termination but not necessarily require the re-purchase.

> Help us build this list of terms. Send in your successful terms, and we will publish them anonymously. **Mail** them to:
> PSMJ Buy/Sell Agreement Terms,
> 10 Midland Ave, Newton, MA 02458, or
> **fax**: 617-965-5152, or **e-mail**: info@psmj.com

Figure 10-1

4. **Disability** – The agreement should provide, if desired, the valuation and terms for payment of value in the event of the long term or permanent disability of an owner. It is assumed that any owner will be expected to be an active, contributing employee of the company. Disability is often defined according to the terms of a company's specific disability insurance policy.

5. **Termination** – Since it is possible that an owner/employee's active employment with the company may be involuntarily terminated, the buy/sell agreement provides for the terms under which any shares of stock are redeemed by the company from the terminated employee. Receipt of value may be accelerated under involuntary termination provisions as a deterrent to the termination of an owner/employee.

6. **Retirement** – Agreements provide for the conditions entitling the owner/employee for retirement. Such retirement may be either upon the voluntary notice of retirement or under provisions which mandate the termination of shareholding upon the achievement of a certain age. Involuntary retirement provisions for employees who are not owners involve age discrimination laws and need to be reviewed by an attorney.

Retirement of share and the receipt of value for those shares may be accompanied by additional benefits such as continuance of health insurance and professional liability insurance coverage. Some residual holding of shares may be allowed. The goal is frequently to assure availability of shares for younger employees by mandating sale of shares by older owners. Continued employee status may be allowed.

7. **Voluntary Departure** – Voluntary termination of employment requires redemption of shares from the terminating employee. The firm should maintain the option, but not the obligation, to repurchase such shares as a right of first refusal. Value may be reduced if this event occurs before official retirement. Alternatively, extended terms may be required to prevent a terminating employee from using the value of shares to establish a competitive business. Often the payment of value is tied to adherence to the terms of any non-compete agreement.

8. **Legal Proceeding and Associated Cost** – Provisions are often included in a shareholder agreement which dictate the responsibility for any costs associated with upholding the agreement. These costs may include legal fees and/or accounting fees in the event of a dispute of share valuation procedures.

9. **Spousal Considerations** – Various legal jurisdictions establish certain community property rights of spouses. Shareholder agreements in community property states may require spousal consent to the agreement and usually have terms, which prevent the spouse of an employee from coming into actual possession of any shares. Both estate and divorce considerations are important.

10. **Term/Limitation of Agreement/Amendment** – It should be recognized that an agreement is not expected to remain constant in perpetuity. Providing for periodic amendments will force reconsideration of certain provisions or allow for the termination of the agreement under certain circumstances. An agreement with an automatic termination provision which may inadvertently leave the parties without an agreement should be avoided.

11. **Limits of Activities of Partners** – Agreements will frequently limit the activities of partners especially as it relates to outside business activities of potential competitive circumstances. It is frequently expected that an owner/employee will devote substantially full-time effort to the business.

12. **Right of Refusal for Sale of Stock** – Many owners may be concerned with the ability to maintain a certain percentage ownership of outstanding shares. Preemptive rights can be used to protect percentages of ownership. This concern may require the establishment of a right to purchase certain amounts of shares, which are offered for sale by another owner. Such concerns are especially relevant when all sales are not mandated to be through the firm itself.

13. **Deferred Compensation** – Various firms may establish certain deferred compensation programs for owners and/or employees. This provision is one which is best set forth in an employment agreement. Certain clauses in an agreement can establish

Continued on the next page

Figure 10-1 (continued)

specific rights of owners as it relates to deferred compensation programs.

14. **Timing Impact of When Stock Is Bought / Sold** – The formula used to value shares may result in differing values at different moments in time. The agreement usually provides a specific definition of timing of value calculations under various conditions. For example, agreements usually provide for the valuation in the event of the death of a shareholder to occur as of the day before death to prevent any insurance proceeds from being included in valuation. Death is not the only reason valuations occur. They are also required to deal with "fairness" issues within a firm's ownership structure as it transitions.

15. **Prohibition on Pledging Value** – Since it is usually the desire of an organization to prevent shares from coming into possession of any individuals or entities not employed by the company, there is frequently a provision which prohibits the use of value as a collateral for any loans, etc. Default in any such loans could lead to an outside, non-signatory party coming into possession of stock. Certain specific exceptions to pledging value may be allowed to permit bank loans for an initial purchase of shares. Also, pledging may be mandated to support a loan to the corporation.

16. **Non-Compete During and/or After Ownership** – Since shareholding may be accompanied by a strong commitment to long-term employment by the company, there are frequently provisions in a shareholder agreement which serve as the equivalent of a non-compete agreement. Ownership may also suggest accessibility to proprietary information.

17. **Professional Liability After Ownership** – As a long-term protection for owners, terms are frequently included into a shareholder agreement which mandate the continuance of professional liability insurance covering a former shareholder for acts performed while an agent of the company.

18. **Bankruptcy of a Partner** – Since legal bankruptcy proceedings may require liquidation or dispensing of assets, in order to prevent shares from being encumbered or becoming the property of a non-identified owner, the declaration of bankruptcy by an owner usually requires a repurchase of shares under specifically defined conditions and value. Owners want the buy/sell agreement to include provisions which protect other owners against the fraudulent conveyance of shares by one owner facing bankruptcy.

19. **Minority Rights of Shareholders** – It may be in the interest of the shareholders to establish certain occasions when a super majority or unanimous vote of shareholders is required to undertake certain action.

20. **Voting Powers** – Under certain circumstances, it is desirable to establish specific powers to be maintained and held by certain senior identified shareholders. These conditions need to be stated as clauses within any agreement. For example, new shareholders may be subject to approval by all founding firm owners.

21. **Life Insurance** – To protect their estates, owners may require that the company maintain certain levels of life insurance. Similarly, to protect itself, the firm may require the cooperation of shareholders in the acquisition of such life insurance coverage. The agreement may also allow for the transition of life insurance interests in the event of the termination or retirement of a shareholder.

22. **Permitted Number of Owners** – In order to assure that both management status of ownership is maintained, specific provisions may limit the number of owners. This may either be by limitation to a specific number or limitation to a number established by a formula.

23. **Legal Jurisdiction** – Any agreement usually specifically states the legal jurisdiction under which the agreement is to be enforced and interpreted. Typically the governing jurisdiction is the State in which the corporation is organized.

24. **Special Rights/Concerns of Founders** – Founders of firms may need to have special provisions apply to them only, different than the provisions applied to newer shareholders. These may include special share valuation formulas, retirement benefits and provisions, or employment provisions. These special conditions may be of extra significance and

Figure 10-1 (continued)

concern if the founding partner continues to hold such a significant portion of shares that normal provisions could not practically apply.

25. **Interest Calculations** – Where any agreement terms provide for payments to or from shareholders or the company, specific terms with respect to interest on those timed payments should be detailed. Without this detailing, imputed interest and its special tax implications could be applied to the agreement.

26. **Notification Provisions** – Where official notification or communication needs to be provided to shareholders, the agreement should provide for the procedures to be used to effect that notification. Such notification can include the time and place for meeting of shareholders, intended changes in shareholdings by any shareholders or adjustment in share value.

27. **Outside Accountants** – The agreement should state when any value or other calculations are to be made as a result of financial statistics prepared or reviewed by outside accountants rather than internal staff. There should be stated procedures established for the selection of those outside accountants.

28. **Outside Sale** – When the potential exists for the sale of the business to an outside party, it may be appropriate for all shares to be subject to purchase upon the vote of a super majority of current shareholders and shares. A valid outside purchaser may only be interested in an acquisition when 100 percent of shares are made available for sale. They may not wish to have minority shareholders.

29. **Nepotism Considerations** – To avoid potential disputes, it is appropriate to consider including within an agreement specific provisions or even prohibition of hiring of employees with specified relationship to shareholders.

30. **New Shareholders** – The agreement can specify the conditions under which new shareholders can be added to the existing group of shareholders. These can include selection criteria, super majority votes or other provisions.

31. **Management Provisions** – Who will manage the firm and how managers are selected should be part of the agreement. The responsibility of management should be spelled out in this agreement so that owners know which decisions require management input.

Acknowledgment:

This publication was prepared with the valuable assistance of attorneys at the law firm of Baer Marks & Upham LLP, where James E. Frankel heads the Construction Industry Practice Group. Mr. Frankel can be reached at 212-702-5700 or by e-mail at frankel@baermarks.com.

Figure 10-1 (continued)

1. *Demand excellence*—There is no substitute for doing a great job and allowing for the time that it requires. Establish a standard of excellence by implementing a comprehensive quality control system in your firm. Be sure communication is clear at the start of a project so both your firm and the client understand the scope of work they'll get for the agreed price. Deliver what others only promise.

2. *Ignore jealousy*—Jealousy can undermine the successful entrepreneur. Focus on achieving project success, not just on doing the job better than competitors.

3. *Watch your back*—When you get to the top, others will try to knock you down. Remain vigilant! Be sure that your staff, marketplace, ideas, or processes are not being stolen (or in the case of the last two, cheapened) by a competitor.

4. *Think ahead*—Think of the product life cycle, strive for new ways to satisfy your clients, and be one step ahead of your peers.

5. *Share*—Be a professional. Share nonproprietary information with your peers, and they will do the same, to the benefit of both of you.

6. *Take pride in your work*—In interacting with your peers, being strong does not necessarily mean being hostile; it simply means having pride in your worth.

7. *Continue learning*—Don't underestimate the power of insights from business leaders like Tom Peters, Donald Trump, and Lee Iacocca. In addition, keeping a finger on the pulse of your marketplace, activities and outlooks of competitors, and the workings of industries outside A/E/C all will give you a competitive advantage.

SUCCESS CHALLENGES

1. Is your staff sharing information among themselves in a consistent, focused direction?

2. Is your firm strong enough to turn away work that does not coincide with its market and strategic business plans?

3. Have you decided whether or not to have a leadership transition plan? (See Chapter 1.) Does everyone in the firm know your criteria for becoming a leader?

4. Is your firm's purpose clearly understood by all parties in the firm? Are you reinforcing that purpose daily with your actions?

5. Are you becoming a better leader through continued training?

6. Are you going to, with the help of the first chapter, write your small-firm strategic plan?

Chapter 11

Do's and Don'ts of Success

This chapter abstracts certain essential recommendations from the preceding material. These are presented as do's and don'ts. However, a strong word of caution applies. There are sometimes good reasons for not observing a do and for ignoring a don't. These are clearly stated in each case, and it is up to you to consider your unique circumstances and come to a reasonable decision.

Some normally accepted extras (fancy offices, cars, etc.), contrary to popular belief, don't really affect your success or profitability as a design firm. You may rationalize that these items are the norm in design practice, but firms that follow the norm generally don't meet with success.

Most design firms are traditional businesses doing traditional work. They have unoriginal marketing plans, follow tired advice from books and seminars on the industry, achieve lower-than-normal profits, struggle with ownership transition, achieve mediocre levels of design, employ small numbers of low-paid professionals, and struggle for years to maintain profitability, size, and a smooth flow of transition. The firms that stand out are the ones that reject the status quo.

DO'S

Hire a Top Accountant A good accountant is geared toward improving your net worth and your bottom line, and is one of your most valuable resources in the marketplace. Each small-firm entrepreneur needs someone with whom to discuss and devise strategies to improve business performance. See Figure 11-1 for tips on hiring a good accountant and utilizing her services effectively. Figure 11-2 instructs you on how to evaluate your present accountant.

Become a Business Consultant Stop thinking of yourself simply as an architect, an engineer, or an interiors or landscape planner. Start thinking of yourself as a business consultant. When you do, you immediately

Obtaining and Utilizing a Good Accountant

1. Hire an accountant (or accounting firm) who understands the design business, including its contracts and procedures, and who has worked for four or five other design businesses.

2. If you choose an accountant firm, choose one from which you can obtain principal involvement on your work. Just as your clients prefer you, as a principal, to be involved in their projects, you should request the same of your accountant firm.

3. Hire an accountant who is knowledgeable in both tax and business strategy. Don't hire an accountant who can only fill out your forms; hire someone who can advise you on business decisions so that she can act as a consultant to you.

4. The accountant should understand your tax situation and banking relationships within the local area. Most importantly, an accountant should be from your geographical region and understand the nuances of specific banking regulations in your area.

5. Hire an accountant whose business is located nearby. If your accountant is one or two hours away, you won't seek her advice as often as you should.

6. The accountant should be willing to visit your firm at least once per quarter; this will help her gain a true understanding of your project management procedures.

7. Make friends with your accountant. Having a personal relationship helps ensure that your accountant is concerned about the progress of your business. You don't want to be viewed as just another client.

8. Make sure your accounting firm is not overburdened with work to the extent that you get short shrift. Be certain the staff is competent, that they can handle your work expeditiously, and that they respond swiftly when you call

Figure 11-1

turn a corner and run headlong into enhanced client service and greater profitability.

A business consultant analyzes a client's industry, anticipates the client's needs, and becomes a trusted adviser. Go to your clients with more information than they have about their facility. Teach them what they need to know. This is the role of a business consultant—and it's a heck of a lot more profitable than that of a designer who performs a tremendous amount of upfront research work for free in hopes of landing the job!

Could you imagine anyone at McKenzie Consulting walking into a potential client's office, presenting a business plan tailored specifically for the client, and *then* asking for their business? When you frame your services as valuable insight and experience with the client's industry, you bring to the table knowledge that's worth paying for. This is the edge you have over competitors—your unique perspective and knowledge. Don't give away your smarts for free!

Evaluating Your Present Accountant

Accountants' financial reports are not always effective. Here are some common problems:

■ Expenses are listed in alphabetical order on the income statement instead of being categorized to provide organized statistical information.

■ The accountant is not specific enough. An example of this is an expense listed as "Officers' Salaries" that is not broken down into direct and indirect components. By not being specific, your accountant may be revealing that he is not familiar with the A/E/C business.

■ Bonuses are not separated from salaries. They are shown below the line as a non-operating expense. This makes bottom-line profits meaningless as a measure of firmwide performance.

■ Data are not organized in a format that enables you to differentiate between direct project cost and overhead or to evaluate the effectiveness of project profits.

The reason for these problems is simple. Your accounting firm is using a basic format instead of one specifically suited to design firm accounting. Using this basic format may save a few dollars, but the results will not be effective in comparing with other firms in your profession.

Another way you can spot poor accounting firm performance is when the accountant assures you, "This method will absolutely keep you from an audit." While overaggressiveness in tax matters is not recommended, using an audit-proof method is generally too conservative. Tax laws are subject to interpretation and multiple methods of reporting. Your accountant should be taking the most favorable action to save tax dollars, not just to avoid an audit.

Discuss your firm's individual needs with your present accountants. If they cannot meet your needs, seek other accountants. Remember, you pay them for meaningful information tailored to your specific needs as a design firm.

Figure 11-2

Source: "Need a New Accountant?" *Professional Services Management Journal,* December 1984.

Figure 11-3 profiles a professional in the A/E/C industry who regularly sells his brainpower. This is one unique take on becoming a business consultant. John Landry has translated years of experience into a lucrative expert-witness testimony business, and he believes this is a potential revenue stream for A/E/C firms who have the interest and the information.

Hire the Best Staff When you look at your employees, do you see leaders who inspire you to greatness? Most business owners find a proportion of employees who are less capable than they are— that is, who are followers. Learn from successful entrepreneurs such as Southwest Airlines' Herb Kelleher and EarthLink's Charles Brewer. Read what they say and look at

Taking Advantage of a Business Niche

Firm: *John P. Landry & Associates, Inc.*

Specialty: *Architectural Expert Witness Testimony in Construction Defect Litigation*

Address: *5973 Avenida Encinas, Suite 202*
               Carlsbad, Calif. 92008

Starting in 1987, John P. Landry & Associates has seized its opportunity to take advantage of a unique niche in the A/E Industry by specializing in the analysis of construction defects in architectural structures. Firm principal John Landry explains, " This is a hybrid world of attorneys and architectural experts working together to achieve an equitable and fair remedy for construction defects.." Landry goes on to say, "Our niche has been created because this hybrid environment puts most Architects beyond their comfort zone. Our firm is one of a very few specializing in this work and we see very little emerging competition in the Los Angeles to San Diego market."

The construction defect litigation niche exists as a result of lawsuits filed by plaintiff attorneys seeking remedies/repairs for construction claimed to be defective. Such lawsuits in the Los Angeles to San Diego market usually involve the following project types: single-family residences, condominiums, and apartments. Typically, the plaintiff attorney files a lawsuit against the developer of the project. The developer in turn files a cross-complaint lawsuit against most parties involved in the construction, such as, architects, engineers, general contractors, and subcontractors. It is quite common for 20 to 30 parties to be involved in a single lawsuit of this type, and each party will have its own attorney and team of experts. Landry states, "We are almost always hired as the architectural expert for the developer/general contractor. Developer cases usually involve very large money claims by the plaintiff ($5 to $30 million), which results in complicated, document-intensive cases for the developer's expert team. For example, one of our developer, single-family cases (over 200 homes) has approximately 70,000 photographs generated by our firm alone during site inspections of the existing construction."

Over the past 14 years, Landry has been an architectural expert in over 450 construction defect cases for plaintiff and defense, including architect, developer, general contractor, and subcontractor. "To me the challenge is to determine the exact cause of the defective construction in a professional, objective, nonadvocate manner so as to assess responsibility fairly and equitably. The process is a real-life detective story and that is very interesting to me," Landry says of his niche in the A/E Industry.

For those wishing to benefit from the opportunities in this niche, Landry advises that careful consideration be given to basic requirements: strong technical skills and knowledge of codes and manufacturers' literature, solid design experience in wood-frame construction, strong computer and graphic skills, and excellent communication and presentation skills. A high-quality service firm in this niche market can anticipate repeat business, word-of-mouth marketing, significant financial performance, reliable cash flow, and recession-resistant revenues.

Finally, Landry emphasizes his success at delivering accurate quality service for large, complex construction defect cases is the result of the custom computer database analysis system designed and programmed by his firm. The program, trade named VERDICT, contains 17 modules to assist the expert and staff at each stage of the expert witness process. Landry says, "VERDICT is a hands-on computer program forged out of our real-life experiences in the 450 cases we have completed. This program can handle anything in construction defect litigation from unit lists and defect lists to complex analysis of depositions and trial exhibit preparation." Architects interested in this niche market or the VERDICT program may contact the firm at 760-930-0407.

Figure 11-3
Source: John P. Landry & Associates. Used with permission.

the people they hire. They search for the best and put them in positions where they can excel. (See Chapter 5 on how to hire the best.)

Encourage Leadership Development In Your Firm Once you've identified top-notch performers and brought them into your firm, begin nurturing leadership characteristics. Firms that have taken the time to create leadership guidelines find their star employees not only staying with the organization but also rising quickly to the top. (See Chapter 1 on creating a list of leadership attributes and its benefits to the firm.)

Get Good Quality Control Advice Don't allow disputes, lawsuits, or other conflicts to sidetrack you or your firm from performing at top levels. By getting good quality control advice, you can handle mistakes before they occur instead of letting them get out of hand. See the section in Chapter 4 entitled "How to Set Up a Quality Control Program for the Small Design Office."

Start quality control management in the initial formulation of the scope of services. Be certain quality control is thought of when writing and signing contracts so that everyone in the firm understands the terms and the meanings of each contract item. Good quality control starts with project planning, including:

- Clearly defining the scope of services.
- Contracting so that the budget and schedule are integral parts of the contracts, clearly understandable to both the client and your team.

Quality control checking at the end of the project does not compensate for missing the boat on quality control at the beginning of a project. Have a quality control plan for technical aspects of the job, such as standard details and procedures for putting together drawings in a similar and consistent manner. Use standards whenever possible. (See Chapter 4.)

Develop Your Own Contract Many successful firms develop their own contracts. If you use a standard association contract, go through it clause by clause (for each project) with your legal counsel to make sure it reflects your project goals and echoes your business standards. Figure 11-4 contains an example of a customized contract. Standard contracts do include much necessary detail, but they are best used as guidelines for tailoring your own contract. See Figure 11-5 for a delineation of profitable contract terms.

ARIZONA
ENGINEERING
COMPANY

Civil and Environmental Engineering
Land Surveying

Client Contract

Client Name & Address:	
	Proposal Date:
	Proposal Number:
	This Proposal Will Be Open for Acceptance Until:

Identification of Project:

Scope of Services (Basic Services):

Payment for Basic Services:

Retainer Amount and Terms:

Payment for Additional Services:

Special Conditions:

The Terms and Conditions on Page 2 of this form, including rates & payment provisions, are a part of this Agreement.

Submitted By Arizona Engineering Company	Accepted For:
	Accepted By:
By: Charles Dryden, President	Signature Date

419 North San Francisco Street
Flagstaff, Arizona 86001

Telephone.   520-774-7179
Facsimile: 520-779-1041

Please return one copy, bearing your original
signature, to Arizona Engineering Company

Terms and Conditions

- You'll tell us everything you know about the Project, and about what you want us to do for you.
- You'll give us all the information you have about the project.
- You'll make sure we have access to the Project site if we need it to do our work.
- We'll try not to damage anything at the Project site while we're there working, but damage is possible, and our fee doesn't include the cost of repairing any damage.
- We may tell you how much we think it will cost to construct something, but we don't guarantee that the actual cost won't be different from our estimate.
- We don't guarantee that there won't be changes in the project scope of work or project schedule that result from submitting the project for review by public agencies. Such changes may be the occasion for re-negotiating our fee.
- We'll decide who in our firm will work on the project.
- If our fee is based on an hourly or daily basis, we will bill at the rates prevailing when we do the work. Our normal minimum charge is 2 hours. Our current billing rates are as follows:

E-4, Principal	$160.00 per hour
E-3, Associate/Gen'l Mgr.	$115.00 per hour
E-2	$90.00 per hour
E-1	$75.00 per hour
E.I.T.	$60.00 per hour
A-5, Office Manager	$52.50 per hour
A-2, Clerk/Typist	$32.50 per hour
S-5, Sr. Survey Manager	$90.00 per hour
S-4, Survey Manager	$75.00 per hour
S-3, Survey Crew Chief	$60.00 per hour
S-2, Instrument Operator	$47.50 per hour
S-1, Survey Technician	$37.50 per hour.

- We will review our hourly billing rates annually, in January, and we will advise you of any changes that may affect work currently being performed for you.
- If you ask us to work outside normal business hours, we'll charge 1.5 times our regular rates.
- We'll charge 2.0 times our regular rates for services related to litigation or arbitration, including preparation for litigation or arbitration. This multiplier does not apply to non-binding mediation.
- Subconsultant services will be marked up 20 per cent unless Page 1 of this contract specifically establishes a different markup rate.
- Reimbursable expenses, including travel, meals and lodging, expedited shipping, printing, and title reports will be billed separately and are not included in our lump sum or daily fees unless Page 1 of this contract specifically states that they will be included.
- We'll bill you monthly or when the work is complete. It's up to us. We won't provide backup documentation with our bill. If you take exception to any part of our bill, including the amount of the bill or our estimate of the work complete, you'll let us know in 10 days or less. By not doing so, you agree that you won't dispute any part of the bill, or withhold payment in whole or in part.
- You'll pay us in 30 days or less. If you don't pay us in 30 days, you'll owe us interest at the rate of 1.5% per month, and we can stop work until you pay us in full.
- If damages or losses result from something you do or fail to do, you'll make sure that we don't have to pay for them.
- If damages or losses result from something we do or fail to do, our financial responsibility will be limited to ten times our fee or $50,000.00, whichever is less.
- We currently maintain insurance policies in the amounts set forth below. If you require higher insurance limits or special certifications, the cost of obtaining such insurance will be a reimbursable expense.

Worker's Compensation	Statutory
General Liability	$1,000,000/$2,000,000
Automobile Liability	$1,000,000/Accident
Professional Liability	$1,000,000/$2,000,000

- In an effort to resolve any conflicts that may arise during surveys for, or design or construction of the Project, or following the completion of the project, we mutually agree that all disputes between us arising out of or relating to this agreement will be submitted to non-binding mediation unless, at the time of the disputes, we mutually agree otherwise.
- If either of us sues the other to enforce this agreement, the one who loses will pay attorney fees and expenses for the one who wins.
- Drawings and documents prepared by us are for this project only. We don't accept any responsibility for damages or losses that result if they are re-used, in whole or in part, without our written permission.
- This contract is between you and Arizona Engineering Company. No one else is entitled to use the documents we prepare for this project without our written permission.
- We'll keep original drawings, but you can have reproducible copies if you ask for them.
- Our work may not be perfect. However, it will conform to generally accepted engineering and surveying principles and practices.
- Either of us may terminate this agreement at any time, with or without cause, by giving the other thirty calendar days' written notice. If either of us fails to live up to the terms of this agreement, the other may quit on seven days' notice. If you decide to abandon the Project, you can tell us to stop work on seven days' written notice.
- If this agreement is terminated for any reason, you'll pay us for all the work we've done so far, plus five per cent, which we mutually agree to accept as the cost of stopping work and putting everything away.
- Any changes to this agreement will be in writing. If we advise you in writing of conditions that in our opinion justify changes in this agreement, specifically including changes that may result in increases in our fees or changes in the project schedule, you agree to notify us in writing within 5 business days of any objections or exceptions to the proposed changes. In the absence of such notification from you, you and we agree that our letter advising you of changes will constitute a written change to this agreement.

Arizona Engineering Company Terms, 1-01-2000 Revision (Contract Page 2)

Figure 11-4. Sample of a custom contract.

PSMJ | Resources, Inc.

PSMJ Resources, Inc. 10 Midland Avenue Newton, MA 02458 **Call** 800.537.PSMJ **E-mail** info@psmj.com

29 TERMS TO INCLUDE IN A/E CONTRACTS

Over the past twenty-five years, PSMJ has observed design firms using various terms to improve their contracts with clients. While we do not provide legal services or advice, we share with you below, as an exclusive PSMJ subscriber benefit, 29 contract term ideas. Study these suggested terms, and rewrite them to meet your own firm's specific circumstances. You may not get everyone of them into your next contract, but each new one will improve your firm's approach to the "business of design." As always, check with your attorney before finalizing any contractual change.

1. **Prepayment**: "Upon acceptance of this contract by the client, a payment of $_____ will be required to initialize the project."

Explanation: Cover working capital obligations on the project. If the project will take three months or less to complete, request 100 % of the fee up-front. If it will last longer, request a lesser percentage of the fee up-front, etc.

2. **Fee in Escrow**: "Upon acceptance of this contract by the client, a deposit of $_____ will be placed in an interest-bearing escrow account in the name of XYZ Associates. These funds, including interest, will be released to XYZ on _____, 2001, or upon completion of 75% of the work on this contract, whichever occurs first."

Explanation: Use this clause if you fail to get prepayment. It allows you to earn interest on funds, which will eventually be paid.

2a. **Evidence of Funds**: "As a condition of the Architect's obligation to commence or continue with its services, the client shall furnish upon request during the course of the project evidence satisfactory to the Architect of available funds to satisfy the client's obligations hereunder."

Explanation: Make sure your client has the money to pay you if you are not going to receive payment up-front or if payment will not be held in escrow.

3. **Job Cancellation Fee**: "Because of potentially significant revenues from other projects forgone by XYZ Associates to take this project, if the project is cancelled by the client, a cancellation fee will be immediately due and payable according to the following schedule: 0 to 30 days, $____; 31 to 60 days, $____, etc."

Explanation: In the event a project is cancelled, get the client's commitment to pay for opportunities you lost by committing to work on the project. This cancellation fee will decrease the longer the project has run, as you should have earned a greater portion of expected revenues.

4. **Project Restart Fee**: "Because of substantial cost incurred by XYZ Associates to stop and restart a project once it is underway, should this project's progress be halted at any time for 30 or more days by the client, for any reason, a project restart fee of $____ or 10% of the total fee earned to date, whichever is greater, will be due and payable immediately."

Explanation: The longer you work on a project, the longer it takes to get back up to speed after a stop. The longer the stoppage, the more potential for changes. Seek some compensation for events beyond your control.

5. **Construction Contingency**: "A contingency fund of ___% [usually 5% to 8%] of the total estimated construction cost of this project will be established by the client. The purpose of this fund will be to pay for any unanticipated changes that occur during the course of the design and construction of the project."

Explanation: Insist the client secure extra funds in the initial financing to cover contingencies that may not be anticipated at the beginning of the project. The funds to cover these contingencies may not be easily secured down the road.

> Help us build this list of terms. Send in your successful terms, and we will publish them anonymously. **Send** them to: PSMJ Contract Terms, 10 Midland Ave, Newton, MA 02458, **fax:** 617-965-5152, or **e-mail:** info@psmj.com

Figure 11-5

6. Automatic Escalator: "After ____, 2001, all fees and hourly rates quoted within this contract may increase by ___% annually thereafter."

Explanation: Most firms put a clause in their contracts stating that after some date, all fees will be subject to renegotiations. This is not the same as specifying a specific percentage increase. "Renegotiations" could result in decreased fees to the design firm.

7. Limit of Liability: "It's understood that the total liability of XYZ Associates for any claims arising out of the services performed under this agreement shall be limited to a maximum of the net fee received by XYZ Associates, not including reimbursable sub-consultant fees and expenses."

Explanation: This is simply a more reasonable limit of liability than that of the total fee.

8. Late Penalty Schedule: "All invoices not paid promptly will be subject to the following late payment penalty: 30 to 59 days overdue, $500.00; 60 to 89 days overdue, $750.00; etc."

Explanation: This clause will help you get paid faster. It may also bypass usury laws by not being referred to as an interest penalty.

8a. Suspension of Services: "If the client fails to pay an invoice within seven days of the date payment is due, the Architect shall be entitled, upon three days' notice, to suspend further services until all accounts due have been paid."

Explanation: The best payment leverage is to cease working, which also minimizes the extent of the potential lost time and effort.

9. Sample Invoice Format: "All invoices will be formatted and submitted as in the attached example provided in Appendix A."

Explanation: Define the invoicing format and procedure according to what is best for you as opposed to the client. This sets the stage for additional fees should the client want to vary from the "standard."

10. Certification Indemnification: "The client shall indemnify XYZ Associates from claims arising out of any certifications which are required to be signed on behalf of the client during the course of the project."

Explanation: Discourage requests for signing of certifications by establishing the client's associated liability.

11. Certification Fees: "As an acknowledgement of the significant liabilities incurred by XYZ Associates when signing certifications, a certification fee of $5,000 will be due for the first certification required on this project, $4,000 for the second certification required, etc., with a minimum fee of $500.

Explanation: If you must sign certifications, get compensated for the associated risk. The per-certification fee should decline with each additional certification required.

12. Limitation on Design Alternatives: "XYZ Associates will...[use one of the following: (1)...limit the number of design alternatives provided under this contract to three; (2)...limit to ___ hours the time expended in design; or (3)... stop developing project design] by ___, 2001, upon which time the design will be considered complete."

Explanation: Make sure you're not designing all the way through the project, or if you are, get paid for the effort.

13. Premium for Client Team Member Reorientation: "There will be a client team member reorientation fee of $10,000 paid for each project team member from the client who is added or replaced prior to 25% completion of the project, $20,000 for each team member added or replaced prior to 50% completion, etc."

Explanation: New project team members in the client's office cost you time and money. Prepare for such a likelihood (and discourage when avoidable) by passing the cost to the client. The obvious down side to this clause is that the client may want you also to sign off rights to change team members.

14. Job Site Signage: "Because of its standing as a professional design firm, XYZ Associates has complete authority over all content, graphics, and placement of all job site signs with the exception of those required for the purpose of maintaining worker safety and the security of the facility."

Explanation: It is in your best interests to maintain control over project signs from the standpoint of maximizing marketing opportunities and maintaining your professional identity.

Continued on the next page

Figure 11-5 (continued)

15. **Graphics Control**: "Because of its standing as a professional design firm, XYZ Associates has complete control over graphic content and presentation of all studies, reports, and other documents produced under this agreement."

Explanation: Same as #14 above.

16. **Lien Provisions**: "The client acknowledges that it has secured legal rights to the property upon which the project will be built or that such right will be secured by _____, 2001, and shall furnish a description of the property to the architect prior to the Architect's commencement of services. The client further acknowledges that non-payment of fees owed under this agreement will result in a mechanics lien being placed on the property upon which the project is/will be located."

Explanation: Even though most state statutes allow you to do this anyway, it never hurts to have it clearly spelled out in the contract.

17. **No Back-up for Reimbursable**: "No back up data or copies of bills will be provided for reimbursable expenses invoiced under this agreement. Should back-up data be requested, it will be provided for an administrative fee of $100 per monthly invoice requiring verification, plus $1.00 per bill or cost item supplied."

Explanation: Supplying back-up for reimbursable expenses takes time. The typical A/E/P firm doesn't have staff resources to squander on non-billable activities.

18. **No Exact Reimbursable**: "The client will pay 15% of each total monthly invoice for professional services submitted by XYZ Associates as a reimbursable fee to cover all typical reimbursable expenses, such as postage, fax, phone and mail, but excluding models, renderings, or copies of drawings or specifications in excess of ___sets."

Explanation: This clause greatly simplifies your accounting and saves money. It also eliminates the need to keep track of mountains of detailed back-up.

19. **Client Signatures at Various Stages in the Project**: "Beginning with the date of project initiation, all drawings produced under this agreement will be signed by an authorized representative of the client each 60 days during the project, or at more frequent intervals when appropriate."

Explanation: Document any design changes mandated by the client. You will need to minimize future misunderstandings on client wants and needs. Notice that the above was written to provide signatures at a date, not a phase or percentage of completion, but leaves open the possibility of sign-off at the end of a phrase. It's too easy to end up in an argument with your client over what defines or constitutes completion of a phase. Hence, PSMJ recommends never tying payment of fees to "phase completion."

20. **Ownership and Copyright of Documents**: "All drawings and documents produced under terms of this agreement are the property of XYZ Associates, and cannot be used for any reason other than to bid and construct the above-named project. The client shall be granted a revocable license to use the drawings and documents for the purpose of constructing, maintaining and operating the [project], and shall not use such documents for any other purpose without the Architect's consent. The client shall indemnify and defend the Architect from any claim, loss or damage arising out of the client's failure to abide by the terms hereof."

Explanation: Documents used for other than their original purpose may result in liability to the original design professional.

21. **Fee for Prints after Five Years**: "After five years from the date of project completion, or on _____, 2002, a document reproduction fee of $_____ [typically $500 to $1,000] per sheet will be charged.

Explanation: The minute you bill the client for anything, it may have extended the applicable statute of limitations along with your potential liability. Seek compensation for this risk. Furthermore, unless a firm physically surveys a project on which it provides prints, it does not know what physical changes have been made after construction, rendering prints obsolete.

22. **Higher Fees Paid for Changes**: "Any changes requested in the attached scope of services provided under this agreement will be billed at a multiplier of 1.25 times customary billing rates."

Figure 11-5 (continued)

Explanation: Project changes mean a costly remobilization, a greater potential for errors and omissions, and disruption of other project schedules. Seek compensation at higher rates than normal.

23. Stamp Only after Payment: "XYZ Associates will not stamp drawings produced for any phase of this project under the terms of this agreement until all invoices billed up to that point in the project have been paid in full."

Explanation: This is one more attempt to get paid expeditiously.

24. Stamp on Drwings: "XYZ Associates shall not be liable for any plans or specifications produced under this agreement until such drawings are stamped as approved by all relevant building department officials."

Explanation: This clause is used to help liability.

25. Contract Validity: "This contract is valid only if signed on or before _____, 2001, unless formally extended by both parties."

Explanation: Don't make open-ended commitments that you may not want or be able to live up to in the future. This clause also helps to define the time of project completion.

26. Free Publicity: "XYZ Associates has the right to photograph the above named project and to use the photos in the promotion of the professional practice through advertising, public relations, brochures or other marketing materials. Should additional photos be needed in the future, the client agrees to provide reasonable access to the facility. The client also agrees to cite the name of XYZ Associates as the designer in all publicity, presentations, and public relations activities which mention the name of or depict the facility."

Explanation: This doesn't cost your client anything, yet can mean a great deal to you.

27. Third Party Legal Defense after a Specified Period of Time: "After September 1, 2005, any legal cost arising to defend third party claims made against XYZ Associates in connection with the above-named project shall be borne by the client."

Explanation: If you are at fault, your errors would certainly have been discovered in five years of operating the facility, so why should you be bothered with third party claims that you obviously weren't responsible for.

28. Royalty Clause: "In recognition of XYZ Associates' significant contribution to the long-term real value of the above-named project and property through the rendering of unique design services, a term will be added to the legal deed on the property by the client at the time of closing providing XYZ Associates a royalty of $_____ each and every time the property is sold subsequent to the initial closing for a period of 99 years."

Explanation: Since you create real value, you may be entitled to a share of the project's profits as it changes hands in future years. This must be written into the first deed on the property by the client at closing.

29. Hazardous Waste: "Any hazardous waste or asbestos required to be removed, encapsulated or otherwise contained during the course of this project will result in compensation to XYZ Associates equaling 3.0 times above normal customary hourly billing rates for any plans, specifications, or construction observation services provided. XYZ Associates will additionally be indemnified from any and all liability associated with removal, encapsulation or containment of hazardous waste or asbestos."

Explanation: Discourage involvement with hazardous waste and asbestos, but get paid well if it is required by the client.

Acknowledgement:
This list was prepared with the valuable assistance of Attorneys Burton Winnick and Stanley A. Martin of the firm Gadsby & Hannah, LLP. Mr. Winnick and Mr. Martin can be reached at 617-345-7000 or by e-mail at bwinnick@ghlaw.com.

Disclaimer:
PSMJ is not in the business of rendering legal advice and intends these contract terms and conditions to be used only after consultation with a competent attorney knowledgeable in contract law in your area of professional practice and in your locale.

Figure 11-5 (continued)

Unfortunately, many small firms do not have the resources to develop their own contracts. You should realize that it takes each association seven to ten years to develop its own standard contract. Over this period, circumstances in the market are changing. While standard association contracts are not (and have not been for the last 15 years) used by the most profitable firms in PSMJ Resources' Financial Statistics Surveys, there are many instances in which using the standard association contract is better than using your own. To decide which type of contract is appropriate for you, consider the following:

- If you cannot afford an attorney to review your contract, use the standard association contract.
- If your clients insist on standard association contracts or require you to spend exorbitant amounts of time negotiating nonstandard items on your own contracts, perhaps you should use the standard versions.
- If your firm's primary goal is neither profitability nor liability protection, perhaps it may be more equitable for you to use a standard association contract, which is coordinated with all other aspects of the contract, including general conditions.
- If you cannot write your own contract terms or don't desire change, by all means stay with the standard association contracts.
- Although standard association contracts have a good history, are well recommended by liability companies, and serve a valid purpose in the marketplace, the most profitable firms have found that it is better to use standard association contracts as foundations on which to build, the goal being to create their own better contract.
- The standard association contract is a vanilla pudding contract because it must cover a wide variety of circumstances; therefore, it cannot possibly relate to a particular firm as well as a customized contract can.
- If you are crossing out more than 20 percent of the paragraphs in a standard contract, it may be time for you to consider developing your own contract.

Teach Selling to Every Project Manager Make sales an integral part of your project managers' duties. Do not retain project managers who cannot bring in clients. Teach project managers selling tips for presentations. Here is advice you can offer them:

- Remain natural. Don't dress up extraordinarily for a presentation. Dress naturally and comfortably in a businesslike manner. A regular suit and tie is fine—don't go overboard and buy a special presentation suit.

- Learn to talk on your feet. Successful project managers practice public speaking. They go out into the community and become involved in the local chamber of commerce, business clubs, and so forth.
- Learn to use the tools of presentation—projectors, whiteboards, laptop computers, flip charts, and so on. Practice!
- Don't overdo presentations by having too many people performing the actual presentation of material. A maximum of three other people should be involved. Bringing more people to the presentation requires tremendous coordination that can undermine the project manager's confidence level.
- Collect as much data and research on a presentation as possible. Confidence is the key to selling and, if a project manager collects all the data himself, he'll have more confidence in the use of that data in the presentation.

Change Your Voice Mail Message Daily Don't present callers with a stale voice mail message they've heard time and time again. These busy days, voice mail is often (unfortunately) the first contact you make with a client or future client. It only takes a moment to change your voice mail message every morning. A daily message serves many purposes:

- It tells callers you care about their messages.
- It gives callers an accurate report of your availability and whereabouts.
- It provides a refreshing change of pace from the same droning message callers encounter time after time at other firms.

Here's an example of a daily voice mail message: "Hello, this is John Smith. Today is Tuesday, February 8th. I will be out of the office all day, but I will be checking my voice mail. Please leave me a message so I can return your call. If you need to speak with someone immediately, press 0 and ask for Mary Jones. Thanks!"

Focus on Service Service is *the* key to success. Clients remember bad service as well as good. Bad service can undermine any strategy you take in a professional design firm. See Chapters 2 and 4 for more detail.

Be Distinctively Different Position your firm in a way that gives you a distinctive difference in the marketplace. See Chapter 2 for details.

Call Clients Regularly Most successful firms have regular, established relationships with their clients. They are friends with them and remember them after the project is done. Project managers should get friendly with clients, to the point where they can genuinely call them friends. Obviously, a business relationship differs from a personal one. It's seldom that a client friend is as close as a personal friend. However, the idea is to build professional yet personal friendships—open and honest relationships that will encourage or obligate the client to choose you as their design professional.

Build relationships with clients—there is no downside to getting friendly.

Listen, Read, and Think Many people read the magazines directly related to their profession only. Successful design professionals listen carefully, read widely, and are infinitely curious about things outside of their environment. Very successful design CEOs read novels and other publications totally unrelated to the design environment. When was the last time you read a book on leadership, such as *On Becoming a Leader,* by Warren Bennis, or *Leadership Is an Art,* by Max DePree? Do you keep up with international business and political news? Although such subjects are outside the architectural/engineering professions, they may prompt you to think about how your firm can make improvements and seize opportunities.

Welcome Change "If it ain't broke, fix it." This is contrary to what most of us are taught, but highly successful firms tend to fix things before they break. Most firms wait until after the fact. Successful firms never accept the status quo. For example, if a presentation or a particular contract has worked for three clients, most firms would decide to use them for the next three clients; the successful firm would improve or change them in the belief that even better results can be obtained the next time around.

Challenge the Norm—Relinquish Tradition When everything seems normal, go outside the norm and challenge it in the marketplace. As in the example above, the successful firm challenges its strategy. Rethink your strategies to ensure that they keep your firm ahead of the rest. Welcome change; don't just create standard operating procedures. The asbestos market is a good example. When most people ran away due to fear of liability, those who stayed analyzed the asbestos market, challenged traditional approaches, developed strategies, and dove in, looking at the positive side—the opportunity to be nearly alone in a niche.

Respect and Treat your staff as superiors or at least as equals, because
Praise your Staff they are important in building your small firm's reputation.
See Chapter 5 for tips on how to motivate your staff.

Have an A documented ownership transition plan is a critical part of
Ownership your firm's operations. In the worst-case scenario, your
Transition Plan ownership transition plan will prevent legal complications
in the event of your death. A more typical benefit is smooth,
predetermined transfer of ownership between parties who
have agreed to the terms important to you.

DON'TS

Don't Have Many firms have partners. Partners are accepted as the
Partners norm in the design industry. However, some firms argue
against partners. Their arguments include the point that a
single leader drives the firm, keeping total control of the
entity. This allows the firm to react and move quickly to capture new opportunities instead of wasting time arguing
about whether or not to pursue such a direction.

Most successful small firms have a limited number of
partners. One small (35-person) interior firm in St. Louis had
four partners requiring equal amounts of compensation and
had struggled for years dealing with the four-partner environment; there were partner meetings every week, conflict
between the partners, factions within the firm, and unpro-
ductiveness that drove down the partnership earnings and
the resulting profitability of the firm. Only when two of the
partners were eliminated did the firm achieve a 33 percent
net profit.

This firm learned from experience that it needs only two
people to manage and make decisions. Too many opinions
inevitably cause problems. Choose few partners and choose
them wisely.

Figure 11-6 presents the disadvantages of partnerships.
If you do have a partnership, see what you can do to improve
it. Tips for improving your partnership appear in Figure 11-7.

Don't Hire a Using firm earnings to pay your personal secretary is con-
Personal trary to the service mentality design firm principals must
Secretary embrace to be successful in today's economy. Rather than
dedicate one full-time employee's entire efforts to serving
your administrative needs, why not employ an assistant
whose main priority is client service? If you have an assistant who monitors your email inbox, fields your calls, and
fulfills your requests with the goal of providing flawless service to your clients, you have justifiably added an important
member to your team.

The Disadvantages of Partnerships

Regardless of their formal structure, as a single proprietorship, partnership, or corporation, most professional service firms operate internally as a partnership. Here are some limitations to this form of organization:

- Because a partnership is a voluntary association of individuals, participants are likely to become oversolicitous of the feelings of their associates. Areas of disagreement are covered over rather than resolved. Unresolved issues can cause frustration to the point where one or more partners leave.
- Partners may end up creating their own independent operations that may not work in unison or in harmony. Truly strong partnerships are not just an amalgamation of individual professional practices but a unified effort.
- Because partnership relations are complex, there is a natural reluctance to admit new partners if that will result in complicating the ownership/operations environment. Key employees may be lost if they see that final recognition of their value—partnership—is not open to them.
- The partnership organization can lead to indecisive management. Partners are reluctant to act without complete consultation or even without unanimous agreement. Even minor policy decisions may be delayed unreasonably. The organization gives the appearance of being either indecisive or unaware of problems.

Given the drawbacks of a partnership-style organization, your firm can follow these steps to avoid its pitfalls:

1. Establish a strategic planning process that ensures that all partners are committed to the same goals and objectives. Emphasize resolving issues and disagreements by means of a common vision of your firm's future and each individual's participation in its achievement.

2. Assign management functions to one individual with specific authority to act. He would make all but major policy-setting decisions, and thus allow the firm to take fast, decisive action when necessary, without elaborate consultation requirements.

3. Separate income derived from partnership from income earned as an employee. Partners receive a fair and appropriate return on their investment as owners. They also receive, separately, compensation as a result of individual performance as employees. Partnership percentages are separate from job responsibility and titles.

4. When appropriate, include those outside the partnership in decision making. Professionalize the management of the organization. For example, the board of directors in a corporate format can include people who provide special expertise and flow of new ideas without the major shareholders losing control of the organization.

5. Commit the partnership to making new partners as soon as they are recognized as capable and key to the success of the firm. Most professionals see equity positions as the final recognition of their achievements.

6. Provide a way for partners to phase out their participation as they approach retirement or as they redirect their attention to other areas of endeavor.

Figure 11-6

Improve Your Partnership

Most design firm principals, like most married couples, never seek outside help to improve the way they work together.

Ask yourself if this quote could be from one of your partners:

I've got a fairly good idea about how to deal with problem employees, but that's not my biggest concern. What I'm wondering about is my partners and me. We hardly ever talk frankly about our own performance or even about how we're getting along with each other. We're not unhappy, but we're not happy either. We're successful, but we're not happy. And I don't think we're alone, either. What can we do to deal with this kind of problem and maybe even improve the quality of our partnership?

Let's say that you, like the person who posed this question, want to improve the quality of your relationship with your partners. What can you do? Here are some immediate suggestions:

1. Make the improvement of your relationship with your partners a top priority. Like a marriage, a partnership is a relationship between people. For any relationship to succeed, it takes work. Too many partners say they're going to improve relations but never do. Like gardeners who plant the seeds but forget to tend the garden, they get out of the relationship what they put into it: not very much.

   What does "making a commitment to improve our partnership" really mean? Time, effort, and energy. It also means:

   ■ Accepting your partners as having a right to be different from you and not trying to make them be more like you.
   ■ Being willing to sit down periodically and talk openly about your relationship with each other.
   ■ Being able to listen to the other person's point of view, especially when it's different from your own thoughts and feelings, especially when there are problems.
   ■ Taking responsibility for the contribution you're making to problems in the relationship rather than blaming it all on the others.
   ■ Being willing to look for solutions to problems that everyone can live with rather than trying to have it all your own way.

   Although the above sounds good in theory, almost everyone knows how hard it is to put into practice. That's why it's important to make a strong personal commitment right up front.

2. Personally reflect on your relationship with your partners. Each partner should think independently about the quality of the relationship between the partners, including problems, and develop suggestions for making the partnership less frustrating and more satisfying for everyone. Each partner should make these suggestions in writing so that important thoughts can be captured for later discussion. Use these questions to stimulate your thinking:

   ■ What do you value in your partners?
   ■ How have they helped the firm and enriched your life?

Continued on the next page

Figure 11-7
Source: "Improve Your Partnership," by Marty Grothe and Peter Wylie,
Professional Services Management Journal, Vol. 9, No. 11.

- What frustrates you about them?
- Have these frustrations gotten in the way of the firm's growth or your personal satisfaction?
- How has your relationship with your partners evolved over the years?
- How are problems between you and your partners dealt with—out in the open, too openly, under the table, or swept under the rug?
- What are some of the sensitive, touchy subjects that should be talked about but never get mentioned?
- What topics have you ducked?
- What do you suppose your partners haven't mentioned to you?
- How are you and your partners viewed by other key people, like clients, junior partners (including those who have left the firm), and employees?

3. Get together with the partners to talk about improving the relationships. Spend at least one day in a quiet, secluded spot where there are no telephones and other distractions. Bring a flip chart to record main points.

   Start by asking each person to focus on thought-provoking questions like: "On a day-to-day basis, how satisfied or dissatisfied are you with your relationship with each of your partners?" "What are your major sources of frustration and dissatisfaction?" "What could we—your partners—do to make your life less frustrating and more satisfying?"

   To ensure each person gets an opportunity to respond fully, apply the following ground rules:

   - When the first person starts talking, everybody else should listen attentively. Particularly avoid such ineffective gestures as interrupting, rolling your eyes, or disregarding the ideas of the person who's talking.
   - When the first person finishes talking, the rest should encourage him to say a little more, asking "What else would you like to add?" or "What you're saying is very interesting. Keep talking."
   - When the first person finishes building on original remarks, the next person should be formally invited to begin speaking.

   After each partner has responded to the first question, move on to the next question and go through the process again.

4. By the time everyone responds to all of the questions, the group will have amassed an enormous amount of information. The important next step is to start working on a few things everyone can agree to even if they don't seem to be the most important things to you. Don't worry at this point if touchy subjects have not surfaced, or about what to do about areas of disagreement. Get the group started working on joint efforts. More difficult projects can be tackled later, and some will even take care of themselves.

5. Ask for help if you need it. If you can't do what was suggested or you try and find that you couldn't do it on your own, don't be afraid to ask for outside help. Rather than a failure, asking for help when it's needed is a sign of maturity and effectiveness.

There are many reasons to improve the quality of your relationship with partners, some of which have to do with productivity and profits. However, the most important reason is that you will get more satisfaction and fulfillment out of your working life. Speaking personally as partners for many years, that's what it's all about.

Figure 11-7 (continued)

Don't Employ Family Members Hire employees on the basis of ability, not relationships, especially familial ones. There is simply no room for this kind of special accommodation in a successful firm. The only exception to this axiom is when a family member has worked for 10 to 15 years in an outside business and comes in with recognizable capability to take over your firm.

Don't Give Clients Your Cell Phone Number In the name of client service, many firm principals or owners readily give out their cell phone number. Before long, their cell phone is ringing off the hook at all hours of the day. To maintain control of your cell phone and initiate contact with clients when you can give them your full attention, pass out a pager number or check your voice mail regularly, using your cell phone only to return calls.

Don't Count on Working Only 40 Hours per Week Successful design firm principals do what it takes to get the job done. In most cases, this means working an average of 65 hours per week. Late hours, in most instances, is the way to push your profitability up and keep it there.

Don't Develop a Bureaucracy; Keep Standard Operating Procedures to a Minimum Abhor procedures. Get away from paperwork and outlines. Find simple, straightforward ways to do things. Try to:

- Develop performance standards.
- Eliminate office procedures.
- Do away with written documentation and interoffice memos.
- Call directly rather than send e-mail.

Minimize written standard operating procedures (SOP) to avoid overhead time being spent developing elaborate manuals that are rarely used. Instead, replace them with performance standards that allow your staff to be totally creative in accomplishing what must be done. Performance-related standards are better than task- or procedure-related standards; they allow individuals to create their own methods of reaching the stated result or goal. Task-oriented standards are time- and space-consuming and do not allow for the personal creativity that leads to personal satisfaction.

Of course, certain SOPs are necessary, such as a quality control/quality assurance system (QC/QA). For a QC/QA system, it is good to have standard checklists that set the goals for performance to be achieved, but do not outline the procedures. Contract language is another area where firm standards should be developed. Such standards save time, assure consistency of approach, and permit people to learn by following the standards. In general, however, successful small firms keep SOPs to a minimum.

Don't Keep Nonperforming Employees— Fire Them! Have a low tolerance for nonperformance. Identify weak employees and dismiss them. (See the section in Chapter 4 entitled "Fire Incompetents.") This does not mean that you should not take legal steps to document nonperformance. Put in writing warnings, poor performance reviews, and the like well in advance of letting an employee go. Periodically assess the staff's performance and do not ignore nonperformance, hoping it will improve itself.

Don't Focus on Winning Design Awards Many profitable design firms are not well known for design by their peers. They do not seek peer design awards (some even abhor them), they don't pay for design awards, and they don't fund processes to pursue design awards. However, they do go after design awards given by their clients, such as the Urban Land Institute's Awards for Excellence. The Institute is a client group of developers. Successful firms get many awards from their clients but few from their peers.

Don't Join Peer Associations Only It may seem contrary to the professional ethic, but many top firms simply do not support, belong to, or reimburse peer association membership. How can they be successful? The answer is simple and straightforward. Not being part of peer associations is done in the spirit of client service, their clients do not belong to the peer associations either. A client-dedicated company cares less about peer relationships than about client relationships. Peer relationships among architects and engineers are high on the list of important items for most design professionals, but they have little use as a tool to enhance firm profitability. If you are active in your peer associations, at least remember that you are not networking in this milieu. Seek membership in the groups your clients join.

Don't Not Spend on Technology While technology is certainly not the answer to increasing profitability in your firm, it is an aspect of firm life that cannot be ignored. Plan to spend 5 to 10 percent of annual revenues on technology. This assures that your staff has the technology necessary to get the job done.

Don't Have Fancy Offices Amazingly, many architects and engineers spend considerable money on elaborate office environments to make sure that their office's image is better than their clients'. Having an office that makes an overwhelming impression on your client is unnecessary. Not surprisingly, the most successful firms have normal offices located in out-of-the-way places, which reduces overhead. Successful small firms have functional, clean offices, but they don't have first-class design-award-winning offices.

A list of an office's functional necessities versus unnecessary extras appears in Figure 11-8.

Don't Impress Clients with Nice Toys Most wealthy design professionals lead ordinary lives. In fact, most drive Chevrolets. You won't find many Ferraris, Porsches, and other luxury cars in the parking lots of firms achieving great profits. It's not rare to see successful design professionals tooling around in pickup trucks. The point is, don't try to impress your clients with fancy toys; it is much more important to concentrate on cultivating client relationships.

Necessities versus Extras

Necessities	Extras
■ Computers with sufficient memory and software	■ Weekly birthday parties
■ Ample office supplies	■ Fresh flowers in conference or reception areas
■ Email	■ Catered lunches for principals
■ Clean environment	■ Expensive parking spaces in urban settings for principals
■ Proper lighting	■ Private elevator in your building
■ Clean rest rooms	■ Original artwork on walls
■ Access to private telephones	■ Oriental rugs
■ Access to a laptop computer for travel	■ Designer furniture
■ Adequate storage facilities: file space, closet space	■ China
■ Cell phones	■ Outside coffee service
■ Accurate receiving department	■ Candy/vending food service
■ Clean, presentable reception area	■ Directed lighting where generalized lighting will do
■ Palm Pilots	■ Designer curtains
■ Full kitchens	
■ Daily cleaning services for small tasks such as emptying wastebaskets	

Figure 11-8

A FINAL WORD

Much of the advice on success in this book may appear bold and sweeping. Obviously, no firm will fit the exact profile this book suggests. Methods for success were taken from many diverse firms and should be understood in that light. Remember, however, that these concepts, if applied, will make the difference in your firm.

Examine your business strategies and compare them to the strategies suggested here. Consider the success challenges at the end of each chapter to assess whether or not you have the leadership you need to go forward and make the changes necessary for your firm to succeed. Obviously, there is no guarantee for sustained success. Outside factors, such as market changes or leadership transitions, can undermine the success of any firm.

A firm needs to have a directed leader, focused on a vision, who puts his energy into seeing that vision come true. A small firm with such a driven leader, who steers the firm's focus toward a particular market, has a higher probability of succeeding than the typical small firm, which is struggling to forge a reputation and accepts any and all types of projects at varied pricing arrangements and contract terms.

This book has attempted to establish criteria against which to measure your firm's success. Profitability is the one criterion most readily understood, and that is why it is amply used. Profitable firms are directed, focused, and driven by creative leaders.

Do not let this book's definition, however, be the only definition of success. Your small firm can be considered successful if it measures up to your own criteria for success. You can increase the probability of your success by sitting down and starting with the first suggestion in this book. Write a one-sentence vision on which to build your strategic plan. Armed with a mission, you need only to summon the passion—the psychology of success—to carry it out.

SUCCESS CHALLENGES

1. Are you thinking creatively about every aspect of your practice? Are you challenging each traditional item, or are you just working the way it's always been done?

2. Are you overspending on unnecessary items? Eliminate some luxuries, the savings from which could make the firm more profitable.

3. Is your office location really necessary? Should you be in a less expensive office environment rather than in the typical prestigious downtown office, trying to impress clients?

4. Are you taking advantage of technology in a way that will enhance productivity?

5. Have you taken steps to nurture leadership and plan for the future of your firm with an ownership transition plan?

6. Are you continually seeking new ways to be more profitable, or do you follow traditional ways only?

7. Are you reading material from outside your professional field? Are you listening to thinkers, actors, movers, and shakers in other fields and applying their strategies and tactics to your field?

8. Develop five performance-oriented processes to replace five standard operating procedures.

Buy/Sell Agreements

A buy/sell agreement specifies how ownership in a closely held firm will be transferred internally under certain circumstances such as a shareholder's death, retirement, or termination.

Clearly envision and describe your intentions, and write them in a buy/sell agreement that you review and update at least every two years. In this way, you can avoid the unhappy circumstances of after-the-fact disputes, a firm that can't function, or owners engaged in suing each other.

GETTING STARTED

Don't call the lawyers yet. First, know what you want to accomplish and think about what will get you there.

- *Define your objectives*—What kind of company are you trying to create and perpetuate? What are your personal and professional objectives, and your vision for your firm's future?
- *Study terms and agreements*—Look at the terms suggested in this appendix and study the sample buy/sell agreement. Consider how you would handle each issue to support your objectives.
- *Make a checklist of terms to consider*—Use a worksheet to define your questions and concerns.
- *Call your lawyer*—Send him your objectives, your checklist, and your questions. Then go over the checklist with your attorney, who can turn it into an agreement that reflects the unique culture and circumstances of your firm.

DON'T COPY ANYBODY'S TERMS, NOT EVEN PSMJ'S

It might be tempting to copy PSMJ's sample buy/sell agreement or some of the terms we discuss in this chapter. But even though we've been studying buy/sell agreements for more than 15 years, we're not attorneys and we don't know your company; you should consult your own legal counsel before implementing any of the suggestions we make in this appendix.

PSMJ'S RECOMMENDED BUY/SELL AGREEMENT

THIS AGREEMENT was made as of _____, 20____,

BETWEEN _____, a company incorporat-

ed under the laws of the State of _____ and having its head office in

the _____, (hereinafter called the "Company).

OF THE FIRST PART

-and-

those parties who have executed this agreement

OF THE SECOND PART

Whereas the Company was incorporated under the _____
Corporations Act by Articles of Incorporation as amended with an authorized capital of
_____ (   ) common Shares without par value;

AND WHEREAS all of the issued Shares have been issued as fully paid and non-
assessable, to individuals who are employees of the Company (such persons and the
number of Shares registered in their names is as set out in Appendix "A" annexed hereto);

AND WHEREAS the Shareholders wish to create a guaranteed market for the Shares;

AND WHEREAS the Shareholders realize that the harmonious and successful management and control of the Company could be disrupted in the event of the death, bankruptcy, retirement, dismissal, disablement, or resignation of any of the Shareholders of
the Company, or if Shares could pass into ownership or control of a person other than a
person approved by the Board of Directors of the Company;

AND WHEREAS the Shareholders desire to enter into this Agreement among
themselves and the Company to ensure a succession to the ownership and control the Shares, and for the purpose of providing for the sale and purchases
thereof, in the event of the death, bankruptcy, retirement, dismissal, disablement, or resignation of any Shareholder of the Company and when
Shareholders of the Company are reducing the Shares held by them as they
approach retirement;

AND WHEREAS the number of Shares held by each Shareholder may change from time to time and whereas employees who arc not Shareholders on the date of this Agreement may from time to time become Shareholders of the Company;

AND WHEREAS the Shareholders have agreed that, in the event of the death, retirement, dismissal, disablement, or resignation from, employment of the Company of any Shareholder of the Company, the Company will purchase the Shares of the Shareholder in the manner and upon the terms hereinafter set forth;

AND WHEREAS, insurance has been purchased by the Company upon the lives of certain shareholders and the policies have been deposited with the Trustee who, in the event of the death of a Shareholder, will forthwith collect the proceeds of the insurance and use the proceeds to purchase the Shares pursuant to this Agreement;

AND WHEREAS, the Company may, at any time, add further policies of insurance to be held in the same manner as policies herein before referred to and to be subject to the terms of this Agreement and deposited with the Trustee;

AND WHEREAS, the Shareholders desire to enter into certain agreements with respect to the operation of the Company and to grant each other certain rights and privileges in respect of shares;

NOW THEREFORE THIS AGREEMENT WITNESSETH that in consideration of the mutual covenants and agreements herein set forth, the parties hereby covenant and agree as follows:

1.0   <u>DEFINITIONS</u>

    1.1   <u>Board of Directors</u>

        "Board of Directors" when used in this agreement shall mean the Board of Directors of _____, Inc.

    1.2   <u>Date of Withdrawal</u>

        "Date of Withdrawal" means the day upon which employment ceases with the Company or any of its subsidiaries, for any reason whatsoever including those defined in Section 1.13 below.

1.3   Directors

"Directors" when used in this Agreement shall mean members of the Board of Directors of _____, Inc.

1.4   Disablement

"Disablement" refers to a situation or event whereby a Shareholder's ability to practice the profession for which he is hired by the Company is substantially affected by accident, injury, mental or physical illness, alcoholism or drug abuse. The Board of Directors of the Company shall, by a fifty-one percent (51%) or greater vote of Shares, not including Shares held by disabled stockholders, and based on medical evidence which concurs with definitions contained in the Company's disability insurance policy, have the power to decide by resolution that such a shareholder is subject to permanent or temporary incapacity for the carrying on of the role or profession practiced by him on behalf of the Company from the date of such resolution. The Shareholder shall be deemed to be "disabled" for the purpose of this Agreement in accordance with the Company's disability insurance waiting period of 24 months, and such action by the Board may occur after such waiting period has transpired, and the Shareholder's salary shall cease to by paid three months after the date of the Board of Director's resolution.

1.5   Employee

"Employee" means a full-time employee of the Company, or any of its subsidiaries.

1.6   Book Value

"Book Value" means the Total Shareholder's Equity as indicated on the Accountant Prepared "Consolidated Balance Sheet," plus the following three items as indicated on the Accountant Prepared "Consolidated Balance Sheet":

(a) the "Reserve for Bad Debts";

(b) two (2) times the "Work in Process"; and

(c) twenty-five percent (25%) of the "Deferred Income."

1.7 Prime Bank Rate

"Prime Bank Rate" means the lowest rate of interest charged by the Company's bankers of record on the last day of the previous month in California on loans to large customers of good credit.

1.8 Retired Shareholder

"Retired Shareholder" is a shareholder who has reached the age of sixty-five (65) years or who alternatively has retired with permission of the Board of Directors at an earlier age.

1.9 Selling Shareholder

"Selling Shareholder" means the Shareholder, or the estate of the deceased Shareholder, who sells or is selling, for whatever reason, all or a portion of the Shares owned by him.

1.10 Shareholder

"Shareholder" includes only those persons who have executed this Agreement.

1.11 Shares

"Shares" mean common Shares of stock in the Company.

1.12 Withdrawal

"Withdrawal" means the cessation of active full-time employment with the Company for any reason whatsoever, including death or disability. Absence requested by the Board of Directors shall not constitute, for the purpose of this Agreement, Withdrawal.

1.13 Withdrawing Shareholder

"Withdrawing Shareholder" means a shareholder whose employment with the Company has ceased for any reason whatsoever.

1. 14 Trustee

"Trustee" within this agreement shall be the corporation's attorney as designated by the Board of Directors of the Company.

1.15   Effective Date

"Effective Date" is the date first mentioned above in this agreement.

1.16   Fair Market Value

"Fair Market Value" is 1.25 times the book value as defined in Section 11.1.

1.17   Goodwill Value

"Goodwill Value" is the difference between the sale price of the stock and Fair Market Value.

2.0   SCOPE OF AGREEMENT

2.1   All Shares of the Company which have been issued and are outstanding, and all Shares which may be issued in the future, shall be subject to the terms and conditions of this Agreement.

2.2   All current and future shareholders acknowledge the existence of an agreement dated _____, by and between ˙_____and _____ _____ attached as Appendix "C." Such agreement is the only "side agreement" currently in existence under this agreement, and other than those specific terms set forth in it, both parties agree to abide by all other terms of this agreement.

3.0   BOARD OF DIRECTORS SELECTS NEW SHAREHOLDERS AND DISTRIBUTES ALL SHARES

3.1   The Board of Directors reserves the right to invite non-Shareholder employees to become Shareholders by offering to them for purchase a number of Company Shares, at which time the Board will advise the Secretary of the Company in writing of the further distribution of Shares offered and accepted. Such an offer of Shares shall be by a majority vote of all directors in place at the time of such offering.

3.2   The Board of Directors reserves the right to decide how available Shares are to be distributed, except that distribution of additional Shares to members of the Board must be approved in writing by the vote of sixty percent (60%) of the issued outstanding Company Shares.

3.3   The Board of Directors will advise the Secretary of the Company in writing within seven (7) days each time the Board of Directors varies the distribution of the Company Shares.

4.0   <u>BOARD OF DIRECTORS SELECTS NEW SHAREHOLDERS AND DISTRIBUTES ALL SHARES</u>

4.1   As persons become Shareholders of the Company they shall as a condition precedent thereto agree to each and every clause in this Agreement, and sign their name to indicate adherence to the Agreement.

4.2   Upon execution of this Agreement by each shareholder and prospective Shareholder (and the acceptance thereof by the President of the Company on behalf of the Company and all of the Shareholders) he shall have and be deemed to have all the rights and obligations of a Shareholder as fully and to the same effect as if he had been a signatory to this agreement except that the Effective Date thereof as respects such person should be the date upon which he became a Shareholder of the Company.

4.3   Upon receipt of the Agreement signed by the prospective Shareholder, the Secretary of the Company shall cause copies thereof to be prepared and mailed or delivered to all persons who are then parties, whether original or subsequent, to this agreement.

4.4   Notwithstanding anything herein contained to the contrary, the terms and conditions of this Agreement shall be binding upon all transferees of Shares.

5.0   <u>LEGEND ON SHARE CERTIFICATES</u>

5.1   All Share Certificates evidencing Shares registered in the name of a Shareholder shall bear thereon conspicuously the following legend:

"This certificate is issued and the Shares represented hereby are issued and held subject to the provisions of a certain agreement in writing between the Company and the holders of the Shares of the Company made as of the _____ day of _____, 20____.

6.0   <u>FINANCIAL STATEMENTS</u>

6.1   Financial statements shall be prepared by an independent Certified Public Accountant each year and copies provided to each stockholder within three (3) months of the end of each fiscal year. The independent Accountant of Record will be engaged by the Board of Directors subject to approval of a majority of the stockholders. The accountant prepared financial statement will become the basis for all stock value computations.

7.0 SECURITY INTEREST OF TRANSFER PROHIBITED

7.1 The Shareholders agree not to hypothecate, pledge, create a security interest or otherwise encumber, transfer, give, sell or dispose of their Shares, save with the consent in writing of the Company and all of the Shareholders or as provided in this Agreement; provided, however, that any Shareholder may hypothecate, pledge, create a security interest or otherwise encumber his Shares to or in favor of a commercial bank as security for indebtedness to such bank in order to purchase Shares in the Company, if and only if such bank acknowledges to the Company in writing that the said Shares may not be registered in the name of such bank or sold by such bank and are only subject to the provisions of this Agreement.

7.2 A Shareholder may make a gift of some or all of his or her Shares of stock to his or her spouse or issue, or to a trust established for the benefit of said spouse or issue, provided, however, that such gift shall be effective only upon execution by the recipient of a copy of the document attached hereto as APPENDIX "E" and delivery thereof to the Company. Should the recipient of the Shares of stock fail or refuse to execute said document, the Shareholder agrees that there shall be no gift, that any purported gift shall be null and void, and the Company and Shareholders shall not recognize such purported gift. Further, the Share certificate or certificates shall bear the legend set out in Paragraph 5.1 of this AGREEMENT;

8.0 MANDATORY PURCHASE OF SHARES

8.1 In the event of the death of any Shareholder, the bankruptcy of a Shareholder, the disablement of a Shareholder, the withdrawal of any Shareholder at any time after the date hereof, the parties hereto covenant and agree each with each other that the Company will purchase and the estate of the deceased Shareholder, the trustee of the bankrupt Shareholder, the disabled shareholder or the Withdrawing Shareholder, will offer for sale all of his Shares to the Company pursuant to Section 15.0 and 18.0.

8.2 The purchase and sale of the Shares will be deemed to have taken place the day before the time and date of death, bankruptcy, disablement, or withdrawal at the price per Share equal to Fair Market Value as calculated pursuant to Clause 11.0 hereof and upon the terms hereinafter set forth. Such date shall be hereinafter sometimes called the "Effective Date." Any and all insurance proceeds received by the company for death, bankruptcy, or disablement of a shareholder will not be included in the Fair Market Value calculated in Section 11.0.

8.3   The Secretary of the Company shall promptly notify in writing each Director of the death, bankruptcy, disablement or withdrawal of a shareholder.

8.4   The Company shall within one hundred and eighty (180) days of the Effective Date or within 30 days of receipt of insurance proceeds, whichever occurs first, purchase the Shares of the deceased, bankrupt, disabled or withdrawing Shareholder. The price to be paid for said Shares shall be the Fair Market Value of the Shares. The timing of Payment shall be in accordance with paragraph 12.0 herein.

9.0   DISPOSITION OF ACQUIRED SHARES

9.1   As soon as Shares have been acquired by the Company in accordance with paragraph 8.4 above, the Company may attempt to resell all of said Shares in the following manner:

(a)   By offering at least twenty (20%) percent of the acquired Shares to employees who are not then Shareholders provided that the Board of Directors has determined that there are eligible employees to whom Shares should be sold.

(b)   By offering the remainder of said Shares to existing Shareholders.

(c)   In the event the acquired Shares exceed the amounts set forth in paragraphs (a) and (b) above, then the excess Shares will be retained in the Company for later sale.

10.0   DEFAULT IN PAYMENT

10.1   If the Company defaults in payment to any seller or if any purchaser from the Company defaults in payment to the Company, then the balance of such purchase price shall from the day after the due date bear interest at the Prime Bank Rates plus two percent (2%) per annum calculated monthly.

10.2   Any interest payable because of default in payment for Shares shall be paid monthly to the Selling shareholder or the Company.

10.3   Any profit distribution, dividends or other benefits accruing to the Purchasing Shareholder with respect to the Shares purchased from the Company shall be forfeited in the event of default in payment by the purchaser, and shall be retained by the Company. The purchasing shareholder will only have a claim to benefits resulting from the ownership of Shares while his contract of purchase with the Company is in good standing.

10.4   As security for payment of the purchase price and interest owing to the Company the purchaser grants to the Company a lien, charge and security interest upon all of the Shares being acquired by him together with all moneys due and owing by the Company to the purchaser in payment of the balance of the purchase price of Shares being acquired by him from the Company. The purchaser hereby assigns to the Company all moneys thereafter owed by the Company to him (except regular salary) until such time as the balance of the purchase price and interest has been fully paid.

11.0   <u>DETERMINATION OF FAIR MARKET VALUE OF SHARES</u>

11.1   The Secretary of the Company shall within ten (10) days of receiving the Company's accountant prepared financial statements for each fiscal year of the Company, calculate and certify in writing to the Board of Directors of the Company the Fair Market Value of Shares. This Fair Market Value, calculated by the Secretary, may be subject to verification and approval by the Company's independent Accountant of Record and shall be deemed to be the Fair Market Value of each Share and shall be the price per Share used to calculate the purchase price payable pursuant to clauses 8.0, 12.0, 14.0, 18.0 and 19.0. The Secretary in making such determination shall establish the Fair Market Value of Shares as calculated at the year ending February 28, in each fiscal year as follows:

1.25 times the book value as defined in Section 1.6.

11.2   The percent Fair Market Value of Shares as determined by the Secretary is listed in Exhibit "B" attached hereto. Within ten (10) days of receiving the Company's Accountant prepared financial statements for each fiscal year, the Secretary shall redetermine the Fair Market Value of Shares and this Value will be endorsed as indicated below and shall be signed by and binding on all parties to this Agreement.

The endorsement shall be in the following form:

The "Fair Market Value of Shares" of _____ for the fiscal year ending _____, 20___, for the purpose of Shareholder's Agreements dated _____, 20__, shall be _____ per common share.

11.3   Each of the Shareholders covenants and agrees with each of the other parties hereto that he will endorse the Share certificate or certificates representing the Shares owned by him and will deliver them to the Trustee of the Company to be dealt with by the Trustee in accordance with terms of this Agreement. The Trustee will provide each Shareholder with photo copies of his Share certificates and annual Fair Market Value endorsements.

12.0   TIMING OF PAYMENT FOR SHARES

12.1   In the event of an employee's death the Deceased shareholder's estate will receive within twenty-four (24) months of the date (or within 30 days of receipt of insurance proceeds if sooner) without interest, one hundred percent (100%) of the Fair Market Value of each of the Shares owned by the Deceased shareholder at death as specified in this Agreement. Each year the Secretary shall submit a copy of current insurance limits to the Board of Directors within thirty (30) days of annual Fair Market Value determination as set forth in Section 11.0.

12.2   In the event of the involuntary termination or disablement of a Shareholder of the Company, the Selling Shareholder will receive, within thirty-six (36) months of the date of actual withdrawal, with interest at the then existing prime rate, one hundred percent (100%) of the Fair Market Value of each of the Shares owned by him just prior to the Date of Withdrawal. Said purchase price will be paid in thirty-six (36) equal monthly installments including interest at the then existing prime rate; provided, however, if the monthly installments so calculated exceed the last monthly salary paid to the Selling Shareholder by the Company then in such event the thirty-six (36) monthly installments shall be in the amount of the last monthly salary paid to the Selling Shareholder. In such event, the remaining unpaid balance owing to the Selling shareholder will be paid in the thirty-sixth month. If within twenty-four (24) months of the date of withdrawal, the Selling Shareholder engages for hire in the practice of services actively being provided by the company, within 75 miles of any offices of the Company, or if within said period he engages for hire in the practice of services actively being provided by the Company, for any client (existing or within the last sixty months) of the Company, then in such event the payment for the Shares will be reduced to seventy-five percent (75%) of the most recent Fair Market Value or the amount paid for the Shares, whichever is lesser and paid out over a sixty (60) month period notwithstanding any other provision of this agreement.

12.3   In the event of the voluntary termination of a Shareholder of the Company, the Selling Shareholder will receive, within sixty (60) months of the date of withdrawal and interest at the rate of nine percent (9%) per annum, one hundred percent (100%) of the Fair Market Value of the Shares owned by him just prior to the date of withdrawal. Said purchase price will be paid in sixty (60) equal monthly installments including interest at the rate of nine percent (9%) per annum; provided, however, if the monthly installments so calculated exceed the last monthly salary paid to the Selling Shareholder by the Company then in such event the sixty (60) monthly installments shall be in the amount of the last monthly salary paid to the Selling Shareholder. In such event the remaining unpaid balance owing the Selling Shareholder will be paid in the sixtieth month. If within twenty-four (24) months of the date of withdrawal the Selling Shareholder engages for hire in the practice of services actively being provided by the Company, within 75 miles of any office of the Company or if within said period he engages for hire in the practice of services actively being provided by the Company, for any client (existing or within the last sixty months), of the Company, then in such event the payment for the Shares will be reduced to fifty percent (50%) of the most recent Fair Market Value or the amount originally paid for the Shares, whichever is lesser.

12.4   The provisions in Paragraph 14.1 to 14.3 shall control the scheduled retirement of any Shareholder. In the event of an unscheduled retirement of a Shareholder which the Shareholder takes with consent of the Board of Directors, the Selling Shareholder will receive with interest at the then existing prime rate, one hundred percent (100%) of the Fair Market Value of each of the Shares owned by him at retirement (the Effective Date) in cash or in five equal annual installments commencing one year after the Effective Date. The decision to pay in cash or in five equal annual installments commencing one year after the Effective Date shall be made by the Board of Directors. If within thirty six (36) months of retirement, the Retired Shareholder engages for hire in the practice of services actively being provided by the Company within 75 miles of any Company office, or if within said period he engages for hire in the practice of services actively being provided by the Company for any client (existing or within the last thirty-six months) of the Company, then in such event the payment for the Shares will be reduced to fifty percent (50%) of the most recent Fair Market Value or the amount paid for the Shares, whichever is lesser.

13.0   MAXIMUM SHARE OFFERING

13.1   The Board of Directors shall, in calculating the number of Shares to be purchased, exclude Shareholders on retirement or withdrawal programs.

13.2   If within any period of twelve (12) months during the term of this Agreement, the number of Shares to be purchased pursuant to clause 8.0 or clause 14.0, when added to the number of Shares previously offered for sale during such period pursuant to said clauses shall in the aggregate, constitute twenty percent (20%) or more of the issued and outstanding Shares, then in such event before purchase of the additional Shares, the Board of Directors shall have thirty (30) days after receipt of the request to purchase Shares to decide whether to proceed with the purchase of such additional Shares, or defer the purchase as provided in this Agreement. Failure to reply shall be deemed to be an election to purchase.

13.3   If the Board of Directors elects to defer purchase of the additional Shares, the Secretary shall not be obliged during such period to proceed with arrangements for the purchase and resale of the additional Shares, and the terms of this Agreement relating to the sale and transfer of Shares (including the provisions of clause 8.0), shall as regards the purchase of additional Shares, stand suspended until the expiration of twenty-four (24) months from the date of the last purchase of Shares within said twelve (12) month period referenced in paragraph 13.2 above.

14.0   GRADUAL REDUCTION OF SHARES WHEN APPROACHING RETIREMENT

14.1   Each Shareholder covenants that he will commence selling his stock to the Company and the Company must purchase as follows:

(a)   He will sell 1/4 of such Shares of the Company between his 61st and 62nd birth dates.

(b)   He will sell 1/4 of such Shares to the Company between his 62nd and 63rd birth dates.

(c)   He will sell 1/4 of such Shares to the Company between his 63rd and 64th birth dates.

(d)   He will sell, 1/4 of such Shares to the Company between his 64th birth date and his retirement:

To avoid significant cash drains on the Company, at least one year must lapse between the sale of one quarter (1/4) of any such Shares and the sale of additional Shares by the same party unless authorized by the Board of Directors. In recognition of the fact that the Company may be sold after _____ and/or _____ _____ sells his stock in the Company at a value in excess of Fair Market Value as determined by the Company's accountant pursuant to generally accepted accounting principles as of date of sale, the Company will pay _____, Jr. and/or _____ the difference between the Fair Market Value and the sales price, in accordance with the following formula:

(a)   The Company will pay _____, and/or _____ 100 percent of the sales proceeds in excess of the Fair Market Value based on his stock ownership in the event a sale occurs within one year of _____'s and/or _____'s sale of stock to the company. This calculation will begin on the date of 1st sale of any additional stock each time stock is sold by _____, and/or

_____.

(b)   For every year after the first year following _____, and/or _____'s sale of stock to the Company, the sales proceeds in excess of Fair Market Value will be reduced twenty (20) percent for each such year.

14.2   At the discretion of the Board of Directors the final one quarter (1/4) of the Shares owned at age 64, may be retained until the Shareholder retires, terminates his employment, goes bankrupt, or dies, whichever event occurs first. The Board of Directors will decide by resolution each year to allow the retired Shareholder to retain the final one quarter (1/4) of his Shares or to require him to sell them back to the Company.

14.3   Upon the Shares being transferred to the Secretary pursuant to Clause 14.1, the Company, Secretary, and the Shareholders shall perform their obligations with respect to the Shares in the same manner as they would if Clause 8.1 applied to the transfer of the Shares.

15.0 VOLUNTARY SALE OF SHARES

15.1 If a Shareholder wishes to sell any or all of his Shares for any reason other than death, bankruptcy, disablement, or withdrawal he shall give written notice to the Secretary stating the number of Shares he wishes to sell and other pertinent details and such notice shall constitute an offer to sell the Shares to the Company. There is no obligation on the part of the Company to purchase any such Shares except as specified in this Agreement. This notice shall not be revocable except with the written approval of the Board of Directors.

16.0 INSURANCE ON SHAREHOLDER

16.1 Each Shareholder agrees that the Company may insure his life if it so desires so as to provide funds to facilitate the purchase of the Shareholder's Shares by the Company in the event of the death of the Shareholder, and the Shareholder agrees that he will sign appropriate Company applications for the life and disability insurance and shall submit to all necessary physical examinations.

16.2 Immediately after each fiscal year end of the Company, at the time the most recent Fair Market Value of Shares is calculated, the Secretary will prepare a schedule showing the current Fair Market Value of the Shares held by each Shareholder and held by the Company, and a copy of this schedule shall be sent to each Shareholder to be attached to this Agreement as Schedule "A."

16.3 The said policies of life insurance shall be the sole and absolute property of the Company by whom premiums thereon were paid. Any dividend payable upon the policies prior to maturity or the death of the life insured shall be the property of the Company.

16.4 The Company shall pay the premiums as they fall due on the policy or policies owned, and upon request by the Life insured, shall exhibit the premium receipt.

16.5 The insurance company by whom such policies are issued is hereby authorized and directed to supply to the insured Shareholder upon his request, any information respecting the status of any policy on his life, and is requested to immediately advise the insured when a premium is not paid by the Company on the required date preceding the specified number of days of grace.

16.6   If the proceeds of the policies on the life insured shall be more than sufficient to pay the purchase price for the Shares registered in the name of the deceased Shareholder, the balance of such insurance moneys shall be used to repay any salary, bonuses or Shareholder loans owing by the Company to the Shareholder, after which any balance shall be retained by the Company.

16.7   Upon termination of this Agreement or sale of all stock, each life insured shall have the right to purchase the policy or policies of insurance upon their respective lives owned by the Company. If any of the parties shall fail or refuse to purchase the said policy or policies on his life within thirty (30) days after such termination of this Agreement, such policy or policies may be surrendered for their cash surrender value by the Company or be retained by the Company.

16.8   In the event of the death of an insured shareholder, the Trustee shall forthwith collect from the insurance company the full amount of the insurance held by the Company on the deceased Shareholder and hold it in trust for the purchase of the Shares registered in the name of the deceased Shareholder, as stated in clauses 8.0 and 18.1.

16.9   Spouses, children, creditors and parties other than the Company shall have no claim on any proceeds of any life and disability insurance policy owned by the Company on the life of a Shareholder except as provided herein.

17.0   <u>BONUSES, DIVIDENDS AND OTHER BENEFITS</u>

17.1   Any bonuses, dividends or other benefits resulting from the ownership of Shares shall be distributed to the estate of a deceased Shareholder and to selling and purchasing Shareholders in proportion to the number of days of ownership during the fiscal year of the Company in which transfer of ownership takes place, except that during the first three (3) months of each fiscal year the Effective Date shall be the most recent fiscal year ended, February 28.

For example, if the Shares are purchased on July 1, then the Effective date of the transfer of ownership is June 30 and the Selling Shareholder will receive 122 divided by 365 times the accrual basis profits resulting from ownership of the Shares during the fiscal year of transfer, and the purchasing Shareholder will receive 243 divided by 365 times the accrued basis profits resulting from ownership of the Shares during the fiscal year of transfer.

17.2   All Shareholders agree to bind themselves and their estates to the policy in force at the time of any death or disability with regard to bonuses, dividends or any other disbursements recognizing that such disbursements are set by management based on current, not past or future, performance of the Company.

18.0   <u>COMPANY PURCHASE OF COMPANY SHARES</u>

18.1   The Company may, when authorized by the Board of Directors, and subject to the Articles of Incorporation, By-Laws, and clause 18.2 of this Agreement, periodically purchase or redeem Shares at Fair Market Value of Shares and under the conditions stated in this Agreement except where the Company would, after payment for the Shares, be unable to pay its liabilities as they become due, or the realizable value of the Company's assets would after such payment be less than the aggregate of the Company's liabilities.

18.2   To avoid a significant cash drain on Company funds, the purchase by the Company of Shares owned by a Director or a Shareholder selling more than twenty percent (20%) of the issued outstanding Shares in any one Fiscal Year must be approved in advance in writing by the registered owners of at least sixty-seven percent (67%) of the issued and outstanding Shares.

19.0   <u>ISSUANCE OF SHARES</u>

19.1   No authorized but unissued (excluding treasury stock) stock may be issued by the Company without prior written approval of the registered owners of at least fifty-one (51%) percent of the issued and outstanding Shares.

19.2   The subscription price for each Share shall be the Fair Market Value calculated as specified in this Agreement, and calculated without including the total purchase price of the Shares which are subscribed for as an asset of the Company, and without including the number of Shares which are subscribed for in the total Shares issued and outstanding.

20.0   <u>DISCHARGE OF COMPANY'S LIABILITIES TO SHAREHOLDERS</u>

20.1   In the event suit or action be instituted to enforce any of the terms or conditions of this Agreement, the losing party shall pay to the prevailing party, in addition to the costs and disbursements allowed by statute, such sum as the court may adjudge reasonable as attorney fees in such suit or action, in both trial court and appellate courts.

20.2   Upon the death, retirement or disablement of a Shareholder, the Company will assume 100% of all responsibility for professional liability of the departing Shareholder and indemnify, hold harmless, and defend him for such liability, except for any Shareholder who violates the non-compete provisions of this agreement, pursuant to paragraph 21.0 below. This provision will not apply to shareholders departing voluntarily or terminated involuntarily.

21.0   HOLD HARMLESS

21.1   The Shareholders, upon the purchase by the Company of the interest of a retiring, disabled or deceased Shareholder, shall hold the retiring Shareholder or his successors harmless for all liabilities of the Company which have been guaranteed by the retiring, disabled or deceased Shareholder, and shall pay all judgments, attorneys' fees, court costs or other moneys or time lost or expended by the retiring Shareholder or his successors as a result of any proceeding brought against the retiring, disabled or deceased shareholder as a result of the obligation for which he is held harmless under this provision. A written hold harmless agreement, as shown in APPENDIX "D," shall be executed by the remaining Shareholders to evidence the terms of this provision.

22.0   SPOUSAL CONSIDERATIONS

22.1   Death of a Spouse

Upon the death of the spouse of a Shareholder prior to the withdrawal, death or disability of such Shareholder, the spouse's community property interest in the Shareholder's interest in the Company shall pass, if any, to and devolve upon the Shareholder, and each spouse by executing this agreement and in consideration of the benefits to be received hereunder agrees to make and keep unrevoked at death a valid will containing such a provision to this effect; but the non-existence of a valid will containing such a provision shall not relieve the heirs, personal representatives, assigns, and devisees of such spouse of the obligation fully to perform the terms of this agreement.

22.2   Dissolution of Marriage

Each spouse binds himself or herself and all persons ever to claim under him or her that upon a dissolution of the marriage between the spouse and the Shareholder, neither the spouse nor anyone claiming under the spouse will seek to partition the community property of the spouse and the Shareholder as it relates to any of the Shareholder's interest in the corporation.

The spouse of each Shareholder has joined in the execution of this agreement to evidence the spouse's knowledge of its existence and to acknowledge that this agreement is fair, equitable and in the spouse's best interests, and to evidence the spouse's desire to bind the spouse's community interest, if any, in the interest of the Shareholder to the performance of this agreement.

23.0 SETTLEMENT OF DISPUTES

23.1 Any dispute arising out of or in connection with this Agreement, including disputes between or among the corporation, the Shareholders, or any trustee, shall be settled by the negotiation, mediation and arbitration provisions of The American Arbitration Association.

24.0 TERM

24.1 Unless otherwise agreed in writing by the parties, this agreement shall continue in full force and effect until the Shares of a Shareholder are assigned, transferred or otherwise disposed of in accordance with the terms and provisions of this agreement.

25.0 NO WAIVER

25.1 No term or provision of this agreement shall be construed as a waiver by the Company of any provision of its Articles of Incorporation or By-Laws restricting the sale or transfer of Shares of the corporation.

26.0 EMPLOYMENT

26.1 Except as specifically provided herein, nothing in this agreement shall confer on any Shareholder who is an employee of the Company any right to continue in the employ of the corporation, or shall interfere in any way with the right of the Company to terminate his employment at any time.

27.0 ATTORNEY FEES

27.1 In the event suit or action be instituted to enforce any of the terms or conditions of this agreement, the losing party shall pay to the prevailing party, in addition to the costs and disbursements allowed by statute, such sum as the court may adjudge reasonable as attorney fees in such suit or action, in both trial court and appellate courts.

28.0   <u>NOTICE</u>

    28.1   Any notice required to be given in writing hereunder shall be deliv-
           ered or mailed by registered mail to the Company at its then head
           office, and to any Shareholder at the last address of such Shareholder
           shown on the books of the Company. Notice shall be deemed to have
           been received on the date of delivery or if mailed, three business days
           following the date of mailing on which there is regular postal delivery
           in the areas to which it is addressed.

29.0   <u>COMPANY BOUND BY AGREEMENT</u>

    29.1   The Company hereby acknowledges that it is fully aware of the provi-
           sion herein contained and consents to the same and hereby expressly
           covenants and agrees that, so far as the Company may be permitted by
           law or authorized to do so, the Company hereby covenants and agrees
           to observe and perform the covenants and agreements herein set forth.

    29.2   Agreements previously made between the Shareholders of the
           Company and all rights of any parties under and by virtue of said
           Agreement are hereby terminated.

30.0   <u>TERMINATION OF ALL PRIOR SHAREHOLDER AGREEMENTS</u>

    30.1   This Agreement replaces in all respects any and all Shareholder
           Agreements made between the Shareholders of the Company and all
           rights of any parties under and by virtue of the said Agreements are
           hereby terminated, except as noted in Section 2.2.

31.0   <u>COUNTERPARTS TO THIS AGREEMENT</u>

    31.1   Each of the parties hereto agrees with each of the other parties hereto
           that this Agreement may be executed in as many counterparts as are
           necessary or convenient and such counterparts together shall constitute
           an agreement.

32.0   <u>AMENDMENT OR TERMINATION OF AGREEMENT</u>

    32.1   This Agreement shall as between the parties hereto continue in full
           force and effect until the registered holders of more than sixty-seven
           percent (67%) of the issued and outstanding Shares give thirty (30)
           days written notice to the Company and other Shareholders of their
           intention to amend or terminate this Agreement. Upon the expiration
           of thirty (30) days after receipt of such written notice by all parties
           aforesaid, this Agreement shall be amended or terminated.

PROVIDED, however, that no such amendment or termination shall release or discharge any person from his obligation to pay for Shares pursuant to an obligation existing prior to the date of such amendment or termination. The Agreement shall as regards any undischarged obligations of a Shareholder hereunder, continue in full force and effect as to the Shares not yet paid for.

33.0 COMPLIANCE WITH STATUTES

33.1 All clauses of this Agreement are distinct and severable. Any clause, paragraph, phrase, provision, or term of this Agreement which may not be in full accord and compliance with applicable existing or subsequently enacted statutes shall not render other clauses, paragraphs, phrases, provisions or terms of this Agreement void or voidable. The remainder of this Agreement shall continue to bind and obligate all parties.

34.0 BENEFIT

34.1 The provisions of this agreement shall inure to the benefit of, and be binding upon, the parties hereto, their heirs, trustees, legal representatives, successors and permitted assignees.

35.0 MARGINAL HEADINGS

35.1 The marginal headings in the paragraphs contained in this agreement are for convenience only, and are not to be considered a part of this agreement or used in determining its content or context.

36.0 INTERPRETATION

36.1 Whenever any words are used in this agreement in the masculine gender, they shall also be construed as being used in the feminine gender, and singular usage shall include the plural, and vice versa, all as the context shall require.

37.0 WHOLE AGREEMENT

37.1 The terms of this Agreement constitute the entire agreement between the parties, and the parties represent that there are no collateral agreements or side agreements not otherwise provided for within the terms of this instrument.

38.0 **DUTIES OF PERSONAL REPRESENTATIVES**

38.1 The executor, administrator, trustee or legal representative of a deceased or disabled Shareholder shall make, execute and deliver any documents necessary to carry out this agreement.

39.0 **COVENANT NOT TO STEAL EMPLOYEES, CLIENTS OR TRADE SECRETS**

39.1 Upon the termination of employment of any Shareholder, the party agrees to not solicit, encourage or tamper with the Company's existing employees or clients or trade secrets.

40.0 **COVENANT TO DEVOTE FULL EFFORTS TO COMPANY**

40.1 All Shareholders shall devote their entire professional time and energies to the business of the Company and shall not engage directly or indirectly in any other business activity except as otherwise provided or agreed to by the Board of Directors by a 60% vote of Board Members.

41.0 **CONFIDENTIALITY AND PRIVACY**

41.1 Shareholders shall keep secret all financial and legal matters of the Company plus the names of or any information relevant to any past, present or prospective customer or business associate of the Company, as well as any or all knowledge as to these persons, and as to any loans, financing, sales or other matters which a Shareholder may acquire.

42.0 **ESTATE TAXES OR CAPITAL GAINS**

42.1 Each Shareholder and the spouse of each Shareholder agrees to hold harmless the Company for any estate, income or capital gains taxes in connection with any transaction occurring either directly or indirectly related to this agreement.

43.0 **MARRIAGE OF ANY SHAREHOLDER**

43.1 Within 30 days of the marriage of any shareholder, the shareholder agrees to endorse together with his new spouse the amendment shown as Exhibit "C" binding the spouse to this agreement. Failure of a new spouse to endorse this agreement within 45 days of marriage to a Shareholder will allow the Company at its option to purchase some or all outstanding Shares owned by the Shareholder, pursuant to Section 12.2.

44.0   <u>SALE OF THE COMPANY OR OTHER SUCH MAJOR DECISIONS</u>

    44.1   Major decisions such as the sale or merger of the Company to another Company require an affirmative vote of seventy-five percent (75%) of all outstanding Shares of the Company.

45.0   <u>SUCCESSORS AND ASSIGNS</u>

    45.1   This Agreement shall inure to the benefit of and be binding upon the parties hereto, their respective heirs, executors, administrators, successors and assigns.

46.0   <u>LEGAL JURISDICTION</u>

    46.1   This Agreement shall be governed by and construed according to the General Laws State of California, notwithstanding the fact that certain international legalities may require a special addenda to become part of this Agreement from time to time.

IN WITNESS WHEREOF the undersigned have executed this Agreement acknowledging Appendices "A," "B," "C," "D" and "E" under seal and have by so executing made themselves party to this Agreement, all as of the day and year first above written.

SHAREHOLDERS OF RECORD

By _____
Shareholder   _____   _____
                                         Spouse   Date

By _____
Shareholder   _____   _____
                                         Spouse   Date

By _____
Shareholder   _____   _____
                                         Spouse   Date

By _____
Shareholder   _____   _____
                                         Spouse   Date

APPENDIX "A"

STOCK PERCENTAGES/SHARES OWNED

As of _____, 20___, the following individuals own the following Shares with each share possessing a Fair Market Value of _____ pursuant to this agreement representing the percent of ownership outlined below:

Shareholder	# of Shares	Fair Market Value	% Ownership

_____

Signed: Accountant of Record

_____

Signed: Corporate Secretary

APPENDIX "B"

ADDENDUM AGREEMENT

Addendum Agreement made this _____ day of _____,
20___, by and between _____ (the "New Shareholder"),
and _____, Inc., a corporation (the "Company"),
who are parties to that certain Agreement dated _____, 20_____,
(the "Agreement"), between the Company and its shareholders.

W I T N E S S E T H

WHEREAS, the Company and the Shareholders and their respective spouses
entered into the Agreement to impose certain restrictions and obligations upon themselves and the Shares of stock of the company; and

WHEREAS, the New Shareholder is desirous of becoming a shareholder of the
Company; and

WHEREAS, the Company and the Shareholders have required in the
Agreement that all persons being offered stock must enter into an Addendum Agreement
binding the New Shareholder and the New Shareholder's spouse to the Agreement to the
same extent as if they were original parties thereto and imposing the same restrictions
and obligations on the New Shareholder, the New Shareholder's spouse and the Shares
of stock to be acquired by the New Shareholder as were imposed upon the Shareholders
under the Agreement,

NOW, THEREFORE, in consideration of the mutual promises of the parties,
and as a condition of the purchase of stock in the Company, the New Shareholder and
the New Shareholder's spouse acknowledge that they have read the Agreement. The
New Shareholder and the New Shareholder's spouse shall be bound by, and shall have
the benefit of, all the terms and conditions set out in the Agreement to the same extent
as if they were original parties to the Agreement. This Addendum agreement shall be
attached to and become a part of the Agreement.

_____   _____
New Shareholder   Date

_____   _____
Spuse of New Shareholder   Date

Agreed to on behalf of the Shareholders and the Company

By:_____
   Its Chairman of the Board

Date:_____

APPENDIX "D"

INDEMNIFICATION AGREEMENT

AGREEMENT entered into this 1st day of _____,
20____, by and between _____,
_____, and _____ (collec-
tively "the SHAREHOLDERS").

WHEREAS, the SHAREHOLDERS have executed a certain AGREEMENT
("THE AGREEMENT"), a copy of which AGREEMENT is attached hereto as APPEN-
DIX "A";

WHEREAS, the SHAREHOLDERS are all the shareholders of
_____ _____, INC., a corporation "the
COMPANY").

WHEREAS, _____ has guaranteed certain
obligations and liabilities of the COMPANY from time to time;

WHEREAS, the AGREEMENT provides for the execution by the SHARE-
HOLDERS of a written hold harmless agreement with regard to those obligations and
liabilities guaranteed by a retiring, disabled or deceased SHAREHOLDER upon the purchase by the COMPANY and/or the SHAREHOLDER of the interest of a retiring, disabled or deceased SHAREHOLDER; and

WHEREAS, _____ is
_____ and the COMPANY and/or the SHAREHOLD
ER are purchasing _____'s interest in the COMPANY
upon _____'s retirement, disablement, or death:

THEREFORE, in consideration of the premises, the SHAREHOLDERS,
excluding _____, for themselves, their heirs,
executors, administrators, successors and assigns, do hereby jointly and severally,
covenant and agree with _____, his heirs, execu-
tors, administrators, successors and assigns, as follows:

1. The SHAREHOLDERS, excluding _____,
    will indemnify and hold _____ harm-
    less against any and all liability, loss, costs, damages, attorney's fees and
    other expenses, and reasonable value of time lost or expended, which
    _____ _____ or his heirs, executors, admin-
    istrators, successors and assigns may sustain or incur by reason of, or in

consequence of the execution by _____ of any guaranty of or for the benefit of the COMPANY, and any renewal, continuation or successor thereof, including but not limited to, sums paid or liabilities incurred in settlement of, and expenses paid or incurred in connection with claims, suits or judgments under such guaranties, expenses paid or incurred in enforcing the terms hereof, in procuring or attempting to procure release from liability, or in recovering or attempting to recover losses or expenses paid or incurred, as aforesaid.

2. The spouse of each SHAREHOLDER has joined in the execution of this agreement to evidence the spouse's knowledge of it and to evidence the spouse's community interest, if any, in the interest of the SHAREHOLD-ER to the performance of this agreement.

3. Any dispute arising out of or in connection with this agreement shall be settled by arbitration which shall be held.

4. In the event arbitration or suit be instituted to enforce any of the terms or conditions of this agreement, the losing party shall pay to the prevailing party its attorney's fees, court and arbitration costs.

5. The laws of the State shall apply to this agreement.

6. This agreement may not be changed or modified orally. No change or modification shall be effective unless specifically agreed in writing.

IN WITNESS WHEREOF, the parties have executed this agreement on the date first set out hereinabove.

SHAREHOLDERS   SPOUSES

APPENDIX "E"

AGREEMENT

The undersigned, in consideration of the agreement of the _____, Inc. ("the Company") and its Shareholders to allow and consent to the receipt of certain Shares of stock of the Company from the spouse or ancestor of the undersigned (said spouse or ancestor referred to hereinafter as "the SHAREHOLDER"), and pursuant and with reference to a certain BUY/SELL AGREEMENT dated _____, 20____ ("the BUY/SELL AGREEMENT"), agrees as follows:

1. The recipient shall be bound by all the terms and conditions of the BUY/SELL AGREEMENT.

2. Upon the death of the spouse or child, or upon the dissolution of marriage of the Shareholder and the spouse, the recipient shall sell the Shares of stock to the Shareholder, or, if the Shareholder is unwilling or unable to purchase all of the Shares, to the Company, under the same price, terms and conditions as would apply under the BUY/SELL AGREEMENT had the Shareholder died.

4. The recipient may not hypothecate, create a security interest or otherwise encumber, transfer, give, sell or dispose of the Shares, except to the Shareholder, save with the consent of the Company and all of the Shareholders.

Executed this _____ day of _____,20_____, in
_____, _____.

_____
Recipient

Preparing Your Marketing Plan: Techniques and What to Include

Your marketing plan details the way your firm's resources and energy will be mobilized to create the future. It defines tasks, assigns responsibility, allocates costs, and provides a measuring device to evaluate the effectiveness of your firm's marketing efforts. Make it innovative, imaginative, and resourceful.

Before you do your actual writing, stimulate your creativity with these techniques:

1. *Brainstorm*—List all the ways you could improve your business. No idea is too wild. Ask for input from employees, clients, colleagues, and friends.
2. *Become a client for a day*—Observe and absorb what interests your clients. "Reading the client's mind" is crucial to developing and keeping new business.
3. *Review your markets*—Devise profiles for all clients, current and potential.
4. *Distinguish your most potentially profitable clients from the rest*—Target that group.
5. *Divide the market into segments*—Break the markets down into manageable pieces according to a set of criteria appropriate to your firm's strengths. Identify which of these segments are the most profitable and rank them accordingly.
6. *Benchmark the competition*—Watch how they market. Devise strategies to play against their strengths and weaknesses.
7. *Match your initial brainstorming list with your targeted markets*—Choose eight to ten tactics from your list of ways to improve the business that will support the targeted clients and markets you have chosen.

8. *Write the plan*—Include the following:
   - Goals or objectives
   - Target markets
   - Strategies
   - Redefinition of services and capabilities
   - Marketing budget
   - Timetable for implementation
   - Delineation of responsibilities
   - Evaluation method

GOALS/OBJECTIVES

Where do you want to take the business? List your goals, both primary and secondary, in this section. Attach a timeline for measurement purposes, such as: "to increase customer base by 10% by (date)."

Be specific. Include goals that may be particular to a certain target market (intended customer group) and complementary to your overall objective. For instance, "to increase sales within market X by 10 percent by the end of 2004."

TARGET MARKETS

Identify your intended customer groups, but don't limit your target markets to prospective customers. Include everyone who should know about your product or services and the advantages of working with your firm. Other sources to consider: current clients, vendors, employees, referral sources, networking leads, the media.

STRATEGIES AND TACTICS

Strategies Ask yourself how you want to be perceived in the marketplace and what you are going to do (in general terms) to communicate that image to the public. Bear in mind that your strategy is the road you'll take to get your firm from point A today (your self-assessment) to point B tomorrow (your goals/objectives).

Tactics Tactics are the nuts and bolts of your marketing communications plan—the "to do'" list that includes activities from each of the following areas: public relations/community relations, networking, advertising, promotions, direct selling, and collateral materials (printed materials that represent your company).

Avoid focusing all your marketing efforts on just one area. Putting all your eggs in one basket is risky. Integrating activities will stretch your budget, as some are less costly than others. Also, when you engage in a variety of marketing activities, your firm will be perceived as much larger than it actually is.

REDEFINITION OF SERVICES AND CAPABILITIES

Revise the description of your services. Focus on knowledge rather than product. Identify the unique value that you can deliver to your clients—superior service, personal attention, and so on.

MARKETING BUDGET

Don't skimp here. Your budget must be adequate to achieve your objectives.

TIMETABLE FOR IMPLEMENTATION

Incremental measurements will allow you to spot strategies and tactics that need revision or replacement. A timetable keeps everyone on track, provides deadlines for task completion, and is a measurement device for the evaluation process.

DELINEATION OF RESPONSIBILITIES

Be very clear about who is doing what. Marketing is a team effort, something in which everyone on your staff participates. Include an ownership component in your plan—an assignment of responsibility for each proposed activity.

EVALUATION METHOD

Include a section on how you'll evaluate individual projects, as well as the overall plan. It's acceptable not to achieve all your objectives, but you must be able to determine the "why" in order to fine tune your plan for the future.

FINAL THOUGHT

As you write and implement your plan, keep these points in mind:

- Be consistent in terms of the image you want to project.
- Stick to your objectives.
- Don't bite off more than you can chew. Do as much or as little marketing as you feel is appropriate for your business but never abandon your marketing efforts.

Writing a marketing plan is a time-consuming activity, but one that will pay off in business growth and success for years to come. Keep your plan in a highly visible location where you and your staff can refer to it often.

Is Your Cover Letter Making a Difference?

Do you want to give your firm a better than fighting chance at the proposal stage? Then start the process off right with a cover letter that works.

How often have you dashed off a meaningless proposal cover letter that no one reads? Well, stop! The cover letter might be the most important page in the proposal.

WHY IS A COVER LETTER IMPORTANT?

Most review board members thumb through a proposal, glance at eye-catching graphics, then quickly skim the cover letter.

Here's what a typical letter tells a reviewer:

- The firm is pleased to submit the proposal.
- The firm is uniquely qualified.
- The project is very important to the firm.
- The firm is excited about the opportunity to work with the company.
- Call if there are any questions.

What is the focus of such a letter? *The firm.*

Ironically, by the time he or she has finished reading that cover letter (20 to 60 seconds), the reviewer has formed an opinion about the firm—usually less than flattering and largely based on the physical appearance of the proposal and the message of the cover letter.

So knock 'em dead right from the start! From the following eight elements, assemble your killer cover letter, focusing on the prospect.

In the sample cover letter on page 307, the numbered sections correspond to the numbered elements in this appendix.

ELEMENTS OF A KILLER COVER LETTER

❶ **Subject line:** Make this an action/solution statement addressing your prospect's number one hot button issue. Always include the subject line: it grabs the reader's attention.

❷ **Salutation:** Address the letter to someone you know on a first-name basis.

❸ **Grab 'em section—the "what":** In your first paragraph, refer to the hot button issue. Then, in words, look your prospect straight in the eyes and assure him or her that your priority is to resolve that issue.

Use short words and sentences. Keep this and all paragraphs to five or six lines. Address the reader as though you are talking with her in person. Keep it simple.

❹ **Hold 'em section—the "how":** Start your second section with a "How we will" headline: "How we will solve _____" (fill in the blank with the specific issue). Or use a more generic approach: "How we will meet your need."

Under the headline, write a paragraph that:

- Tells the prospect *exactly* how you will solve the hot button issue.
- Refers the prospect to proposal page numbers that offer more information about your solution.
- Reveals or reemphasizes the main benefit from your approach.

❺ **Sell 'em section—the "why":** Begin with a new headline, promising more benefits. "How you will benefit from this approach," or "What you will get from this plan." Use bullets under the headline to tell the reader what else she will get from going with your plan. Each bullet should present a new benefit and refer the reader to a page in the proposal.

When she has finished reading this section, she will know why she should select your firm for the project.

❻ **Statement of enthusiasm:** Tell your prospect you have set aside a specific week in which to meet with her in the event you are selected for an interview. Then thank the prospect for her consideration. This approach lets your reader know that you really want to work with her on this project.

❼ **Signature of principal**

❽ **Postscript.** By including a P.S. with the principal's home phone, cellular phone, or pager number, you're reemphasizing that you want the project, and you're letting the reader know that you're available at all times.

OUR DESIGN FIRM UNITED, INC.

February 15, 2001

Elizabeth Hoover, CEO
The Client
Anchor Plaza Parkway
Anywhere, U.S. 12345

❶ RE: **How you can open the (school name) school before August 16, 2002 by choosing the (firm name) project plan.**

❷ Dear Elizabeth:

❸ We understand your need to have the (school name) school ready for the new academic year. In response, we have developed a work plan to ensure that the school goes fully operational before August 16, 2002.

❹ **How we will meet your need**
We will meet your deadline by placing a design team on-site with your staff, full time. The team will include (names, positions, responsibilities). (See page 23.) This in-person, ongoing collaboration will save you approximately three months on the schedule. (See pages 11-15.)

❺ **What you will get from this plan**
In addition to having your school open on time, you will receive three more important benefits:

● You will save 12 % on construction materials. Our selection process consistently places clients' school costs 12% below the county average per square foot. (See page 28.)

● Your children will do better. In schools we design, children's grades typically increase by 4%. (See page 5.)

● Your school board will know exactly what they'll spend. Before the budget approval meeting, we will let them know the maximum costs for the project. (See page 33.)

❻ In the event that you select us for an interview, we have set aside the week of March 11th to meet with you. Thank you very much for considering us to be part of your team.

Sincerely,

Our Design Firm United, Inc.

❼ _____

John Williams
Principal

❽ P.S. Please contact me on my cellular phone at 555-443-1234.

THREE MORE SUCCESS SECRETS TO A KILLER COVER LETTER

1. Use "you" and "your" much more frequently than "I," "us," and "our." Put yourself in your prospect's shoes. What does she care about: your firm or her business?

2. Write a letter draft *before* you create the proposal. Knowing the client's bottom-line benefits up front will help you organize your proposal around selling those benefits.

3. Bind the letter into the proposal. This way, your letter will always be where the prospect can see it. It will remain an integral part of your pitch to the review board.

Source: "Does Your Cover Letter Make a Difference?" *PSMJ Best Practices*, November 2000. Barry Yoakum, a PSMJ consultant, provided the sample cover letter.

Recommended Reading

Attitude Is Everything, by Keith Harrell. Cliff Street Books (March 2000).

The Book of Leadership Wisdom: Classic Writings by Legendary Business Leaders, by Peter Krass, editor. John Wiley & Sons (November 1998).

The Customer-Centered Enterprise: How IBM and Other World-Class Companies Achieve Extraordinary Results by Putting Customers First, by Harvey Thompson. McGraw-Hill Professional Publishing (December 1999).

First, Break All the Rules: What the World's Greatest Managers Do Differently, by Marcus Buckingham & Curt Coffman. Simon & Schuster (May 1999).

How to Master the Art of Selling, by Tom Hopkins. Warner Books (November 1994).

Intellectual Capital: Realizing Your Company's True Value by Finding Its Hidden Brainpower, by Leif Edvinsson & Michael S. Malone. Harperbusiness (March 1997).

Kotler on Marketing: How to Create, Win, and Dominate Markets, by Philip Kotler. Free Press (April 1999).

Leadership Is an Art, by Max Depree & James O'Toole. DTP (September 1990).

Lincoln on Leadership: Executive Strategies for Tough Times, by Donald T. Phillips. Warner Books (February 1993).

The New Strategic Selling: The Unique Sales System Proven Successful by the World's Best Companies, by Stephen E. Heiman, Diane Sanchez, Tad Tuleja, Robert B. St. Miller. Warner Books (January 1998).

Partnering Intelligence: Creating Value for Your Business by Building Smart Alliances, by Stephen Dent. Davies-Black (October 1999).

The Project 50 (Reinventing Work): Fifty Ways to Transform Every "Task" into a Project That Matters! by Tom Peters. Knopf (September 1999).

Rewards That Drive High Performance: Success Stories from Leading Organizations, by Thomas B. Wilson. AMACOM (April 1999).

Spin Selling, by Neil Rackham. McGraw-Hill (December 1998).

Swim with the Sharks without Being Eaten Alive, by Harvey Mackay. William Morrow (1988).

Technoleverage: Using the Power of Technology to Outperform the Competition, by F. Michael Hruby. AMACOM (January 1999).

Top Performance: How to Develop Excellence in Yourself and Others, by Zig Ziglar. Fleming H. Revell (1986).

The 22 Immutable Laws of Branding: How to Build a Product or Service into a World-Class Brand, by Al Ries & Laura Ries. Harpercollins (October 1998).

Who Moved My Cheese? An Amazing Way to Deal with Change in Your Work and in Your Life, by Spencer Johnson. Putnam (September 1998).

Index